THE CHILD AT SCHOOL

A PAEDIATRICIAN'S MANUAL
FOR TEACHERS

*Lessons from Childhood: Some Aspects of the
Early Life of Unusual Men and Women*
with C.M. Illingworth
(Translated into Japanese)
Edinburgh, Churchill Livingstone, 1966

*The Treatment of the Child at Home: a Guide
for Family Doctors*
Oxford, Blackwell Scientific Publications, 1971

*The Normal Child: Some Problems of the Early
Years and their Treatment*
(Translated into Greek, Spanish,
Japanese, French)
London, Churchill Livingstone, 5th edition, 1972

*Babies and Young Children. Their Management,
Feeding and Care*
with C.M. Illingworth
London, Churchill Livingstone, 5th edition, 1972

*Development of the Infant and Young Child,
Normal and Abnormal*
(Translated into Japanese)
Edinburgh, Churchill Livingstone, 5th edition, 1972

Common Symptoms of Disease in Children
(Translated into Greek, Spanish, Italian)
Oxford, Blackwell Scientific Publications,
4th edition, 1973

Basic Developmental Screening
Oxford, Blackwell Scientific Publications, 1973

THE CHILD AT SCHOOL

A PAEDIATRICIAN'S MANUAL
FOR TEACHERS

BY

RONALD S. ILLINGWORTH

MD, FRCP, DPH, DCH

Professor of Child Health, University of Sheffield
Paediatrician, The Children's Hospital, Sheffield
and the United Sheffield Hospitals

A HALSTED PRESS BOOK

JOHN WILEY & SONS

NEW YORK

© 1974 Blackwell Scientific Publications
Osney Mead, Oxford,
3 Nottingham Street, London W1,
9 Forrest Road, Edinburgh,
P.O. Box 9, North Balwyn, Victoria, Australia.

First published 1974

Published in the U.S.A. by
Halsted Press, a division of
John Wiley & Sons Inc,
New York

Library of Congress Cataloging in Publication Data

Illingworth, Ronald Stanley, 1909–
    The child at school.

    "A Halsted Press book."
    Includes index.
    1. Developmental psychobiology.   2. Child
development deviations.   I. Title.
RJ131.I745   613'.04'32024372   75–14463
ISBN 0–470–42657–8

Printed in Great Britain

CONTENTS

17 Common Symptoms and Diseases   244

Abdominal pain, acute
Abdominal pain, recurrent
Acne
Anaemia
Asthma
Ataxia
Constipation
Cough
Cystic fibrosis of the pancreas
Dental caries
Diabetes mellitus
Diarrhoea
Ear pain, ear discharge
Eczema
Flat foot
Frequency and urgency of
    micturition
Funnel chest
Glands, enlarged
Haemophilia
Headaches and migraine
Heart disease
Impetigo
Knock knee

Lassitude
Limping and limb pain
Mouthbreathing
Muscular dystrophy
Nasal discharge
Nausea
Oedema of the face
Pediculosis
Pigeon chest
Pruritus
Rheumatoid arthritis
Ringworm
Scabies
Tinnitus
Tonsils and adenoids
Tuberculosis
Urticaria
Vertigo
Vomiting
Vomiting of blood
Warts
Weight loss
Worms

18 Common Infectious Diseases   274

Incubation period and infectivity

Specific infections
    Chickenpox
    Colds
    Diphtheria
    Dysentery
    Enteric group
    Gastroenteritis
    German measles
    Glandular fever

Infective hepatitis
Measles
Mumps
Poliomyelitis
Scarlet fever
Whooping cough

Prevention
    Immunisation
    Tetanus
    Quarantine

19 Accidents and First Aid   283

Accidents
    General
    Factors involved
    Prevention
Head injuries
First Aid
    Abrasions, cuts, bleeding
    wounds

Bites
Bleeding nose or tooth socket
Broken tooth
Burns and scalds
Foreign body in the eye, ear,
    nose
Poisoning
Stings

PREFACE

I have written this book in order to try to help teachers to understand more of the children for whom they are responsible. I hope that it will help them to understand better the reason for a child's behaviour, backwardness, thinness, fatness, smallness, madness or handicap. I hope that it will make them think about punishment, and about blaming the parents or the child for his shortcomings. I hope that teachers will not take this amiss, and that they will not be annoyed at the suggestion that they do not know enough about children. They don't—and neither do paediatricians. The danger of writing about the behaviour of children lies in the implication that one knows all the answers. None of us do—for however many years of experience we have, and however many thousands of children we see, we continue to learn about them—or should do.

I have for years thought that there is a regrettable fence between the teacher and the paediatrician. It is a pity, because each has so much to contribute to the other. Our interests overlap, and if in this book I have strayed too far on to the teachers' side of the fence it would not be surprising if I were to have revealed my ignorance —and I hope that forbearance will be shown. Often, when our interests have overlapped, I thought that it would be useful for the teacher to read about the paediatricians' experience.

Many will think of obvious gaps in this book. Many of these are deliberate because the subjects are adequately covered in textbooks —such as books on psychology—or because the teacher will know more about them (e.g. sex education) than I do. Many subjects were omitted because I thought that they were irrelevant to the teacher, or because I lack the experience to write about them. Others, I fear, may have been omitted because I did not think about them. I have deliberately not discussed the work of the school medical service; I thought that it would be better not to discuss it in view of the reorganisation of the Health Service.

I have avoided generalisations about the development of the child after the first year. The subject is covered by many psychology texts: I avoided it because the development is so profoundly affected by the environment, culture, neighbourhood, personality and intellectual endowment—and I preferred to discuss instead those factors which affect behaviour and development and the general performance at school. I felt that the teacher would want to know why children behave and function as they do: the teacher has to cope with the product of the parents and their problems and attitudes, and the result of ill health and handicaps. I have tried to discuss these in simple non technical language—and for this reason may well be accused of being superficial: but I have throughout included references for further reading, knowing that many of the papers, being in medical journals, would not normally be seen by teachers. I set out with the intention of avoiding references to articles or books published more than ten years ago: but I soon found this impossible, for many of the older papers were of fundamental importance.

I wish to thank the innumerable writers of papers and books which I have quoted in this book. I have tried to acknowledge them all, but if I have failed, I am sorry. Finally, I wish to thank the thousands of children, including my own family, who have taught me so much and given me the experience which I have tried to verbalise in this book; and I wish to thank Mrs S. Smart for so carefully and uncomplainingly typing the script.

Sheffield, October 1973

CHAPTER 1
FACTORS WHICH AFFECT THE
CHILD BEFORE BIRTH

INTRODUCTION

Numerous conditions, including well over 50 drugs, may have an adverse effect on the fetus during pregnancy. I shall confine this chapter to conditions which may have a permanent effect on the child, and which are therefore of interest to teachers.

Important factors operating before conception may have a long-lasting effect on the child to come. There are hundreds of *genetic or hereditary diseases*. Many of these, being dependent on both parents having the gene of a particular disease, are 'recessives'. Examples are phenylketonuria and fibrocystic disease of the pancreas. When one child has the disease, there is a one in four chance that other children in the family will have it. Some diseases are sex-linked, being confined to one sex (like haemophilia). Some are dominant, and one in two children will have the disease. More often a child is found to have an abnormality at birth, but there is no previous relevant family history—but it is none the less genetic. There is sometimes a familial tendency to multiple pregnancy (e.g. twins), or to having children of low birth weight. Much of a child's personality and intelligence is genetically determined, though environmental factors are also relevant. Others factors include the intelligence and personality of the parents and their upbringing: for a couple who as children were brought up in happy loving homes are more likely to have happy children than a couple brought up without love. Parents brought up in childhood without love are apt to be unable to give or receive affection, and so their children are apt to be unloved and to react accordingly. Even the method of discipline and punishment used in childhood is liable to affect the next generation: children subjected to corporal punishment are apt to use the same method for their children—using the argument that 'the rod did me no harm'—not realising that the use

1

of the rod on them has made them the sort of parents who want to use the rod on their own children.

I do not propose to enter here into the controversy about the genetics of intelligence and the proportion of intelligence which is inherited and the proportion which is dependent on environment. Burt (1969) pointed out that while the mean IQ of children of professional parents was 120, and that of unskilled manual workers was 100, that of children of unskilled labourers was about 90: and that in the non-manual classes the proportion of children endowed with ability to go to a university is nearly five times as large as that in the manual classes; yet as the manual classes greatly exceed the non-manual classes, the number of children in the manual classes possessing an IQ which should enable them to secure entry to a university is well over five times that of the non-manual classes— yet less than half of the children of the manual classes with a suitable IQ enter for a university.

A psychological factor of importance is the number of years of married life before conception. An only child born after 15 years of married life is apt to be overprotected and spoiled. Other factors of psychological relevance are the age of the parents and the number of other children and the parents' desire for a child of a particular sex. The child of the desired sex may be spoiled and the subject of favouritism, and the child of the undesired sex may be rejected.

THE PLACE IN THE FAMILY

Terman showed that 60 per cent of gifted children, having an IQ score of 140 or more, were first born. Several studies have shown that the IQ score tends to be lower in later born children in large families: but environmental factors may be partly the explanation: for later born children are likely to have less time devoted to them by their mothers, and their mothers are older. It is said that eldest, youngest and only children tend to be more intelligent than intermediate ones (Lynn 1959, Stone 1969). Again, this must be due to environmental circumstances, for it could not be explained on genetic grounds. The mean IQ score of the first born in families of two or three is higher than that of his younger siblings. The higher mean IQ of first born children may be related to social class —couples of the upper classes having smaller families than those of lower classes. In two child families, the mean IQ is higher when there is a longer interval between births. The mean IQ of twins is probably around 95.

It is difficult to draw conclusions from the various studies of the relationship between birth order and psychological features.

SOCIAL FACTORS

Malnutrition in pregnancy is associated with a low birth weight: and the fetus may suffer malnutrition as a result of an inadequate placenta. The number of brain cells in the fetus is determined largely in the latter part of pregnancy, so that malnutrition may permanently affect the child's brain. The smaller of twins has on average a lower IQ than his co-twin, and this may be due partly to the effect of malnutrition in utero. Furthermore, there is a significant correlation between the size of the child at birth and his subsequent weight and height. Postnatal factors are also related to the child's growth.

The older mother is more likely than a young mother to give birth to a mongol, to twins, to a child with hydrocephalus, to a child with hare lip and cleft palate or congenital heart disease. The older father is more likely than a young one to be responsible for the birth of a child with achondroplasia (dwarfism), a particular deformity of the skull (craniostenosis) or congenital deafness.

The spacing of births is of some importance. The shorter the gap between births, the greater the likelihood of jealousy. Twins are particularly liable to be seriously jealous of each other. It is said that the narrower the gap between births, the lower is the mean IQ of the younger child.

The mean birth weight of children of mothers who smoke during pregnancy is less than those of non-smokers: and children of women who smoke tend to be smaller in the early school years than those of non-smokers.

The mean IQ of children in large families is said to be less than that of children of small families: but it is difficult to equate other social factors which might be responsible for this.

Obvious social factors which may have long term effects on the child are illegitimacy, or forced marriage because of premarital conception. The age of marriage is also relevant: one in four women marrying between the ages of 16 and 18 are divorced by the

20th anniversary, while the figure for those marrying between 23 and 27 is 1 in 16.

There are some surprising seasonal, geographical and racial factors relevant to the child. There is an increased incidence of spina bifida in spring and summer conceptions; in Finland fewer twins are conceived in the winter and more in the summer: there is a seasonal factor in the case of congenital dislocation of the hip and congenital heart disease. In America a hot summer is followed by a slightly increased incidence of births of children who will turn out to have schizophrenia. There is a marked geographical variation in the case of some diseases: the incidence of anencephaly (the birth of a grossly defective baby) is 50 times greater in Belfast than in Lyons. There are considerable racial differences in the incidence of spina bifida, polydactyly and other deformities.

INFECTIONS IN PREGNANCY

Though it had long been known that maternal syphilis if untreated would infect the child, modern knowledge of the importance of prenatal infections stemmed from the observation that cataracts in children may be related to rubella (German measles) in early pregnancy. It is now known that when a mother develops rubella in the first three months of pregnancy, there is an approximately 1 in 4 or 1 in 5 risk that the child will have an abnormality —a cataract, congenital heart disease, deafness, mental subnormality, hepatitis, purpura or certain other conditions. The earlier in pregnancy the infection occurs, the greater the risk to the fetus. After the fourth month of pregnancy, there is hardly any risk to the fetus. It commonly happens that only one of these abnormalities is found: sometimes the only abnormality is partial deafness in one ear, not recognised until school age: but some children are less fortunate, and have a combination of abnormalities. The reason why these abnormalities occur in combination is that the eye, the ear and the heart are all developing at the same time in early pregnancy, and the rubella virus may damage all three. (In the case of thalidomide children, the limb buds are being formed between the 26th and 33rd day after conception, and thalidomide taken by the mother at that time damaged the limb buds and so led to limb deformities.) A baby born with the rubella syndrome excretes the virus for up to a year, and so is infectious; the virus has been isolated from a cataract several months after birth.

Other viruses causing illness in early pregnancy rarely have any lasting effect on the fetus—though some cause abortion. Toxoplasmosis, a protozoal infection common in all domestic animals and an infection which most of us have experienced without knowing it, may affect the fetus if the mother acquires it in early pregnancy: it causes hydrocephalus, mental deficiency and eye changes in the child. Another ubiquitous virus which may cause serious defects in the fetus is the cytomegalovirus. Certain other viruses—such as smallpox, vaccinia, chickenpox or poliomyelitis may infect the fetus. A child may be born with certain infections, such as syphilis, tuberculosis or malaria, in addition to the infections mentioned above.

Various hormones from the endocrine glands pass through the placenta into the fetus. Babies of diabetic mothers are usually unduly large, and are liable to have a low blood sugar and low blood calcium in the newborn period: disturbances of the thyroid or parathyroid gland in the mother may affect the baby: and most full term babies, boys and girls, have some enlargement of the breast, as a result of hormones received from the mother, while girls may have bleeding from the vagina a few days after birth for the same reason.

Numerous drugs taken by the mother may adversely affect the fetus. This matter is so important, and so many drugs may affect the fetus that a woman should avoid all medicines in pregnancy unless they are essential. Even salicyclates (such as aspirin) can occasionally do harm. Many drugs have no specific effect, and may cause a variety of anomalies: others may have a selective effect, like thalidomide, which predominantly affected the growth of the limbs, though it did affect other parts of the body as well. Phenytoin (used for epilepsy) slightly increases the risk of a cleft palate. Several drugs (such as sulphonamides, phenothiazines or salicylates) may sometimes cause jaundice: some drugs, such as antiepileptic drugs, tolbutamide (used for diabetes), thiazide diuretics and anticoagulant drugs may cause haemorrhages in the fetus: some drugs (for instance streptomycin, gentamicin, kanamycin) may cause deafness: chloroquine or chlorpromazine may damage the eyes; antidiabetic drugs may cause a dangerous lowering of the blood sugar in the fetus so that at birth the baby needs urgent treatment: tetracycline will make the baby's teeth yellow when they erupt: drugs taken to reduce the blood pressure may affect the fetus: drugs taken for thyroid disease may give the baby a goitre: corticosteroids present possible dangers to the fetus: certain hormone preparations, notably progestagens, or the contraceptive pill inadvertently taken during pregnancy may cause abnormalities of the female genitalia: vitamin excesses may damage the fetus: and drugs of addiction may have a serious effect, for the baby is born drug dependent. At birth he is suddenly withdrawn from the supply of the drug which he has been receiving in utero, and suffers serious withdrawal symptoms requiring expert treatment. Heroin taken by the mother lowers the birth weight, and the child may have extreme irritability and fits: cannabis may cause limb deformities: morphine addiction may cause a low birth weight and fits. Methadone causes respiratory depression: the symptoms of this and barbiturate addiction may be delayed for two or three days after birth. During labour all general anaesthetics pass to, and affect, the fetus: all analgesic drugs given to the mother have some depressant action on the respiratory centre of the baby. This is a mere brief outline: many other drugs may affect the fetus: and as I stated earlier drugs are best avoided in pregnancy unless they are essential. Nevertheless it must be emphasised that in *most* cases the drugs mentioned carry only a very small risk of affecting the fetus: the facts outlined were unearthed only by extensive statistical studies of large numbers of women and children. For use in experimental pregnant animals there are over 1,500 known teratogens.

Irradiation of the maternal pelvis in pregnancy may damage the fetal brain. Children born by women who were in early pregnancy at the time of the atomic explosions in Japan, and who were within a certain distance from the epicentre, were mentally defective. It is calculated that irradiation is responsible for about 10 per cent of all childhood malignant disease.

Maternal toxaemia and high blood pressure have been said by some to carry a slight risk of persistent abnormalities in the child, including tics and overactivity at school age: but when other variables have been equated—birth order and social class—it is probably insignificant. It has been claimed that severe myopia (short sightedness) in children is related to a history of pregnancy toxaemia. If the mother has phenylketonuria (an inborn error of metabolism) the fetal brain is damaged and the child is likely to be mentally subnormal, though dietary treatment in pregnancy may possibly prevent this.

There is an important relationship between pre-term birth (prematurity) and certain features of later childhood. The cause of premature delivery is not always understood; but it may be due to toxaemia, multiple pregnancy (twins etc.) or illnesses during pregnancy, particularly infectious diseases and thyroid disease, and may be genetic.

Social factors related to premature labour and to the delivery of a low birth weight fetus include smoking in pregnancy, poverty, malnutrition, and work late in pregnancy. Women under 20 and over 34 are more likely than others to produce low birth weight babies, as are women with a low IQ and mothers of illegitimate babies; but social factors are intermingled; for instance, women of low social class tend to have a low IQ and to have larger families. Heroin addiction is in some countries a major cause of low birth weight. Sometimes labour is induced because of pelvic disproportion or maternal disease. One must not ascribe a child's poor performance at school to prematurity: one has to look further back to the physical and social factors which caused the prematurity and to environmental variables after birth, especially that associated with a low social class. A prematurely born baby is more delicate for the first three years than a full term baby: and for this and prenatal reasons he is apt to be overprotected by his mother and so to have related behaviour problems.

The pre-term baby is more likely than the full-term baby to have physical and mental handicaps. He is five or six times more likely to have cerebral palsy—and the smaller his birth weight the greater the risk. A baby with a birth weight of 1250g has about a one in two chance of being spastic, though not necessarily seriously so. The smaller the baby is at birth the lower the mean IQ. Drillien (1963) followed 110 babies who weighed 3lb (1360g) or less, 72 of them for over five years: one third were unsuitable for school, one third of those in an ordinary school were retarded, and a third were doing work appropriate to their age. At school 70 per cent were unusually restless and overactive; of 51 with siblings, 76 per cent were intellectually inferior to their full-term brothers or sisters. Twins fared less well than singletons.

She eliminated the possibility that the poor performance of

those prematurely born could be due to social factors. Takkunen *et al.* (1965) found that the mean IQ of 110 children who at birth had weighed 1750g or less was 94·8. Dann, Levine and New (1964) found the same mean IQ, 94·8, in 100 children who had weighed 1000g or less, while that of their siblings was 106·9. Douglas (1960) followed 400 prematurely born children for 8 years and 350 for 11 years. In all respects the prematurely born children fared less well than controls. The factors studied included powers of concentration, attitude to work and response to discipline. He equated social variables in the two groups. Weiner *et al.* (1968) compared, at the age of eight to ten years, 417 children of low birth weight with 405 children born at term, using 10 subtests of the Wechsler intelligence test for children, eliminating the variables of social class and parental attitudes. The ex-premature babies scored less well on all the tests. Lubchenko and colleagues (1972) found that of 133 infants weighing 1500g or less at birth, 66 per cent at the age of 10 years had handicaps, half of them moderate or severe; 85 per cent of the smallest babies were handicapped. Churchill *et al.* (1966) showed that 51 children with mental subnormality had had a significantly lower birth weight than 51 children with an IQ of 110 or more, matched for sex, age, social class and area of residence. It is thought that with improved methods of management the outlook for the small preterm baby is now better than it was some ten years ago.

Babson and colleagues (1969) found that girls weighing 9lb or more at birth, and boys weighing 9lb 6oz or more at birth, had a lower mean IQ on follow up than did children of average birth weight. It has been shown that the mean IQ of children who were post-mature babies is less than the average.

There is no certain evidence that *psychological stress* during pregnancy may affect the fetus, but it certainly does in the case of experimental animals in which it has been produced in a variety of ways, including overcrowding or conditioning processes prior to pregnancy. Ader (1971) reviewing the problem, wrote that 'although the experimental analysis of prenatal effects is a complex affair, these prospective studies on animals provide ample evidence that prenatal factors are capable of modifying behavioural and physiological development as well as subsequent psychophysiologic function'. Stott (1962) reviewed the relationship of stress in pregnancy to delinquency and other problems in later childhood.

Others have related stress in pregnancy to low birth weight or schizophrenia in the children. Joffe (1969) wrote a good critical review of experimental work in animals and of studies on human beings, and described the difficulties in interpreting the studies.

If a mother has a really *difficult pregnancy*, with troublesome prolonged vomiting or toxaemia, or a difficult labour, her attitude to the child, whom she may regard as the cause of all the trouble, may be different from that of a mother who has an easy, normal pregnancy and labour. The former may have a subconscious attitude of rejection. Alternatively, if a woman has a difficult pregnancy, resulting in medical advice that she should not become pregnant again, she may well overprotect and overindulge the child. Interpretation is difficult, because of all the variables. If a woman has a psychological disturbance in pregnancy, and her child subsequently exhibits psychological symptoms, it is impossible to prove that the psychological disturbances in the child are not due to an inherited personality trait.

I have discussed elsewhere the problems of 'birth injury' and 'brain damage'. I have emphasized that far too many abnormalities in children's behaviour or brain functioning are ascribed to 'birth injury' without adequate thought. I have pointed out that an abnormal presentation at birth, such as a breech delivery, cannot confidently be considered to be the cause of a child's abnormality: one should look behind the factor at birth to the factors which caused the abnormal presentation, the prematurity, the anoxia. In the case of a breech delivery, the usual cause is the fact that the child is 'small for dates'—and that implies that something has adversely affected the fetus in utero: it is that something which is the likely cause of the defect in the child.

SUMMARY

Numerous factors affect a child before birth—many of the factors operating before conception: these include hereditary and psychological factors.

Significant factors during pregnancy include social conditions, nutrition, smoking, drugs taken by the mother, infections in pregnancy, toxaemia, and conditions causing prematurity or postmaturity.

REFERENCES

ADER R. (1971) in STOELINGA G.B.A. & VAN DER WERFF TEN BOSCH J.J. (eds). *Normal and Abnormal Development of Brain and Behaviour.* Leiden University Press.

BABSON S.G., HENDERSON N. & CLARK W.M. (1969) Preschool intelligence of oversized newborns. *Pediatrics,* **44**, 536.

BARKER D.J.P. (1966) Low intelligence and obstetric complications. *Brit.J.Prev. and Soc.Med.* **20**, 15.

BURT C. (1969) Intelligence and heredity. *New Scientist,* **42**, 226.

CHURCHILL J.A., NEFF J.W. & CALDWELL D.F. (1966) Birth weight and intelligence. *Obstet. and Gynec.* **28**, 425.

DANN M., LEVINE S.Z., NEW E.V. (1964) A long term follow up of small premature infants. *Pediatrics,* **33**, 945.

DOUGLAS J.W.B. (1960) Premature children at primary schools. *Brit.Med.J.* **1**, 1008.

DRILLIEN C.M. (1963) *The Growth and Development of the Prematurely Born Infant.* Edinburth, Churchill/Livingstone.

JOFFE J.M. (1969) *Prenatal Determinants of Behaviour.* Oxford, Pergamon.

LUBCHENCO L., DELIVORIA-PAPADOPOULOS M., BUTTERFIELD L.J., FRENCH J.H. METCALFE D., HIX I.E., DANICK J., DODDS J., DOWNS M. & FREELAND E. (1972) Long term follow up studies of prematurely born infants. *J.Pediat.* **80**, 501, 509.

LYNN R. (1959) Environmental conditions affecting intelligence. *Educ.Res.* **1**, 49.

STONE F.H. (1969) Birth order, intelligence and personality. *Develop.Med. Child.Neurol.* **11**, 647.

STOTT D.H. (1962) Abnormal mothering as a cause of mental abnormality. *J.Child.Psychol.* **3**, 79.

TAKKUNEN R.L., FRISK M. & HOLMSTRÖM G. (1965) Follow up examination of 110 small prematures at the age of 6–7 years. *Acta.Paediat.Scand.*, Suppl. 159, p. 70.

WEINER G., RIDER R.V., OPPEL W.C. & HARPER P.A. (1968). Prematures. Correlates of low birth weight. Psychological states at eight to ten years of age. *Pediatric Research,* **2**, 110.

CHAPTER 2
THE BASIS OF BEHAVIOUR

Why is he like he is? Many teachers must ask themselves (and their colleagues) this question about some of their badly behaved or peculiar pupils. In this chapter I shall attempt to supply some of the answers: it is intended to serve as a basis for the chapter to follow, in which I discuss individual behaviour problems. In the previous chapter I have described prenatal factors which affect the child. In this chapter I shall discuss factors after birth which affect the child's later behaviour.

A child's personality and intelligence is partly inherited and partly the product of his environment. A child's behaviour problems arise from a conflict between his ego, developing mind and personality and the personality and attitudes of his parents—and perhaps of his peers and teachers. Life would be easier for many children and many parents if difficult parents were to beget only placid easy going children—but that would be inherently unlikely. Life would be easier in school if difficult teachers had as pupils only placid easy going children.

There are many features of the developing child which cause annoyance or even infuriate their parents. The young child's negativism, aggressiveness, quarrelsomeness, fighting with his siblings, noisiness, untidiness, carelessness with his clothes, over-activity, inability to sit still, disregard for truth, apparently unreasonable jealousy, utter selfishness, lack of sense of time, dawdling, wailing, attention seeking, constant questioning and failure to see that his mother is tired (or that his father wants to read the newspaper and relax after a day's work) all lead to friction and annoy their parents. Mothers become annoyed and irritable when they are hurried or worried or tired or anaemic or unwell or have premenstrual tension. When tired they become less tolerant and lose their sense of humour, snapping at their children or reprimanding them, so that their behaviour becomes worse rather than better. Some people when feeling irritable deliberately provoke—so that they can convince themselves that it is not they who are in the wrong but the other person, who rose to their provocation. Some people when feeling irritable enjoy a fight. A mother with a difficult personality trait is apt to be particularly irked by that same personality trait in her adolescent.

There are many problems of childhood which are basically genetic, but which for their development depend on an environmental trigger. Asthma is due partly to an inherited tendency to allergy, but attacks are precipitated by infection or psychological factors. Migraine is largely a genetic condition, but various environmental factors, including articles of diet, fatigue or emotion may precipitate attacks. Schizophrenia is partly genetic in origin, but environmental factors may precipitate its development. Stott (1962) gave evidence that psychological stress in pregnancy may predispose a child to react to an adverse environment by delinquency.

THE MOTHER'S LOVE FOR HER CHILD

It is almost superfluous to say that the great majority of parents love their children: but not all do. The problem of child abuse is an increasing one. Ten thousand cases were reported in the United States in 1969.

In a symposium on child abuse (baby battering) (Solomon *et al.* 1973) it was found that most battering parents had themselves been battered; and that the parents had themselves almost invariably suffered a 'disastrous rearing experience'. Features in the background of child abuse were premarital conception, youthful marriage, unwanted pregnancy, illegitimacy, forced marriage, social and kinship isolation, emotional problems in marriage and financial difficulty.

PARENTAL ATTITUDES

It has already been suggested that some parental attitudes to a child are attitudes present long before his birth and often before his conception. After birth his mother's attitude to him may be affected by his appearance and his behaviour in the newborn period, or by his sex, if he is not of the sex desired. In the animal kingdom animals examine their young at birth and leave the abnormal ones to die. Sheep do this. Seals protect their normal young but make no attempt to prevent their abnormal young being washed away by the sea. One has seen babies with a hare lip or other deformities rejected by the mother or father. If a normal looking baby cries excessively, and is difficult to feed, his mother may react adversely to him and develop a degree of subconscious rejection which she will feel towards him for years. If animals are separated from their mother immediately they are born, before the mother has licked them, they are rejected by their mother. The goat, for instance, will kick the kid to death even though it has been returned to her three or four hours after birth. When a child has to be kept separate from his mother for a few weeks after birth, because of a serious defect, his mother may reject him when he is returned to her.

OVERANXIETY AND OVERPROTECTION

Overanxiety and overprotection, though not synonymous, are closely similar attitudes which overlap and so may be discussed together. They are very common. They are due to various factors. If the mother greatly wanted the child, and had bleeding during pregnancy, or other serious illness threatening the child's life, or if the child were born prematurely, she is apt to be overanxious about him in his early years. If he is an only child, especially if she is elderly or has lost her husband, or for other reasons she cannot have another child, she is likely to be unduly anxious about him. Overanxiety can be due to the death of a previous child or to the child having had a serious illness; or it can be caused by the child's suffering from a troublesome complaint such as asthma, or having been conceived accidentally or otherwise long after the other children have grown up: and there may be anxiety because there is a hereditary disease in the family. It may be due simply to the fact that the child is of the desired sex after a succession of children of the opposite sex. It may be due to the mother being unhappy with her husband, and so depending on her child for the affection which she so much wants. Psychiatrists say that overanxiety occurs because the mother had an unhappy childhood, or because the parents are rejecting the child and conceal their rejection by over-protecting him. Almost all children with a mental or physical handicap are overprotected by their parents—or at least by their mother.

Overanxiety about a child is shown in health and disease. The mother is constantly afraid of him catching cold, saying to him, 'Don't catch cold,' as if by a feat of the will he can keep the virus away from his nose: she says, 'Don't get your feet wet'—as if in some remarkable way wet feet would enable the virus to settle in his respiratory tract. For the same reason she will not allow him to swim. She obtains permission for him to be excused from games, ostensibly because he is delicate, but in fact because she is afraid that he will get hurt, and she gets him excused from physical exercise for the same reason. She keeps him indoors if it is cold or wet or misty. She fusses over every trivial symptom. She is worried about his bowels. I have seen several children aged six to eleven who were never at home allowed to go to the lavatory alone: they had to use a potty in the bedroom so that the mother could see whether they had passed enough. The mother takes the child to school, long after he is old enough to go alone or with friends. Like G.K. Chesterton's mother she will not let him choose his own friends; or she vets the books which he wants to read or the films which he wants to see. Like the mother of John Ruskin or Orde Wingate, she may even keep him away from school so as to prevent him becoming contaminated by other children. A mother of an eleven-year-old girl told me that she never let the girl go out to play with her friends in case she should pick up the Sheffield accent. I knew a doctor and a dentist who as children had their temperature taken every night for 15 years in case they had an infection. Some parents help the child every night with his homework. If he criticises other children or his teachers they always support him without hearing the other side of the story. When he has any difficulty they rush to help him and convince him that he cannot do things for himself, and that there is no need for him to try. In front of him they tell the teacher how sensitive, how highly strung he is. Every morning the mother dresses him to get ready for school—when he is six, eight or even ten years old. She gives him too much pocket money, so that he never fails to have anything that he wants. She does everything possible to secure his approval.

She fails to realise that it is a disaster to protect a child from all stress. John Ruskin's parents were determined to bring John up without any stress and he was never allowed to go to school. His mother deliberately deprived him of all pleasure; if he were given toys, she immediately confiscated them. When finally he went to Oxford his mother went to live there, leaving her husband in London, in order that she could see John every day to make sure that he was well. John grew up to be a psychopath: he could not enjoy sex: he became insane. Even experimental animals, such as mice or dogs, if prevented from taking part in aggressive play in the early hours after birth do not know later what to do when attacked. It is the natural reaction of parents to separate their small children when they are fighting or quarrelling or being rude to each other, instead of leaving them to reach agreement amongst themselves. It is a mistake, for they are learning at home something which otherwise they or only children have to learn painfully when they start school. Overprotection at home is a potent cause of unpopularity at school. Children as they grow older need to be allowed to make decisions for themselves—and to make mistakes, so that they can learn from their experience. It is one thing to protect them from serious accidents, which they are not mature enough to anticipate: it is another thing to prevent them experiencing any trivial discomfort which would teach them to be more careful, to learn the consequences of foolhardiness.

ATTITUDE TO ILLNESS

The parents' attitude to illness is of the greatest importance to the welfare of their children. The whole of a person's attitude to illness is established in childhood. If parents overprotect their child, and show and express anxiety about every trivial symptom which their child has, putting him to bed, calling the doctor in, giving him medicines and keeping him away from school without any good reason, they are doing their child great harm. They magnify his symptoms and enable him to dominate the household thereby: he uses his symptoms to attract attention, to get his own way, to evade unpleasant tasks. Parents who have a fetish about their own health, who constantly moan about their own symptoms, and absent themselves from work for trivial reasons, and who watch their childrens' bowel actions, are encouraging their children to be neurotics and hypochondriacs, who, apart from anything else, come to disregard the value of education. The behaviour of parents when they are ill, or think they are ill, has a profound effect on their children's behaviour, and it is an effect from which they may suffer for the rest of their life. Parents should minimise symptoms instead of exaggerating them: they must strike a balance between unkindness and lack of sympathy on the one hand, and over-anxiety and over-solicitude on the other.

A child with neurotic symptoms almost always has a neurotic parent. His personality is partly inherited: but he is brought up in an atmosphere of neurosis in which his neurotic parent constantly talks about her or his symptoms, and above all, exaggerates every trivial discomfort. In addition the neurotic parent is apt to show overanxiety about the child. Consciously or subconsciously he imitates his parent. If a father constantly moans about his stomach pains, his daughter may directly imitate him and complain herself, or, more likely, fear that she will have the same symptoms—and does.

It is not only in neurosis that the child takes after his parent: in cases of more serious psychological disturbance one commonly finds a family history of the same complaint. One in five of new child patients at the Maudsley Hospital had a mentally ill parent. Some mental conditions, such as schizophrenia or manic-depressive psychoses, are inherited.

OTHER ATTITUDES

Perfectionism is a harmful attitude. It is apt to be associated with excessive discipline and to lead to insecurity and unhappiness. A parent may be determined that his or her child will be perfect, and then, as years go by, and imperfections inevitably manifest themselves, he or she may show disappointment in no uncertain way, almost rejecting the child (now an adolescent).

Tolerance and understanding of a child's developing mind are of great importance: ignorance of the normality of such traits as negativism from the age of one to three, with a recurrence in early adolescence, leads to serious difficulties and friction. Acceptance of this trait, combined with a good sense of humour, enables the phase to pass without trouble. G.K. Chesterton wrote that the only man who understood him as a child was his tailor, who knew to measure him afresh each time he needed a new suit.

A *puritanical attitude* to sex is apt to have unfortunate consequences. It may lead to homosexuality, ridicule at school for outmoded ideas, and later failure to marry: or rebellion and sexual excess.

Favouritism is a most unfortunate parental attitude. Its causes are varied. Each parent may have his own favourite. The girl is often the father's favourite, and the boy the mother's favourite. If there is a third child, he is favoured by neither, and is liable to be jealous and insecure. A child may be favoured because he is of the desired sex, or good looking, or more clever than the others, or has a more affectionate personality. A mentally or physically handicapped child is extremely apt to be the subject of favouritism: it makes the other children jealous, and 'spoils' the handicapped one. The favoured child gets his own way more than the others. If he gets into trouble with one parent, the favouring parent comes to his defence, for the child can do no wrong. He gets away with acts for which his siblings are reprimanded. He is given more presents. His parent shows more interest in what he says and what he achieves. The parent does not know that he is showing favouritism: he does not show it deliberately; but it is obvious to everyone else, and particularly to the unfavoured ones. It leads to friction and jealousy in the home. When adolescence is reached and independence is acquired, the unfavoured one grows away from the parent. Serious favouritism by the mother towards her boy is apt to lead to mother fixation and even homosexual tendencies, particularly if the father is weak and ineffective.

SOME OTHER FEATURES IN THE PARENTS

The example set by the parents in innumerable walks of life has a profound effect on the child. Parents who are unkind to each other, especially in front of the child, or who quarrel openly or show hatred to each other, must realise that their behaviour will inevitably have an adverse effect on their child. Children are imitators and are sensitive to atmosphere in the home. One sees children who have attacks of asthma or migraine when they have witnessed domestic disharmony. If parents fail to show love, honesty, unselfishness and politeness to each other and to their children, they cannot expect anything different from their children. If parents feel unable to apologise for loss of temper, they cannot expect their children to do so. If they are insensitive to people's feelings, or to their children's feelings, their children are likely to show the same traits when they grow up. If parents show intolerance towards others, constantly criticise and are foolish in their spending, if they in their conversation denigrate religion, honesty and kindness, they are setting a bad example to their children. It is at home that children learn what is right or wrong, honest or dishonest, kind or unkind.

Parents may be jealous of each other, and often are. A mother may envy her child because he seems to get everything he wants and to have everything done for him, and to get out and enjoy himself whenever he wants, while she is tied to the house. She was perhaps an only child, while she sees her children go out and play together and enjoy themselves in a way which she never could.

Parents feel thwarted at features of the child which they are unable to control. They cannot make the child eat, go to sleep, use the potty, stop twitching the face, sit still or tidy up, and they feel annoyed and upset.

A mother who temporarily or permanently gives up her professional career to look after her small children may feel lonely, bored and thwarted, and becomes irritable. This in turn has a bad affect on her children.

Parental attitudes are not deliberate. They are unintentional. They arise from the subconscious mind. As Leo Kanner, American psychiatrist wrote, they are the crystallisation of their life experience. Noxious attitudes are expressions of their emotional difficulties. They cannot help having these attitudes and personality problems and doctors and teachers must avoid blaming them for them; after all, the parents inherited much of their personality from their parents, and acquired other features of their personality in their own childhood.

THE CHILD'S NEED FOR LOVE AND SECURITY

All children need above all love and security. They need to be loved, and to feel loved, wanted and important. As babies they need to have their basic needs for comfort met. After infancy they want to be accepted, and understood. When children are behaving badly, when they are at their worst, when they are most unlovable, it is then that they most need loving.

Children are made to feel insecure in many different ways. They may be unwanted and rejected, cruelly treated and just unloved. A parent may feel and show positive dislike to one of his children. They may be loved by their parents but for various reasons they do not feel loved—or they do not feel wanted and important. They are upset by criticism, sarcasm, disparagement, derogation, disapproval. They are upset by constant reprimands—and in many homes every day is one long day of remonstrances. Determined efforts to teach discipline, particularly before the child is ready to learn, may lead to insecurity and many resulting problems. In some homes every mealtime is a time of misery for the child: he receives constant admonitions about the use of his knife and fork, about the noise he makes when eating or drinking, or about not sitting still, or about putting his elbows on the table. Children are upset by 'comparisons' and labels—by being told that they are not as kind, or as clever or as useful in the house as an older brother or sister. They are seriously upset by favouritism. It is not enough for a parent to love his child: he must show it. He shows it—or the lack of it—by his facial expression, his tone of voice, even the speed with which he talks. When one talks to a parent about an insecure child's needs, the parent commonly says, 'He is certainly loved. He gets everything which he asks for, everything that money can buy.' But what he wants most is something which money cannot buy. He feels unloved—and when he is punished for something which he has done—usually for something which he could not help, or could not know was wrong, he is all the more convinced that he is not loved. Frequent punishment is a potent cause of insecurity. Lasting love is made up of hundreds of little kindnesses, hundreds of occasions when tolerance and understanding are shown: but when those occasions are missing, children as they get older are likely to grow apart from their parents. Oscar Wilde remarked that children begin by loving their parents: as they grow older, they judge them: sometimes they forgive them. The book by Virginia Axline (1971) entitled *Dibs* gives a vivid account of the profound effect of rejection on a highly intelligent boy. In our book *Lessons from Childhood*, in which we described the early life of famous men and women, we gave several examples of the lasting effect of cruelty in childhood; we mentioned in particular Maxim Gorky, Ivan Turgonev and Martin Luther. Anton Chekhov wrote about the cruelty which he experienced as a child: and added that

B

as an adult he would like to be kind to people but did not know how to be.

A child may feel insecure because he is made to attend a nursery school before he is ready for it. He may feel insecure because of moves from one house to another—and later because of repeated moves to different schools. At school he may feel insecure because of unsuitable clothing, or because of teasing or bullying by other children, or because of the unkindness of a teacher. When he changes for gym or sport he may be embarrassed because of early or late puberty. He may worry because in physical exercise he is ridiculed by the teacher for his clumsiness. In some schools children are weighed publicly at the beginning of term, and the figures are announced for all to hear: an obese child is upset by this. Others are upset because examination marks are read out. Others are told in public that their poor results are due to the fact that they are not working hard enough—when the child knows that he has worked hard, but there are other reasons out of his control which explain his poor performance. Children have a strong sense of what is fair or unfair and unjust. In some schools there is a lack of sensitivity to children's feelings.

Much has been written about the psychological effect of separation of the child from his mother in his first three years. Prolonged separation at this time has been found to correlate with delinquency, and with inability to give or receive affection in adult life. One repeatedly sees children who are rejected by the mother or father, who themselves had an unhappy childhood without love. Emotional deprivation in childhood is liable to affect the next generation. There is some evidence that the child most needs his father after the age of five, and that prolonged absence of the father after that age correlates with juvenile delinquency. Various studies of suicides, drug addicts and alcoholics have shown a high incidence of loss of parents by divorce, death or other means.

Children may suffer because the mother is out at work all day, and they are either left alone in the house, or, when older, come home from school and have to wait outside for the mother to come back from work. Provided that small children are left in charge of a granny or someone who loves them, no harm to the children is likely to accrue. Yudkin and Holme (1963) in their book on the subject wrote that the relevant factors were the age of the child, the duration and frequency of the mother's absences from home, the number of hours spent by the children each day away from the mother, the arrangements for the care of the child, the presence of siblings, the social class, the occurrence of previous separations, the physical conditions in the home and the overall environment. If proper arrangements were made, the authors found little or no evidence of emotional trauma to the children. Douglas and Blomfield (1958) formed the same conclusions. George Bernard Shaw wrote that he never forgot 'the misery of his childhood or his mother's responsibility for it. I would say that she was the worst mother conceivable. We children were abandoned entirely to servants who were entirely unfit to be trusted with the charge of three cats, much less of three children'.

Some mothers have to work when their children are small, for financial reasons. Others understandably do not want to give up their professional life when they have a family. It is difficult for a woman after a 10-year absence from her profession to pick up the threads and resume her work. When prevented from pursuing her profession she is apt, as already stated, to feel thwarted and bored and unhappy—and if she does, this will have a bad effect on her children—and cause insecurity. She may feel guilty about working and leaving her children during the day; but opinions are changing and it is becoming more acceptable for the mother to continue her career when she has children (Wallston 1973). The problem was reviewed by Howell (1973) in a paper with 116 references. The general conclusion was similar to that of Yudkin and Holme (1963) —namely that provided that there is proper substitute care, little harm will result; but that harm will be done if the mother gives up her career and feels thwarted and discontented. Some mothers do not go out to work, but are so heavily occupied with charity and other good works that they have no time for their family, and the children suffer (Gavron 1966).

Emotional deprivation, whatever the cause, is said to affect linguistic skill and acquired knowledge least, and abstract thought most. Ainsworth (1962) showed that deprivation in the first year affects language and abstract functioning more than deprivation in later years. Prugh and Harlow (1967) wrote that recovery from a single brief depriving experience is prompt, but gives vulnerability to future threats of separation. 'Prolonged and severe deprivation beginning early in the first year, and continuing for as long as three years, usually leads to severe effects in both intellectual and

personality function that resist reversal.' Prolonged separation
beginning in the second year may lead to grave personality defects.
They found that impairment in language, in abstraction and in the
capacity for strong and lasting interpersonal attachments, were less
reversible than other problems. Severe emotional deprivation is
one of the causes of defective physical growth.

Various circumstances may lead to emotional deprivation and
therefore to insecurity. They include illegitimacy, institutional
care, divorce and the mother being at work. There are about
75,000 illegitimate births per year in Britain. Ninety thousand
babies (1 in 4 firstborns) are born within eight months of marriage.
In the United States 65,000 babies per year are born to unmarried
girls of 17 or less. Though illegitimacy *per se* does not necessarily
cause insecurity and emotional problems, it may do. A baby
adopted in the early weeks of life suffers no emotional trauma: but
less than a quarter of illegitimate babies are adopted (Dewar 1968).
(Famous persons who were illegitimate included Boccaccio,
Erasmus, Leonardo da Vinci, Borodin, Cezanne, Edgar Wallace,
Ernest Bevin, Sarah Bernhardt, Chancellor Dollfuss and Lawrence
of Arabia.) Approximately 27,000 children are adopted in this
country each year—about three per cent of all live born babies.
Eighty per cent of them are illegitimate though 70 per cent of
illegitimate children are not adopted. Between 30 and 40 per cent
of adoptions are by a parent or relatives. An increasing number of
unmarried mothers are keeping their children: the implications for
the emotional development of the child are obvious. He is brought
up in a fatherless family—and often as an only child. There are
special problems of adoption, including those of religion, colour
and mental or physical handicap—all with possible emotional
difficulties for the child.

In Britain there are about 71,000 children at any one time 'in
care'—either because they have no home of their own, or because
the parents are unfit or unable to look after them. Each year about
50,000 children are taken into care, largely because of the mother's
confinement or illness. There is a strong association between such
short term care and antisocial behaviour (Wolkind 1973).

Bereavement presents severe emotional problems to children.
A study of adult mental patients revealed that a significantly
greater number than controls had lost a parent in their first six
years.

The effect of divorce on children has been the subject of several papers (Brun 1964, Sugar 1970). In this country about one in four teenage marriages when the bride is pregnant end in divorce. (The overall figure for divorce in Britain is 9 per cent.) In the United States the divorce rate has greatly increased in the last 30 years: in 1960 there were 393,000 divorces involving 463,000 children, and in 1967 the number of divorces was 523,000, involving 700,000 children. Approximately 1 in 3 American marriages now ends in divorce. In the United Kingdom the number of divorces in 1958 was 22,000, but in 1968 it was 45,000, and involved 60,000 children (*British Medical Journal* 1971). A leading article in the same journal in 1972 declared that 'if present trends continue, 1 in 4 marriages beginning in 1972 will break up irretrievably before the children of that marriage have left school'. In Egypt in 1970 there were 325,000 marriages and 700,000 divorces.

It is not only divorce in itself, with consequent loss of a parent, which upsets the child. It is the preceding domestic friction, and the succeeding attitudes of the parent who is in charge of the children. Rutter (1971) found that separation from the family is a potential cause of short term distress, but little cause of long term disorder. Later antisocial behaviour is more due to family discord preceding and accompanying the separation. Children may feel that they are the cause of the divorce. A mother given custody of the children may constantly show her bitterness against her husband, depicting him as a monster, and overprotect and spoil the children (Bernstein and Robey 1962). Being anxious to retain her children's affections she showers them with gifts and gives them everything they ask for, and fails to exert discipline. There are often serious financial problems and housing difficulties. Children are upset about continued strife concerning their custody.

Divorce has been correlated with a high incidence of enuresis, poor behaviour at school, accident proneness, depression, delinquency and other behaviour problems. Other common reactions of children to divorce include guilt feelings, insecurity, self-punishment, fantasy-thinking and day-dreaming, and a variety of psychosomatic symptoms such as asthma (Brun 1964). Prugh and Harlow (1962) found that the results depend on the nature and duration of the discord, the age and stage of development of the child, and the quality of mothering before and after the divorce. Bernstein and Robey (1962) showed that boys brought up without fathers develop masculine traits more slowly. Biller (1971) in his review of studies concerning the effect of separation from the father, wrote that the principle factors were the timing and duration of the absence, the availability of father-substitutes, the environment and the attitude of the mother who may overprotect her son. Prolonged absence of the father before the age of four or five is apt to make the boy less masculine—and so affect his ability to make friendships at school.

A wide variety of behaviour problems is related to insecurity. They include excessive fear, timidity, shyness, weeping, jealousy, clinging to the mother, bedwetting, faecal incontinence, head banging, tics, nail biting, stuttering, hostility, aggressiveness, destructiveness, stealing, school phobia and truancy.

THE EGO

From the age of six months the child reveals his developing ego: bound up with it is the normal negativism reaching its peak between one and three years of age, with a recurrence in early adolescence. Determined efforts to make the child of one to three do anything against his will—to eat, go to sleep, use the potty, or to stop thumb sucking—are almost certain to lead to the opposite of the effect desired. He is determined to be recognised as a person of importance, and he wants his own way. He adopts all manner of attention-seeking devices if he does not receive the attention which he wants. If he can get the whole house revolving around what he eats, or around his use of the potty or around his going to sleep, he will love it. If by throwing a good temper tantrum he can get his own way, it will be well worth the energy which he has to put into it. If he can dominate the household by his symptoms or behaviour, he will. The more intelligent the child, the more likely he is to learn ways and means of attracting attention and controlling his parents. Failure to satisfy the child's ego causes insecurity and may lead to any of the many behaviour problems mentioned.

SUGGESTIBILITY AND IMITATIVENESS. HABIT FORMATION

All children are suggestible, and all imitate. If a mother repeatedly says 'is your tummy still hurting you, darling?' it will. All children are imitators: hence the importance of setting a good example.

All children learn habits, good and bad. The brighter they are, the more likely they are to learn habits. Hence parents have to beware of starting bad habits. A good example concerns sleep problems. If a 10-month-old baby discovers that whenever he screams in the evening, he will be picked up and taken downstairs, he will do it every night.

CONDITIONING

All of us become conditioned to a variety of stimuli. If, for instance, we smell delicious coffee when feeling thirsty, our saliva will flow because we have become conditioned to the flow of saliva when taking food. If mealtimes are thoroughly unpleasant for a child, because he is smacked for not eating and forced to take food which he does not want, he is likely to turn against all food and develop a genuine bad appetite. If when the toddler is put on the potty and is compelled to sit on it by brute force when he is trying to get off it, he will turn against the potty and associate the emptying of the bladder or bowel with unpleasantness: and so he refuses to use the potty and withholds his stools, becoming severely constipated as a result.

MATURATION

The child's ability to sit, walk, talk, read, control the bladder or bowel depends largely on maturation of the relevant part of the nervous system. No amount of practice or instruction can cause a child to acquire those skills until the nervous system is ready for it.

A troublesome behaviour problem, overactivity, largely disappears as the child matures.

THE CRITICAL PERIOD

According to Standing (1957) in his biography of Madame Montessori, Hugo de Vries, Dutch biologist, was the first to use the phrase 'sensitive period' in development. By sensitive period one means that stage of a child's development in which a certain stimulus is most able to elicit certain behaviour: and by the term 'critical period' one refers to that stage of development beyond which the stimulus will no longer elicit certain behaviour. There are numerous examples of these critical periods in animals. For instance if a squirrel is not given nuts to crack by a certain age, he will never learn to crack them: if a chimpanzee is not given a whole banana by a certain age, he will never learn to remove the skin.

In human beings there are many comparable examples. It is common knowledge that many highly intelligent adults coming to this country and living here never learn the British accent, while children learn it readily. If a congenital cataract is not removed by a certain age, the child will remain blind. If a cleft palate is not closed by a certain age, speech will remain defective. If a deaf child is not taught to speak by a certain age, it will be extremely difficult to teach him. Madame Montessori's system of education depends on the sensitive period: for instance, she referred to the importance of children being taught colour, sound, shape and texture at the optimum period, $2\frac{1}{2}$ to 6 years. She said that the best age for a child to learn to write is between three and four and a half.

The role of the sensitive or critical period in education is uncertain, but there is good medical evidence that the phenomenon of the critical period, unquestioned in animals, is also applicable to human beings. (See also p. 95.)

ENDOCRINE GLANDS AND BEHAVIOUR

The endocrine glands—the pituitary, the thyroid, the adrenal and the gonads all affect behaviour. Psychological stress alters the level of hydroxyketosteroids in the urine, of growth hormone in the blood, and the plasma cortisol. Children with thyroid deficiency are sleepy and inactive, and those with thyroid excess—thyrotoxicosis—are nervous, trembly and highly strung. If the ovaries are removed from rats, male rats no longer groom them or mate with them, but they do both as soon as the ovariectomised rats are given oestrogens. The normal aggressiveness of male animals is probably due to androgenic hormones, especially testosterone. In experimental animals castration stops aggressiveness and testosterone restores it (Leshner 1973). Removal of the adrenal glands reduces aggressiveness—an action apparently independent of the testes. There are other examples of the effect of hormones from the endocrine glands.

METABOLIC FACTORS AND BEHAVIOUR

If the blood sugar drops to too low a level in a child's blood he is apt to become irritable, bad tempered, aggressive and badly behaved. Many a child returns from school in a thoroughly bad temper. The unwise parent argues with him and reprimands him: the wise parent gives him a meal as soon as possible, knowing that he will be a different child after it.

Phenylketonuria is a hereditary metabolic disorder in which as a result of an enzyme defect there is an excess of the amino acid phenylalanine in the blood. As soon as the high level is reduced by appropriate diet a child's constant crying may completely stop. Numerous medicines given to children, notably phenobarbitone for epilepsy, may profoundly affect a child's behaviour, causing defective concentration, drowsiness or extreme irritability (p. 118 and Chapter 16).

We are learning more about the biochemical basis of behaviour. It seems likely that the amines 5 hydroxytryptamine, noradrena. line and dopamine are concerned with mood regulation. Their breakdown is prevented by monoamine oxidase inhibitors, which are commonly used as antidepressant drugs, and another group of antidepressant drugs (the tricyclic group) appears to potentiate them. Coppen and colleagues (1973) found a striking reduction in the levels of free plasma tryptophane in 24 women with a depressive illness; the plasma level rose on recovery of the patients.

More mysterious is the effect of weather on behaviour. Many adults feel depressed when the weather is bad and the skies are dull, and elated when it is bright and sunny. Some have odd feelings when a gale is blowing. Many react badly with headaches and discomfort to an approaching thunderstorm. Krueger (1973) adduced evidence that some of these symptoms are related to the concentration of positive or negative ions in the air; changes in the ratio have a remarkable effect on plants and animals. The malaise and discomfort caused by the Sharav in the Middle East and the Föhn in the Alps are said to be due to these changes in the ions. Positive ions, as in a thunderstorm, raise the blood levels of serotonin; negative ions reduce the serotonin and have a tranquillising action. Polluted air in badly ventilated rooms may for the same reason cause lassitude and loss of efficiency.

Some are more disturbed than others by ambient sound—not so

much because they are more distractable, but because they are more sensitive to sound. Some are disturbed by infra-sound— sound not heard by most people: and Brown (1973) suggested that the discomfort, bad temper and even vomiting experienced by some in stormy weather (and abroad when the Fern wind blows) may be due to the rise of infrasound which we know occurs in these climatic conditions.

There may well be a biochemical basis for homosexuality, as mentioned in Chapter 15.

THE EFFECT OF THE MIND ON THE BODY, AND THE BODY ON THE MIND

Psychosomatic disease, which basically consists of the effect of the mind on the body, is now an enormous subject and it is not possible to provide a useful summary here: suffice it to say that the mind has a great effect on every organ of the body. Those interested should read the classical paper by Wittkower (1935) and the classical book by Cannon (1963). The mind affects the body—and the body the mind.

CHROMOSOMES AND BEHAVIOUR

Certain chromosome abnormalities are associated with abnormal behaviour—and most of them with mental subnormality. The most striking example is the extra Y chromosome: some boys with this condition are unusually tall and unusually likely to be delinquents.

ILLNESS OR DISEASE AND BEHAVIOUR

It is only to be expected that ill health would affect behaviour. Chronic ill health, such as that due to ulcerative colitis (chronic diarrhoea) or severe asthma, is likely to affect behaviour in various predictable ways—reducing exercise tolerance, causing disinclination for exertion, and perhaps apathy, poor concentration and depression. Epilepsy affects behaviour in a variety of ways. In the first place, the drugs given for its treatment may affect the behaviour and school performance, as already stated (p. 27). Temporal lobe epilepsy is sometimes associated with sudden unexplained unprovoked temper tantrums, or sudden episodes of

inappropriate laughter or automatic behaviour. A child's knowledge that he is liable to fits may cause worry and anxiety. Children
like to conform and to be like other children, and children with
epilepsy know that they are different from others—especially if
they are treated differently (e.g. in sports, physical training,
swimming).

Physical handicaps may greatly affect behaviour. Smallness of
stature may worry a child (Chapter 13). Children with handicaps
are extremely likely to be spoilt, overprotected and the objects of
favouritism. Clumsy children get into trouble because of bad
writing and awkwardness in games. Obese children are teased and
given unpleasant nicknames. Trevor-Roper (1971) in his fascinating book *The World through Blunted Sight*, wrote about the effect
of abnormal vision on children and particularly on art. He wrote
that myopia (short sight) tends to make a child poor at games and
sport, because of poor distant vision, and to be disinterested in the
theatre or cinema, but to show more interest in reading, to be
know-alls, pleasing their teachers but losing their friends, and
achieving greater academic success than their fellows: while long-
sighted children tend to be more interested in sport and other outdoor activities, to be more masculine, aggressive, popular and
extroverts, getting into trouble at school for truancy and inattentiveness because of poor near vision. The deaf child finds that
he is thwarted if he cannot communicate his needs, and adopts
unacceptable ways of expressing them (Burton 1968). The child
with specific learning disorders (especially dyslexia) may respond
to his difficulties by playing truant, or by any of a variety of behaviour disorders. The spastic child is apt to be lonely, and to find
it difficult to make friends.

THE ONLY CHILD

The personality of the only child depends in part on the circumstances which led him to be an only child: these might be his
mother's age or illness or abnormalities of the uterus making
further pregnancies unwise or impossible. The cause may be the
death of a sibling. In these cases the parents are apt to be overindulgent and overprotective. The child is apt to be overpraised,
to receive too much attention from adults, and to become
opinionated. His personality will depend in part on the type of

parents which he has and their attitudes. Some couples, knowing the risk of spoiling an only child, bring him up with unusual strictness—and render him insecure as a result. His mother's over-anxiety may make him timid, fearful and afraid of making mistakes. He misses sibling rivalry, and especially in a rural community may be lonely and isolated from other children. When he goes to school he is not accustomed to other children and is apt to be unpopular. He has to learn painfully at school what a child with siblings learns at home, that he cannot have all his own way: that to secure friendship he must learn to be unselfish and that he must not cheat at games. His teachers, however, are less likely to find him disobedient or hard to manage. He is more likely than others to have food fads.

A colleague of mine coined the term 'second only child' for the child born several years after the previous youngest: he is often unwanted, an accident, and may be rejected: more often he is spoilt, overprotected and overindulged by his parents and grown up siblings. His problems are closely similar to those of the only child of a family.

The first born child tends to be smaller than subsequent children. He tends to speak earlier than subsequent children—a fact which disproves the idea held by parents that children learn speech more from their siblings. In fact he learns more from his parents, and they will have more time to talk to and read to their first born than to subsequent children. Food refusal, termed by parents poor appetite, is almost confined to the first or only child—or to the 'second only child'. Sleep refusal is far more common in the first born or only child than in subsequent children. When he is older he is more liable to have behaviour problems, and later to come into conflict with the law. He is jealous when he is displaced from the important position of being an older child, especially if the gap between him and the next child is a small one. The first child is later given responsibilities, especially if a girl, and the girl may resent having to look after her younger siblings. When she is older, she is kept off school in order to look after her young brother or sister. When there is a fight or a mishap, the older child gets the blame, and is upset at the unfairness of this. He is expected to behave better than the younger ones, and is jealous because they are not reprimanded for acts for which he is punished. He is less likely to be aggressive than the youngest child.

The youngest child is more likely to adopt attention-seeking devices, to have school difficulties: he is likely to be jealous of his older siblings, who may be the objects of favouritism, and who have rights which he cannot have, being younger. He may resent being disciplined by his older brothers or sisters and so become defiant. The younger child is much less likely than the only child to have sleep or appetite problems, or to be overprotected and overindulged—unless he is a 'second only child'.

THE ATTITUDES OF PEERS

Some children are teased by their peers more than others, and some are distressed thereby. It is not easy to state confidently the factors involved. They may be teased because they are fat, weep readily, are clumsy, short tempered, stutter, speak indistinctly, speak with an accent unusual in the school, have an unusual manner of speech, belong to a social class unusual in the school, wear unusual clothes, have prominent teeth or suffer from infantile eczema. They are teased if they are timid and cowardly, failing to stand up for themselves. Yeats, for instance, was teased unmercifully at school and bullied because he never retaliated, and was shy, sensitive and easily rebuffed. Alexander Dumas was teased because he wept so easily. The less bright children tend to tease the brighter child, and particularly the brighter child who is a hard worker and who is not good at sport. I am uncertain whether a dwarf is likely to be teased significantly. I suspect that an unusually tall child is more likely to be teased—particularly because his emotional and intellectual maturity lag so far behind his physical growth. Children, especially girls, may be teased because of the late onset of puberty.

Children tend to be bullied if they cannot stand up for themselves—which so often results from parental attitudes, the parents always having stopped fights at home; it may result from the child having been an only child. Parental overprotection leaves a child convinced that he is incompetent and must always have the help of his parents: as a result life is difficult when he starts school.

Children tend to be the butt of unkind comments if they are unusually ugly, squint, have donkey ears or are fat. Many children destined for fame were acutely conscious of their ugliness. Socrates was said to have a grotesque appearance, with eyes wide apart, a broad nose, and to walk with the strut of a wild fowl. Mirabeau was thought by his father to be grossly ugly—but then his father grossly rejected him. Leo Tolstoy was painfully aware of his ugliness. He could not believe that there could be happiness for anyone as ugly as he. He was said to look like a gorilla, with small sunken eyes, low forehead, a large bulbous nose and enormous ears. He decided to end his life. Turner and Nobel were ugly boys. Anthony Trollope was described as awkward, ugly, illdressed and dirty. He was tortured, bullied and derided at Harrow.

SOCIAL CLASS, POVERTY AND NEIGHBOURHOOD

Many attempts have been made to analyse the features of low class homes or homes in which there is poverty. I have discussed in Chapter 6 the features which are likely to affect a child's school performance. Below is a summary of some of the concomitants of poverty in general.

In infancy
Higher prematurity rate,
lower birth weight,
more abortions, stillbirths,
higher infant mortality and perinatal mortality,
more illegitimacy,
more artificial feeding,
greater use of dummies,
more napkin rashes,
rusks given to babies more.

In general
Lower mean IQ,
poorer school performance than children of middle class with
    same IQ,
more
    delinquency,
    corporal punishment,
    smacking for handling genitalia,
    false modesty,
    enuresis, later toilet training,
    squint,

speech defects,
reading difficulty,
mental subnormality,
rheumatic fever, tuberculosis,
urinary tract infection,
neglected otitis media,
dental caries,
gastroenteritis,
skin infections, scabies, nits,
anaemia,
obesity,
accidents—especially burns, scalds,
laxatives,
dirt eating,
smoking,
clumsiness,
unforthcomingness (Stott),
pocket money,
new bicycles (more second hand ones in middle classes),
smaller height,
later puberty,
later bedtime
larger families: less spacing between births,
less tonsillectomy,
less circumcision,
less breast feeding,
in the home—fewer books,
early school leaving.

THE CHILD AT PSYCHOLOGICAL RISK

This section is largely recapitulation. The factors which make a child at especial risk of developing emotional problems are as follows.
Rejection. Child unwanted. Illegitimate.
The only child.
The second only child.
Elderly mother.
Neurotic parents: or mental disease. Parental depression.
Low parental IQ. Ignorance.

Parent unhappy in childhood.
Parents deaf or blind or otherwise handicapped.
Child with handicaps: chronic disease.
Obesity, smallness of stature.
Bad example at home.
Lack of discipline or excessive discipline.
Domestic friction: divorce. Parents separated.
Unhappy home. Problem family.
Large family. Poverty.
One parent family.
Prolonged separation from mother in first three years.
Bad neighbourhood: gangs.
Mother who reads many books on child psychology.

CONCLUSION

Though we do know the causes of behaviour problems, we cannot say why one child responds to these causes by one problem, such as a tic, while another responds by bed-wetting.

There is much that we do not know about the basis of behaviour. No one knows all the answers. No one knows how to prevent all behaviour problems. We may criticise parents of our patients, or our own parents: we might well have avoided the mistakes which they made—but then we might well make mistakes which they successfully avoided. We must not therefore blame parents for their mistakes. We must certainly not blame the child for his behaviour: we must always look behind the problem—whether it is bullying, tics, overactivity or anything else—to try to understand why the problem has developed. It would be stupid to punish the child for problems which he cannot sensibly be blamed for—problems dependent on his home, his neighbourhood and his heredity. Above all, we must remember that all children, all parents and all teachers have behaviour problems: and in order to deal with them we must try to understand the basis of behaviour and so the background of behaviour problems.

REFERENCES

AINSWORTH M.D. (1962) in PRUGH D.G. & HARLOW R.G. (1962) *Deprivation of Maternal Care*. Geneva, W.H.O.
AXLINE V. (1971) *Dibs: in Search of Self*. London, Pelican.

BERNSTEIN N.R., ROBEY J.S. (1962) The detection and management of pediatric difficulties created by divorce. *Pediatrics*, 30, 950.

BILLER H.B. (1971) Father Absence and the Personality Development of the Male Child. In CHESS S., THOMAS A. *Annual Progress in Child Psychiatry and Child Development*. New York, Brunner Mazel.

BOWLBY J. (1961) *Child Care and the Growth of Love*. London, Pelican.

British Medical Journal (1971) Children of divorce. Leading Article, 1, 302.

British Medical Journal (1972) Plight of one parent families. Leading Article, 2, 667.

BROWN R. (1973) New worries about unheard sound. *New Scientist*, 60, 414.

BRUN G. (1964) The children of divorce in Denmark. *Bull.Menninger Clinic*, 28, 3.

BURTON L. (1968) *Vulnerable Children*. London, Routledge and Kegan Paul.

CANNON W.B. (1963) *Bodily Changes in Pain, Hunger, Fear and Rage. An Account of Researches into the Function of Emotional Excitement*. New York, Harper & Row.

COPPEN A., ECCLESTON E.G., PEET M. (1973) Total and free tryptophan concentration in the plasma of depressed patients. *Lancet*, 2, 60.

DEWAR D. (1968) *Orphans of the Living: a Study of Bastardy*. London, Hutchinson.

DOUGLAS J.W.B. & BLOMFIELD J.M. (1958) *Children under Five*. London, Allen and Unwin.

ECCLESTON D. (1973) The biochemistry of human moods. *New Scientist*, 4 Jan., p. 18.

GAVRON H. (1966) *The Captive Wife. Conflicts of Housebound Mothers*. London, Routledge & Kegan Paul.

HOWELL M.C. (1973) Employed mothers and their families. *Pediatrics*, 52, 252.

ILLINGWORTH R.S. & ILLINGWORTH C.M. (1966) *Lessons from Childhood: Some Aspects of the Early Life of Unusual Men and Women*. Edinburgh, Churchill/Livingstone.

KRUEGER A. (1973) Are negative ions good for you? *New Scientist*, 58, 668.

LESHNER A. & CANDLAND D. (1973) The hormonal basis of aggression. *New Scientist*, 18 Jan.

PRUGH D.G., HARLOW R.G. (1962) *Deprivation of Maternal Care*. Geneva, W.H.O.

RUTTER M. (197) 1Parent-child separation: psychological effects on the children. *J. Child. Psychol. Psychiat.* 12, 233.

SOLOMON T. et al. (1973) Symposium on child abuse. *Pediatrics*, Suppl. 51, 770–812.

STANDING E.M. (1957). *Maria Montessori*. London, Hollis & Carter.

STOTT D.H. (1962). Evidence for a congenital factor in maladjustment and delinquency. *Am. J. Psychiat.* 118, 781.

SUGAR M. (1970) Children of divorce. *Pediatrics*, 46, 588.

TREVOR-ROPER P. (1971) *The World through Blunted Sight*. London, Thames & Hudson.

WALLSTON B. (1973) The effect of maternal employment on children. *J. Child. Psychol. Psychiat.* 14, 81.

WITTKOWER E. (1935) Studies on the influence of emotion on the function of the organs. *J. Mental Science*, 81, 533.

WOLKIND S. & RUTTER M. (1973) Children who have been in care—an epidemiological study. *Clinics in Develop. Med.* No. 46.

YUDKIN S. & HOLME A. (1963) *Working Mothers and their Children*. London, Michael Joseph.

CHAPTER 3
DISCIPLINE AND PUNISHMENT

HISTORICAL

There are many biblical references to punishment of children. In Proverbs XIII, 24 it states 'He who spares the rod hates his son, but he who loves him is diligent to discipline him. Do not withhold discipline from a child. If you beat him with a rod, he will not die'. In Deuteronomy XXI, 18, it is said 'If a man have a stubborn and rebellious son, which will not obey the voice of his father, or the voice of his mother, and that, when they have chastened him, will not hearken unto them, then shall his father and mother lay hold on him and bring him unto the elders of his city and unto the gate of his place: and all the men of his city shall stone him with stones, that he die'. In Kings 2, II, 23 one reads about the punishment administered by Elisha: 'As he was going up by the way, there came forth children out of the city, and mocked him, and said unto him—go up, thou baldhead, go up, thou baldhead.

'And he turned back, and looked on them, and cursed them in the name of the Lord. And there came forth two she bears out of the wood, and tare forty and two children of them.'

In the second millennium BC there was the ancient code of Hammourabi, which stated 'should a house collapse and kill the proprietor's child, the death punishment should be inflicted on the architect's child. Should a woman be stricken and death follows, the daughter of the aggressor should in turn be put to death.' Later the Mosaic law 'Talion' demanded that an offence should be punished by a corresponding penalty—an eye for an eye, a tooth for a tooth. In 1384 in Constance a boy had his tongue torn out because he blasphemed. Later vengeance was replaced by expiation; children had to expiate their sins through suffering so that they could repent.

According to Rolph (1967) in 19th-century schools punishment in advance was an established method. All the likely trouble makers were flogged at the beginning of the day to save time. The idea of

the whipping boy was an interesting one. A whipping boy was kept
by royalty (e.g. by Henry VIII and by the Dauphins of France), and
was beaten if the royal boy committed an offence. In 1801 a boy
of twelve was hung at Tyburn Tree (Marble Arch) for the theft of
a spoon from a lodging house.

In our book *Lessons from Childhood* we discussed the brutal
punishment to which children destined for fame were subjected.
With regard to Martin Luther, his biographer wrote that 'both
parents considered thrashings essential, just as much as eating or
drinking'. For stealing a nut, Martin was beaten by his mother
until the blood flowed. He never forgot the brutality with which he
was treated. Nehru at 6 stole a pen from his father. He was beaten
so severely that 'almost blind with pain and mortification at my
disgrace, I rushed to my mother, and for several days various
creams and ointments were applied to my aching and quivering
little body'. Alfred Lord Tennyson never forgot the brutality with
which he was treated at his school at Louth, and later could not
bear to go near the school. On the other hand it was said about
Lord Clive of India, who was brought up with a total lack
of discipline, that 'a neglected rod altered the fate of three
nations'.

THE NEED FOR DISCIPLINE

All children need to learn discipline. Many feel that lack of
discipline is the cause of much bad behaviour and delinquency.
All children must learn what behaviour is acceptable and what is
not. They have to learn that they cannot have all their own way.
They have to learn to accept needful restraint, to accept a 'No', to
respect the property of others, to respect authority, and to learn
what is safe and unsafe. The child brought up with too little
discipline is spoilt, bad mannered, selfish and insecure: he is disobedient: he is apt to wail when told to do something which he
dislikes: he is apt to be unpopular at school and is more likely than
others to get into trouble with the law or to be accident prone. On
the other hand the child brought up too strictly is also apt to feel
insecure, to be cowed and subdued, or to rebel against authority
when older—and again to be accident prone.

Every child must learn that if he disobeys, something unpleasant will happen: there must be some sanction. The absence of

punishment may be taken as a tacit approval of his bad behaviour (Walters, Cheyne and Banks 1972). Bronfenbrenner (1970) compared American and Russian children. She wrote that 'American children are more likely to cheat, to steal, to ignore another child who needs help. He is left to be brought up by his peers, in an atmosphere of subtle opposition to the standards of adult society, in affluent neglect.' The Russian child is taught more to look beyond himself to the needs of society. One wonders how much of those differences are due to the greater permissiveness in American society.

Too many are afraid to exert discipline because they fear that they will 'repress' their child. In fact firm loving discipline, certainly without excessive strictness, is in the best interests of every child: it helps him to feel secure especially in his relationships with others at school and to face more confidently the vicissitudes of school and later years. All children have to develop independence and self expression; overprotection has to be avoided; but that does not imply that discipline is undesirable. They have to learn the difference between right and wrong—and for that discipline is essential. Many schools today are presented with children who have never learnt the difference between right and wrong; they have been set an appalling example at home: they have never learnt behaviour acceptable to others: they have never learnt to treat others as they would like to be treated.

As Verville (1967) wrote, small children become adept at driving a hard bargain: parents have to beware of the 'peace at any price' policy—giving in to the child when he makes enough fuss. Children have to learn to accept frustration and disappointment in order that they can learn self control and self discipline.

SOME PRINCIPLES

Above all, a child should have his basic needs for love and security met at home. He should then behave because he wants to behave: he wants the good will of his parents whom he loves, and he certainly wants the good will of the teachers whom he likes.

Discipline must not be introduced before the child is ready for it, before he is able to learn the significance of cause and effect, before he can understand the meaning of punishment. Before he is one year old he cannot learn discipline: an average child of three can learn a lot: somewhere in between he should begin to learn. Many parents fail to realise that the more intelligent child can learn sooner, the less intelligent child only later. I have seen troublesome behaviour problems resulting from trying to teach discipline to mentally subnormal children at an age suitable for the normal child. It is interesting to note that according to Newson and Newson (1963), 60 per cent of Nottingham mothers were smacking their children before their first birthday. They noted that there was much more corporal punishment in the lower classes, especially for handling the genitalia. I have often seen a mother smacking her nine- or ten- month- old baby for thumbsucking.

An essential prerequisite for teaching discipline and good behaviour is a good example. One cannot expect a child to obey an order to refrain from an act which he sees his parents do. Parents cannot expect a child to obey an order to apologise to his sister for hitting her when he sees the parents hit her and never sees them apologise for loss of temper.

Wise parents avoid sources of friction as far as possible. For instance, if the children have to wash up after a meal, friction is apt to occur unless an arrangement is made whereby they do it in turns. When there is likely to be friction between two children about which of two pieces of cake is the bigger, the wise parent arranges for one child to cut the cake and the other to choose the portion which he thinks is the better one. If there is friction about the child dirtying his clothes, he should have clothes which he is allowed to dirty.

There must be some sanction: but the wiser the management the less often need it be used—and the less severe need it be. Frequent punishment is always a sign of mismanagement.

A child must understand the reason why he is being told to do a particular task or is being forbidden to do something. He must always have been warned of the consequences of disobedience if a particular sanction is applied. One must always try to understand the child's motive for committing a forbidden act: he must be given a chance to explain what he has done. There is no place for the stock phrases 'Don't answer back', 'I won't hear another word', 'I won't have any back-chat'.

Discipline must be consistent. In many homes a father condones what a mother forbids often to court the child's favour, or to annoy his wife: or a grandmother allows what her daughter-in-law forbids. Some parents alternate overstrictness and punishment with overindulgence because of a feeling of guilt at the severity of a punishment. As already stated, every child must learn that if he disobeys, unpleasant consequences will result. In many families a child is constantly being told not to do this, that and the other, and when he disobeys nothing happens—and so he continues to disobey. Eventually his parent loses his temper and smacks him. Rules should be few, and designed in the early years mainly for safety's sake, but they must be obeyed. For instance, the door banging game, or playing on the stairs, or playing with cord round the neck, or playing with a plastic bag over the head, must always be stopped immediately. There must be a good reason for a rule. One must not dig one's heels in over something which does not matter.

The sanction should be immediate and inevitable, so that the relationship between cause and effect is obvious: but it should not be prolonged, for that is apt to cause unhappiness, resentment and insecurity. There should never be retaliation by the parent. I heard a woman say that if her child bit her, she would always bite him. Admittedly a child has to be able to stand up for himself and deal appropriately with another child who hits him; it would be wrong however for a mother to refuse to help a child who had refused to help her. It must be remembered that a child is less mature than an adult: and that he needs love at all times— particularly when he is behaving badly.

Many parents have gathered that corporal punishment is undesirable and use instead mental punishment, which is often much more harmful. No parent should ever use the weapons of threats of leaving the child, withholding love, putting a child into Coventry. At all times—at home or school—the weapons of ridicule, sarcasm, belittling the child are undesirable: they make a child unhappy and insecure. In the case of the preschool child who is old enough to understand, a smack on the bottom is harmless. Corporal punishment after that age is unnecessary and undesirable. No physical punishment should ever hurt: the child is punished by making it clear that he has lost the approval of the parent whom he loves. A child should not be smacked in front of his siblings. After one smack, nothing more is said. The punishment must not be prolonged. Nothing is said about his heinous offence to the father when he comes back from work—at least, not in the child's presence. It is most important that the father should not be told about the child's crime in his presence in such a way that the child feels that his mother secretly condones and praises the act. Reprimands and remonstrances *must* be kept to a minimum. In many houses they constitute almost the only conversation which the child hears. Constant reprimands if he takes any notice at all can make a child miserable—and have the opposite of the effect desired.

The usual sanction is deprivation. The child is deprived of something as a result of his disobedience or act of wickedness. If a little girl of three cuts a hole in her dress, she is not smacked or reprimanded: she is deprived of the scissors until forgiven, which is soon—but not too soon.

There is now little place for corporal punishment in schools—not only because many feel that it is undesirable, but because of the fear of legal consequences. Castle, in his book *People at School* wrote, 'Looking back, I am inclined to the judgment that no one was improved by corporal punishment, that its effects were purely negative, that on rare occasions when it was brutal, the effects were bad, that it failed to make boys better behaved. It was used most by the weakest teachers. The rod is an uncivilised anachronism.'

Where possible a child should make retribution for his sin. If the boy deliberately tears his sister's book, he will have to give her one of his. One feels that proper retribution should be made by juvenile delinquents, and that they would learn best by this: if they damage someone's property they should be forced to make amends to that person.

PUNISHMENT IS USUALLY WRONG

George Bernard Shaw wrote that 'to punish is to injure'. It has already been explained that numerous behaviour problems are related to insecurity, and that punishment is bound to increase that insecurity. Punishment tends to treat the symptom and not the cause. It is when children (or adolescents or adults) are feeling tired, unwell or irritable that they most appreciate love and tolerance. When a child hits his sibling because of jealousy, the worst treatment is to punish him: it makes him all the more certain that he is not loved and wanted. When a child bullies another, it is senseless to punish him: he bullies because someone is bullying him—physically or emotionally, and punishment is likely to make him resentful and feel that no one understands him (which is probably true). An eleven-year-old girl was referred to me for stealing. She had been seen a fortnight previously by a psychiatrist who in the girl's presence said 'What she wants is a good beating'. From that time onwards her behaviour became impossible. Whenever the mother asked her to do anything or reprimanded her (which was constantly) the girl said, 'Give me a good beating, that's what the trick-cyclist said, isn't it?'. I explained to the mother that what the girl needed was not a good beating, but love. The mother understood. From that day onwards the whole trouble stopped. My colleague, Dr Woodmansey (1966), wrote that the child is told to control his feelings, but the parent does not think that he should. Hostility, he wrote, breeds hostility. 'The mother feels so cross, if bitten by the child, that she feels he should be bitten back—that in some way it will cure his aggressiveness—despite her immediate experience that it has just the opposite effect. Many a parent pleads that it is impossible for him to refrain from chastising his child, but insists that the latter must again be punished if he retaliates. This is to claim a privilege that they clearly cannot both possess, namely the freedom to give vent to anger against the other with impunity. And it is because the adult was denied this right in his own childhood that he cannot now forgo it in favour of the child who will, therefore, in turn withhold it from his children—and so on.'

Punishment is wrong because most of the acts for which punishment is meted out are not the fault of the child at all. Children are apt to get into trouble for forgetfulness, fidgeting, carelessness, inaccuracy in school work, poor concentration, untidiness, unpunctuality, stealing or fighting—when there are obvious explanations for the behaviour which are outside the child's control. Admittedly there must come a time when a child is to be held responsible for his acts—but we should try to understand the reasons for his acts—just as we should try to understand the reasons for the parent's personality and mismanagement—and be more understanding and tolerant. I have already said that children are punished for wetting the bed in their sleep. A friend of mine was put into Coventry by his mother because unfortunately she went into his bedroom when he was asleep and heard him using four-letter words in his sleep, words which she had no idea that he knew. It seemed irrational to me to punish him for swearing in his sleep. Many of the acts for which children are punished arise from the subconscious mind: acts of jealousy are an example. It is not sensible to punish them for such acts. Children are punished for over-activity, bad writing and clumsiness: usually these are no fault of the child (see Chapter 4), and it is stupid to punish them for these acts. It is not difficult to determine whether this opinion is right—for one can readily determine whether punishment makes them better. It does not. Children are called 'maladjusted'— whereas they are reacting normally and predictably to their environment: it is the parents who are maladjusted and not the child.

Many of the acts for which children are punished are not wrong at all. Some of these have been mentioned. When children are called 'naughty' it is more sensible to call them just 'a nuisance'. They are punished, verbally or otherwise, for fighting: but it is normal for small children to be aggressive, and it is normal for them to want their own way and to fight for it. They are punished for thumbsucking or for masturbating.

Much punishment is due to failure to understand the mind of the developing child. Child and parent, teacher and child, find it difficult to put themselves into the place of the other. Adults tend to forget that children, like themselves, are sensitive, get tired, bored, hungry or react unfavourably to unkindness: children can respond only by their emotional behaviour (or by hitting other children), but adults can apply all manner of sanctions, and worse still, can inflict corporal punishment. Children are punished for disasters which they could not possibly foresee: the adult, with his greater experience, could well predict the consequences of what the child was doing. The child, as a result of normal curiosity, does something whose consequences he could not foresee—and gets into trouble.

It must be remembered that children, like adults, are punished more for the consequences of their acts than for the acts themselves. This is irrational, and a form of inconsistency. A child cannot understand why no one prohibits him from doing something which he has done dozens of times, whereas once, unpredictably, something goes wrong as a result of his act, someone is injured and he gets a beating.

Much punishment meted out by parents signifies parental loss of temper. Almost all smackings are due to this. All parents and all teachers have behaviour problems: they become tired or irritable, worried or hurried, and lose their temper—and then they lose their sense of humour, tolerance and understanding, and punish the child. Parents are thwarted at behaviour which they cannot control. They cannot stop the child's tics, they cannot make him eat, go to sleep or use the potty. Parents hate to have their authority questioned—and react violently if their child dares to do it—as an intelligent child should do. I have stated in the previous chapter that some parents (or adolescents) when irritable, provoke. It is easy to see how a vicious circle develops. It must be broken by the parent, who is more mature than the child: it is the parent who should declare the cease fire. Berg (1959) wrote that 'the punisher would appear to be the victim of unconscious forces and mechanisms similar to those of the punished, and therefore a most unsuitable person to treat the latter's symptoms'.

Parents (and teachers) having punished, rationalise their acts. In primitive tribes it was argued that if the tribe did not punish an offender, the outraged god would punish the tribe and destroy its crops. The father argues that he was beaten as a child—and he does the same to his child as a result. Punishment is more the product of emotion than of reason. Some teachers punish to protect their self esteem: they want to be seen as disciplinarians who can keep order.

Corporal punishment is sometimes sadistic in character—the teacher (or parent) acquiring emotional and sexual satisfaction from the act.

Punishment is irrational for another reason. Praise, reward, approval and encouragement are incentives to good action, and much more effective for promoting good behaviour than discouragement, criticism and punishment. The desire to be good is more effective than the fear of doing wrong. Punishment, blame and disapproval are poor deterrents.

Some children want to be punished and acquire the praise and respect of their peers as a result of it. Some acquire a vicarious satisfaction from it—a form of masochism.

REFERENCES

BERG C. (1959) *Fear, Punishment, Anxiety and the Wolfenden Report*. London, Allen & Unwin.

BRONFENBRENNER U. (1970) *Two Worlds of Childhood—U.S.A. and U.S.S.R.* New York, Basic Books Inc.

CASTLE E.B. (1953) *People at School.* London, Heinemann.

ILLINGWORTH R.S. & ILLINGWORTH C.M. (1966) *Lessons from Child: Some Aspects of the Early Life of Unusual Men and Women.* Edinburgh, Churchill/ Livingstone.

NEWSON J. & NEWSON E. (1963) *Infant Care in an Urban Community.* London, Allen & Unwin.

RITTWAGEN M. (1958) *Sins of their Fathers.* Boston, Houghton Mifflin.

ROLPH C.H. (1967) Crime and punishment. *Journal of Royal College of Physicians of London,* 1, 306.

VERVILLE E. (1967) *Behavior Problems of Children.* Philadelphia, Saunders.

WALTERS R.H., CHEYNE J. & BANKS R.K. (1972) *Punishment.* London, Penguin.

WOODMANSEY C. (1966) *Mental Illness in the Family: Its Effect on the Child.* Proc. 22nd Child Guidance Conference. National Association for Mental Health.

CHAPTER 4
BEHAVIOUR PROBLEMS

INTRODUCTION

All children have behaviour problems: all parents have behaviour problems: all teachers have behaviour problems. It behoves us all to know something about problems which are so common. Those interested should read the books by Harry and Ruth Bakwin (1972) *Clinical Management of Behavior Disorders in Children*, and by E. Verville (1967) *Behavior Problems of Children*. I have written in greater detail about behaviour problemsin the young child in my own book *The Normal Child: Some Problems of the Early Years and their Treatment*.

HISTORICAL

In our book *Lessons from Childhood*, in which we described interesting features of the childhood of famous men and women, we mentioned numerous examples of troublesome behaviour in children who were destined for fame. Some were renowned for their temper (like Napoleon), some for their timidity (like Yeats), some for sheer madness (like Shelley), some for their overactivity (like Beaverbrook), some for day dreaming (like Hans Christian Andersen), some for stealing (like Cromwell) and some for their bad behaviour in class (like George Bernard Shaw).

Beaverbrook was an unpopular, quarrelsome, 'lone wolfer': Edisonwas a mischievous problem child, always getting into scrapes, always bottom of his class: Orde Wingate was 'against all and everything'. G.K. Chesterton's teacher at St Paul's said 'We thought him the most curious thing that ever was'. His school-fellow saw him striding along muttering poetry or breaking into inane laughter. Many others were backward at school and the despair of their teachers.

In the sections to follow, arranged in alphabetical order, I have summarised for the teacher some thoughts about the common behaviour problems.

POOR APPETITE

> What is the matter with Mary Jane?
> I've promised her dolls and a daisy chain
> And a book about animals, all in vain—
> What is the matter with Mary Jane?
>
> She's perfectly well, and she hasn't a pain,
> And it's lovely rice pudding for dinner again
> What is the matter with Mary Jane?

> (A.A. Milne: *When we were Very Young*)

Any child or adult loses his appetite when he has an acute infection or when he is ill. Any chronic illness, particularly if it causes inactivity, may reduce the appetite. Loss of appetite should always be investigated so that the cause may be determined.

This section is concerned with the problem of the poor appetite in a well child. This is an exceedingly common problem. It is almost invariably associated with and largely caused by food forcing. The factors involved are various and interrelated. All children are different; some are little eaters and some are big eaters. Some are big children and some are small. If the child is of small build (Chapter 13) he is likely to need and want less food than a big child: a mother becomes worried because her small child eats so much less than the child of the same age but of a much bigger build next door—and so she tries to make him eat more. She is convinced that the bigger a child is, the better he is. All children from the age of one to three or more are passing through the stage of negativism and efforts to force them to do anything are likely to make them do the opposite, and so they refuse: and they love the fuss and anxiety which their food refusal causes.

Mothers believe that growing children should have plenty of protein and vegetables—and so try to get their children to eat meat and greens—and so the children refuse. One child was brought up to me for one reason only—that he would not eat sweets. When I exclaimed that that was excellent, not only because his teeth would benefit, but also because it would save money, she said that she just wanted him to be like other boys. At home he refused to eat sweets despite all persuasion. A boy was brought to me because he would not eat meat. His mother said that she could not get him to eat any proteins—such as meat or fish, and he would not touch those foods at home. When his mother had left the room I asked the boy what he had for dinner at school on the previous day: he had had two helpings of roast beef. Food fads, more genuine than this, develop for the same reason. If a mother makes determined efforts to make a small child eat certain foods, he will refuse. During the era of severe rationing I saw a child who according to his mother would eat nothing else but bacon and egg. As a result he was eating the entire bacon and egg ration of his mother, father, grandmother and grandfather, because they all felt that this alone would keep the boy alive. Rarely a food fad can be due to a genuine distaste for a particular food or even sensitivity to it. I have sympathy with the child who strongly dislikes milk pudding.

Unpleasantness over mealtimes at home may condition a child against food. He comes to associate mealtimes and food with smackings and threats and forcing methods and develops a genuine dislike for food and so a poor appetite. This is a difficult condition to treat.

The personality of the child and his parents is relevant, as with all behaviour problems. The reasons for parental overanxiety have been discussed in Chapter 2. The mother loves her child (usually) and wants him to have good health. She is anxious about his slow weight gain—not thinking that he is of small build, like she is herself, and therefore gains weight less rapidly than other children and therefore needs less food. She is determined to get food into him somehow, and gives him anything which he will take between meals—sweets, milk, bread and dripping, biscuits, cake, fruit drinks and sandwiches, and is then dismayed that he has no appetite at his mealtimes. I have seen several well thriving small children who were being given 20 or more meals a day in an effort to keep them alive. I constantly explain to mothers that it is never necessary to try to make a well child eat, and that efforts to do so always lead to food refusal.

It is important that the teacher should understand the reasons for a poor appetite in a well child. No effort should be made to cause the child to eat. The teacher can hardly discourage the sweet eating habit: it is difficult for the parents to prevent it once they have unwisely started it.

DAY DREAMING: DEFECTIVE CONCENTRATION

Any teacher knows that defective concentration may be due merely to a low IQ: but though the commonest cause, it is not the only one. The association with overactivity is mentioned in Chapter 16. Poor concentration may be due to insecurity, to boredom or lack of motivation. The child may be bored with the subject chosen for him—and perhaps only interested in another subject in which he has a particular bent.

Several famous people caused anxiety in their childhood because of day-dreaming. They included Honore de Balzac, Hans Christian Andersen and Edouard Manet. Lord Beaverbrook's work at school was unsatisfactory because of it.

JUVENILE DELINQUENCY

There is a vast literature on the subject of delinquency. I propose to give only a brief outline.

The legal aspect of juvenile delinquency was changed by the Children and Young Persons Act of 1969. Offenders are subject to adult law at the age of seventeen. An offence cannot be alleged against a child of under ten: but shortly that age will be raised to twelve.

Juvenile offenders can be fined up to £10: discharged absolutely or on condition for three years: ordered to pay costs and compensation: placed under the care of the local authority: placed in hospital or a detention centre for up to three months: or sent to the Quarter Sessions for Borstal training. The parent or guardian can be ordered to enter into a recognizance to take proper care of the child and to control him. The child can be placed 'under supervision'.

In the United Kingdom in 1970 120,957 boys and 10,800 girls under the age of 17 were taken to court for delinquent acts. The peak age for delinquency in the last year at school. The main offences are stealing, burglary, sex crimes and truancy. Delinquency is five times more common in boys than girls. The factors, culled from many sources, mostly named in the reference list, are as follows:

(i) Lack of discipline—or excessive strictness and punishment. Parents are apt to say 'We can't make it out: we have always given him everything that he wants'. Often the child's bad behaviour is encouraged or condoned by the parents who boast in his presence about evasion of the law.

(ii) Lack of love, poor family relationships.

(iii) Unsatisfactory home. The father is disinterested, rejecting, punitive, ineffective, alcoholic, with a poor work record, much absenteeism, invalidism, physical incapacity, unemployed, failing to support his family, a man of poor educational standard, unhappy in his own childhood. Rittwagen wrote that 'often with harsh memories of their own fathers, they can experience neither warmth nor interest in their own unwanted children'.

The mother is liable to be unsatisfactory, feckless and unhappy, with poor health and a large family. Stott (1959, 1966) adduced evidence that stress during pregnancy correlates with subsequent delinquency on the part of the child to be born. There is commonly gross parental discord. There is commonly a family history of delinquency and of mental illness. In one study, 20 per cent of delinquents had a delinquent sibling. 40 per cent had a father with a criminal record.

(iv) Separation from the parents. There is commonly a history of the child having been abandoned by the parents, or having been handed over to another to bring up. There is a high incidence of divorce. In one study of approved school boys 15 per cent were illegitimate, 15 per cent had lost one or both parents, and 25 per cent had separated or divorced parents. Clarke, studying 500 cases of delinquency, found that 42 per cent had a step parent, only one parent, or were adopted or fostered. He found that whereas separation from the mother is more important in the first three years of a child's life, separation from the father is more important after the age of about five.

(v) Personality problems in the delinquent. The personality is partly inherited and partly the product of the environment. An important feature of delinquents is their emotional immaturity. They have failed to grow up. They have retained the primitive selfishness which all small children demonstrate in their early years. They lack self control, moral feeling, respect for property, a conscience. They fail to count the cost of their actions. They blame and criticise everyone but themselves.

Many workers have noted the early antisocial symptoms of future delinquents. Many have remarked that the early features are readily recognisable at school. They have a poor academic record and are frequently absent, often due to truancy. They tend to be unpopular, isolated, aggressive, with difficulty in getting on with their contemporaries. They are more likely than others to get into trouble. They show little respect for authority, tending to be hostile and defiant. They are poor at sport, have few outdoor pursuits, are not interested in team games, social activities such as scouts, hobbies or religion. Baumgartner found that 9 out of 10 coming to court had had serious emotional difficulties before the age of 11, and almost half showed signs by eight or sooner. Douglas (1966, 1968) studied nervous and troublesome children who had been in his long term follow up investigation from infancy. He wrote that 'even at the age of eight, the children who were later going to get into trouble do badly in their work and tests, and in particular score much lower than would be expected from their attainment and non-verbal intelligence. Teachers pick out these as being both nervous and aggressive.'

Finally boredom, insecurity, a quest for excitement or something to do, a desire to get away from home, are important. Acts of delinquency are often precipitated by a stressful situation at home or school or amongst associates.

(vi) Physical handicaps. The frequency of these has been noted by many workers. The handicaps include visual and auditory defects, speech defects and poor physique. Epilepsy is not a factor. An extra Y chromosome is associated with unusual tallness and delinquency.

(vii) The IQ. This is usually less than the average.

(viii) The neighbourhood and social class. Delinquency is more common in the lower classes and in poor neighbourhoods. It is more common in boys than in girls.

It can be said in summary that delinquency is the culmination of many years of unsatisfactory home life; it is the product of heredity, of unsatisfactory parents and of the effect of poverty and the neighbourhood.

The outlook for delinquents is not good. Robins (1966) wrote an interesting and somewhat depressing long term study of 524 men and women who 30 years previously had attended child guidance clinics, comparing them with 100 who as children had

C

not attended such clinics, but were matched for age, sex, race, IQ and neighbourhood. Antisocial symptoms were powerful predictors of adult outcome. Seventy-one per cent of the adults had been arrested at some time, and 86 per cent were sociopaths. Antisocial children were more often arrested or imprisoned as adults, had more marital difficulties, poorer occupation and economic status, poorer social relationships, army records, physical health, more alcoholism, more hospital admissions, more debts, more sexual promiscuousness, a higher accident rate, a higher death rate from violence. For antisocial boys there was a 71 per cent risk of future arrest: for antisocial girls a divorce rate of 70 per cent. Half the men and a third of the women were alcoholics. Those more likely to have a later sociopathic personality were boys referred to the child guidance clinic for theft or aggression, truancy, sex crimes and problems of discipline. Those referred for temper tantrums, sleeping and eating problems were less likely to be in trouble as adults. Children who had been fearful and withdrawn were no more likely to develop psychiatric illness than controls. There were no characteristic findings in childhood which correlated with adult manic-depressive psychoses or anxiety neurosis, but there was an association between symptoms in childhood and adult schizophrenia or hysteria.

Further reading

BAUMGARTNER L. & BECK B.M. (1955) Juvenile delinquency. Am. J. Dis. Child. 89, 62.
CLARKE J. (1962) Juvenile Delinquency, M.D. Thesis, University of Manchester.
DOUGLAS J.W.B. (1966) The school progress of nervous and troublesome children. Brit. J. Psychiat. 112, 115.
DOUGLAS J.W.B. (1968) All our Future. London, Peter Davies.
RITTWAGEN M. (1958) Sins of Their Fathers. Boston, Houghton Mifflin.
ROBINS L.N. (1966) Deviant Children Grown Up. Baltimore, William Wilkins.
STOTT D.H. (1950) Delinquency and Human Nature. Carnegie United Kingdom Trust.
STOTT D.H. (1966) Troublesome Children. London, Tavistock Publications.

DRUG ADDICTION

I have no personal experience of this problem, and would prefer anyone reading this section to know this. Smoking is discussed under another section. Good reviews of drug addiction are those by Block (1972) and Friedman (1972).

'Glue-sniffing' or 'solvent-sniffing' is a common problem in Canada and the United States (Glaser and Massengale 1962, Press and Done 1967, O'Brien *et al.* 1971): it is common in the 7 to 8 years old. In Denver 130 juveniles, of an average age of 13, were arrested in a two-year period on account of glue-sniffing. It is common in New York slums. In some Winnipeg schools (1968) 2 per cent of the pupils indulged in this practice. It is related to delinquency and economic deprivation. Bass (1970) discussed 110 sudden deaths in American sniffers in the 1960s. The deaths were mainly due to volatile hydrocarbons, especially trichloroethane and fluorinated refrigerants.

The term glue-sniffing is not a good one. A better term would be solvent sniffing. The solvents and similar materials include glues, nail polish removers, stain removers, petrol, lighter fluid, plastic cements in building kits, aeroplane glues, lacquers, aerosols, enamels and paint thinners. The addict may squeeze the glue into a handkerchief and sniff it. Others put the nail polish remover into coca-cola and drink it. The solvents contain a variety of poisons, and therefore the effects are many and varied. The solvents include carbon tetrachloride which causes liver damage: benzene which damages the bone marrow and blood: toluene and trichlethylene which damage the liver and kidney: naphtha, which breaks down the red cells (haemolysis), petrol (which may damage the liver, or cause lead poisoning): and central nervous system depressants, causing disorientation, intoxication, unsteadiness, coma and death. Several of the solvents cause symptoms resembling acute alcoholic intoxication, with euphoria, hallucinations, ataxia and confusion. Many of the solvents, when used frequently, cause a deterioration in school work. Some deaths have resulted from plastic bags put over the head so that the drugs can be inhaled.

Cannabis

Cannabis is the most popular drug of addiction after nicotine and alcohol. It is much less dangerous than either. It is not addictive, and does not cause aggression like alcohol does (*Med. J. Australia* 1973). It is said that in 1972, 24 million Americans had experimented with it. When smoked cannabis has been described as smelling of 'burnt leaves or rope with a mild sweetish odour'. There has been much discussion as to what harm the drug causes. In one discussion (Committee on Youth 1972) it was concluded that there is no evidence that it causes brain damage. An important feature is that unlike drugs of addiction, which commonly have to be taken in increasing doses because of the development of tolerance, cannabis is associated with 'reverse tolerance'—smaller doses being found to be effective. There are no withdrawal symptoms. A test for the concentration of cannabis in the blood has been devised in Sweden.

The evidence that it leads to the use of the 'hard' drugs is conflicting. There seems to be little doubt that most 'hard' drug addicts have previously tried the 'soft' drugs: but we do not know how many of those who experiment with cannabis later experiment with the hard drugs. Once they experiment with a hard drug they are in great danger. It is probable that adolescents of a particular personality type are more likely than others to try cannabis —and more likely than others to try a hard drug. The home upbringing may well be a factor, but we cannot pin-point the relevant features of the home: perhaps unwise permissiveness, insecurity and a poor example set by the parents are important in this connection. The example and influence of friends is highly relevant— but the choice of friends is influenced by the nature of the home background. The greatest danger of cannabis smoking is contact with the pusher, who tempts the adolescent to try a hard drug.

A Committee of the American Academy of Pediatrics (1972) reviewed the present state of our knowledge of the effect of the drug. The potency varies, and the drug is not standardised, so that accurate scientific study is difficult. Hashish is usually about five times stronger than marihuana. It is reported that the limited research findings available do not indicate any harmful physical effects when moderate amounts are smoked. The effects are a fast pulse, large pupils, a feeling of coldness, reddening of the eye and dryness of the mouth. With unusually high amounts there may be some unsteadiness and motor weakness.

With the usual quantities the immediate effects are relaxation, a sense of well being, talkativeness, inattentiveness, altered perception of time and space, impaired memory for recent events, hilarity, uncontrolled laughter and increased suggestibility. Decisions tend to be postponed. Athletic performance falls off. In higher than usual doses there may be hallucinations and paranoia. In a Canadian study (Klonoff et al. 1973) of 81 test subjects, it was shown that cannabis caused a transient impairment of all mental processes, including concept formation, memory, tactile form discrimination and motor functions. Cannabis does not cause violent crime, like heroin does. It is said that a car driver under the influence of marihuana suffers a deterioration in his driving standards, speed estimation, distance perception and ability to respond in an emergency (Davis 1972). It has been suggested that cannabis smoke may predispose to cancer of the lung, like cigarette smoke, and interfere with immune mechanisms.*

The Committee of the American Academy of Pediatrics commented that social usage may become a habitual means of avoiding all anxiety, and that this might interfere with normal psychological development and ability to face the stresses of life. 'A drug such as marihuana can provide a more immediate means to avoid stress and challenge, but not a useful one for learning how to cope.' The American Academy has recommended that the possession of the drug for personal use should be regarded as a misdemeanor rather than a felony. Faber (1972) criticised the law for not distinguishing marihuana from the hard drugs. He added that though it may not be entirely benign, society's action in trying to control it is much more harmful. Professor Henry Miller, Vice Chancellor of the University of Newcastle-upon-Tyne, discussed the legislation of cannabis in the *New Scientist* (1973), and expressed the view that the present harsh laws concerning it were irrational. He pointed out that cannabis has not been known to kill anyone, while nicotine kills 40,000 a year in Britain and contributes to the death of a further 150,000; while there are 350,000 chronic alcoholics in Britain, and alcohol causes a high mortality, playing a part in two thirds of all crimes of violence, and at least half of all road fatalities: yet alcohol and smoking are legal.

For reviews, not referred to above, see the papers by Lewin 1972, Leuchtenberger *et al.* 1973 and Paton 1973.

Barbiturates

Barbiturates cause more suicides than any other drug. Their action is potentiated by alcohol. They reduce concentration and school work suffers (see Epilepsy, Chapter 16). Tolerance develops fairly rapidly. Withdrawal causes a feeling of weakness, nausea, irritability, insomnia and may cause convulsions. Lundberg (1973) wrote that nearly 5 per cent of admissions to a large South

* NAHAS G.G., SUCIO-FOCA N., ARMAND J., & MORISHIMA A. (1974) Inhibition of cellular-mediated immunity in marihuana smokers. *Science.* **183**, 419.

California hospital in 1972 were for barbiturate-related diseases. Decrying the widespread use of drugs for depression, stimulation, overactivity and the like, he added:

'The toll of human suffering and death resulting from licit and illicit use of barbiturates is immense.

'So someone is anxious, or hurts a little, or can't sleep, or isn't excited? So what? Everybody is anxious, or hurts a little, or can't sleep, or is depressed from time to time. Why complicate the issue with psycho-active drugs? We must learn to cope with reality without mind—and mood—altering chemicals.'

Phenmetrazine and Amphetamine

Phenmetrazine, previously used as an appetite suppressant for obesity, under the trade name of preludin, is an important problem in Sweden: there may be as many as 10,000 addicts to it in Stockholm (Connell 1971). Amphetamine and phenmetrazine are particularly dangerous drugs of addiction, for they may cause serious brain deterioration. They cause initially a sense of well being, euphoria, alertness and decreased fatigue, but they may cause a feeling of tension and tremulousness. There is excitement, loss of appetite, sometimes rapid speech, superficial thought, fatigue, a dry mouth, dilated pupils and sweating. Later there may be severe depression, hallucinations and paranoia. The picture may closely resemble that of schizophrenia. If injected, there is a danger of hepatitis and other serious illness from infected needles. There is a pronounced tendency to the development of tolerance and drug dependence. Withdrawal symptoms include a voracious appetite, depression and prolonged sleep.

Withdrawal of another appetite suppressant, fenfluramine ('Ponderax') may also cause depression.

Alcohol

Adolescents should realise that alcohol is a drug. It is estimated that one in every 15 who take alcohol become chronic alcoholics. There are 350,000 alcoholics in the United Kingdom and nine million in the U.S.A. It is thought that at least a half of all road deaths are related to alcohol.

Hallucinogens

The hallucinogens include LSD (lysergic acid diethylamide), mescaline, peyote and many other drugs.

LSD is taken by mouth as tablets, capsules, sugar cubes or other means. It causes excitement, auditory and visual hallucinations, severe impairment of judgment (causing accidents), headache, depression, excitement, laughter, panic reactions, suicide, homicide and unpredictable behaviour. Repeated use causes impairment of memory, severe psychoses resembling schizophrenia, and personality deterioration.

Heroin

Heroin is taken by injection or inhalation. Tolerance rapidly develops. It causes euphoria within a minute or two, with loss of fear and tension, followed by drowsiness, lethargy, oblivion, and a dulling of a sense of reality. It causes drowsiness, nausea, constipation, urinary retention, stupor, loss of appetite, pinpoint pupils, watering eyes, a slow pulse and slow respirations. It is injected into the arm or leg, but needle marks may be found between the fingers or toes, under the tongue, around the ankle or on the penis. Hepatitis is a common result, because of infected needles.

Addicts have commonly passed through stages of glue-sniffing, amphetamine or barbiturate addiction before taking to heroin. In the United States it costs an average of 30 to 40 dollars a day for an addict to obtain his supplies of the drug. It is said that 70 per cent of burglaries and muggings in New York are caused by the need to obtain money for drugs. Prostitution is another result. It is estimated that in New York alone there are 50,000 to 100,000 heroin addicts. It is the leading cause of death in New York between the ages of 15 and 35: the average age of death for heroin addicts is 27. Each year in New York between 400 and 800 infants are born to addicts: the infants are drug dependent, and would suffer severe withdrawal symptoms unless treated appropriately.

Cocaine

Cocaine is taken by injection or sniffing. It causes euphoria, excitement, loss of appetite, with paranoia, delusions of persecution and hallucinations.

Methedrine

Methedrine, taken by injection, causes excitement, talkativeness, loss of appetite, insomnia, psychoses and depression.

Mixed Drugs
There is now an increasing tendency to adopt the highly dangerous practice of taking several drugs at the same time, in a mixture.

Discussion
Drugs tend to lead to crime in various ways. Addicts commit crimes in order to obtain the money with which to purchase the drug. The drugs allow character traits to reveal themselves, partly by loss of inhibitions: they have a direct effect on the brain: and they may lead to accidents because of the associated unsteadiness or confusional states.

The causes of drug addiction are numerous. Kepler (1971), Kramer (1972) and Minkowski (1972) wrote that the usual features of the background of the addict are as follows:

Low socio-economic level.
Membership of a minority group.
Residence in a large city.
Broken or disturbed family background: rejecting unloving parents.
Permissiveness of society.
Peer group approval for the use of drugs.
Disturbed inadequate personality.
Cynicism about hypocrisy of society, materialism, social injustice: rebellion against authority.
Boredom with education.
Surfeit of pocket money.
The need for kicks, thrills, adventure: experimentation and curiosity.
Aim to prove one's courage: inferiority complex: search for security and praise amongst peers.
Loneliness. Feeling of being unloved, unwanted, rejected, inadequate. Pursuit of pleasure. Release of stress.
Attention seeking.
Desire to facilitate sexual desire and performance.

It has been emphasised that many children and adolescents experiment with drugs for a short time only: and that it is usual for them to try several different drugs.

References

BASS M. (1970) Sudden sniffing deaths. *J. Am. Med. Ass.* 212, 2075.

BLOCK R.W. (1972) A guide for the management of drug abuse. *Advances in Pediatrics*, Vol. 19. Year Book Publishers.

Committee on Youth (1972) Statement on marihuana. *Pediatrics*, 49, 461.

CONNELL P.H. (1971) in DALEY R. & MILLER H. (eds). *Progress in Clinical Medicine*. London, Churchill/Livingstone.

DAVIS J.H. (1972) Marihuana and automobile driving. *J. Am. Med. Ass.* 221, 714.

FABER R.G. (1972) Marihuana. *J. Am. Med. Ass.* 222, 1423.

FRIEDMAN J.J. (1972) Drug abuse problems in the pediatric age group. *Pediatrician*, 1, 8.

GELLMAN V. (1968) Glue sniffing among Winnipeg school children. *Can. Med. Ass. J.* 98, 411.

GLASER H.H. & MASSENGALE O.N. (1962) Glue sniffing in children. *J. Am. Med. Ass.* 181, 300.

KEPLER M.O. (1972) The abuse of drugs. *Clinical Pediatrics*, 7, 386.

KLONOFF H., LOW M. & MARCUS A. (1973) Neuropsychological effects of marijuana. *Can. Med. Ass. J.*, 108, 150.

KRAMER J.P. (1972) The adolescent addict. *Clinical Pediatrics*, 7, 382.

LEUCHTENBERGER C., LEUCHTENBERGER R. & SCHNEIDER A. (1973) Effects of marijuana and tobacco smoke on human lung physiology. *Nature*, 241, 137.

LEWIN R. (1972) Marijuana on trial, *New Scientist*, June 1972, p. 1.

LUNDBERG C.T.D. (1973) Barbiturates—a great American problem. *J. Am. Med. Ass.* 224, 1531.

Medical Journal of Australia (1973) Marihuana—a red herring? Leading Article, 2, 203.

MILLER H. (1973) Drugs and public morality. *New Scientist*, 59, 442.

MINKOWSKI W.L., WEISS R.C. & HEIDBREDER G.A. (1972) A view of the drug problem. *Clinical Pediatrics*, 7, 376.

O'BRIEN E.T., YEOMAN W.B. & HOBBY J.A.E. (1971) Hepatorenal damage from toluene in a glue sniffer. *Brit. Med. J.*, 2, 29.

PATON W.D.M. (1973) Cannabis and its problems. *Proc. Roy. Soc. Med.* 66, 718.

PRESS E. & DONE A.K. (1967) Solvent sniffing. *Pediatrics*, 39, 451.

ENCOPRESIS—FAECAL SOILING

Faecal incontinence is a most unpleasant and difficult problem to treat. It may have persisted from birth: it is more common in problem families of a low social class. It may develop as a result of emotional stress, sometimes in association with gross constipation. Sometimes it is associated with urinary incontinence. Bellman (1966) in his 151 page monograph, reported an incidence of 1·5 per cent in 7- to 8-year-old Stockholm children: all had lost the symptom by the age of sixteen. In two thirds it developed on starting school, or on being separated from the mother, or on the birth of a sibling. It was more common in boys than girls: IQ scores were average: there were usually other symptoms of insecurity. The mother was commonly tense, anxious and overprotective.

When the soiling is due to gross constipation, the rectum is loaded with a huge mass of hard faeces, and liquid material passes round the edge and leaks out of the anus. The mother then thinks that the child has diarrhoea and incontinence. I have seen such children treated with constipating medicine. It is noteworthy that although the rectum is enormously distended with the huge mass of faeces, the child does not have any sensation of this. He could not pass the faeces if he tried. It is dealt with by means of enemas and efforts to retrain the bowel. It may arise as a result of over-enthusiastic and punitive toilet training in early years. I do not recommend the treatment which the parents of one of my patients had tried for soiling. They had tried corks of various shapes and sizes—without success.

When the cause does not lie in constipation, the matter is more complex and treatment is more difficult. It is usually associated with insecurity, and there are usually other behaviour problems.

Bemporad *et al.* (1972) studied the family background of 17 patients. The usual picture was that of a domineering mother who was too much involved in the child's daily life. There was a high incidence of language disorders and neurological immaturity suggesting that there was an organic basis, but with an unhappy family background. They wrote:

'We found that persistent encopresis is a specific syndrome that occurs predominantly in boys who exhibit signs of maturational deviation and a history of coercive toilet training. These children do not seem to have incorporated sphincter functions under control of the ego or superego but continue to view their toilet functions as intimately related to their relationship with their mothers. The symptom seems to be used as a hostile and attention-seeking maneuver in the course of a hostile-dependent relationship.'

References

BELLMAN M. (1966) Studies on encopresis. *Acta. Paediat. Scandinav.*, Suppl. 170.
BEMPORAD J.R., PFEIFER C.M., GIBBS L., CORTNER R.H. & BLOOM W. (1972) Characteristics of encopretic patients. In CHESS S. & THOMAS A., *Annual Progress in Child Psychiatry and Child Development*. New York, Brunner Mazel.
OLATAWURA M.O. (1973) *Acta. paediat. Scandinav.* **62**, 358.

ENURESIS (URINARY INCONTINENCE)

Enuresis was discussed in the papyrus ebers in 1550 BC. It was suggested that it should be treated by juniper berries, cyprus and beer. Since then hundreds of treatments have been recommended. In an African tribe the child was first whipped, and then a large frog was fastened to his waist to frighten him. Others have recommended roast mouse, hare's brain cooked in wine, hare's testicles, powdered acorn, the dried bladder of a sow sprinkled on to the bed, the dried comb of a cock sprinkled on to the bed, cooked hedgehog, blistering the sacrum, stinging the glans penis with a nettle, a rubber bag in the vagina inflated with air, and many other ideas.

Urinary Incontinence: Bed Wetting

There is a vast literature on enuresis, and there is disagreement between child psychiatrists and paediatricians. Psychiatrists tend to ascribe enuresis always or nearly always to psychological problems. Paediatricians divide enuresis into two types—primary and secondary. In the primary type the child has never been dry at night. In the secondary type the child has acquired control of the bladder and then, after an interval of one or more years, has started to wet the bed again.

The primary type is largely related to delay in the maturation of the relevant part of the nervous system. There is usually a family history of the same complaint. Just as some children are earlier or later than others of the same intelligence in sitting, walking, talking, reading or other skills, so some are later than others in acquiring control of the bladder. If one of identical twins has enuresis, the other almost certainly will, but if one of non-identical twins does, there is only a small likelihood that the other child will. Most children are more or less 'dry' by day by two years of age, and by night by three: but 10 per cent still wet at least occasionally when they start school. This type of enuresis is not normally associated with daytime incontinence, but it is associated with day time urgency. Just as a normal two year old cannot wait when he first feels the desire to urinate, so the primary enuretic, who is late in maturing in control of the bladder, often retains the primitive urgency which the normal two year old has now lost. There is a higher incidence of enuresis in families of unskilled workers.

Psychological factors are commonly superimposed on primary enuretics. The boy is scolded by his mother, punished for wetting the bed, and perhaps ostracised by his siblings because he smells. Furthermore delay in toilet training, and failure to give the child a chance to empty the bladder when he wants to, will delay control. Dr Fred Miller, paediatrician at Newcastle-upon-Tyne, wrote as follows after studying 1,000 families from birth onwards:

'The social correlations were such that it is reasonable to think that most enuresis occurs in a child with a slow pattern of maturation when that child is in a family where he does not receive sufficient care to acquire proper conditioning. We doubt if the continuous type of enuresis is caused by major psychological difficulties at the outset, though we acknowledge that psychological difficulties can occur as an overlap.'

Secondary enuresis is nearly always a behaviour problem, developing as a result of stress and insecurity, especially in the young child who has recently acquired control of the bladder. Occasionally it is due to a urinary tract infection or other ailment which causes frequency of micturition.

The treatment must include treatment of the cause, if that is possible. Scolding for it must cease: it is particularly irrational to scold a child for something which he does in his sleep. For the same reason efforts to shame a child out of bedwetting cannot possibly achieve anything but harm.

Of the hundreds of treatments which are used or have been used for enuresis, two are worthy of mention: the electric buzzer, and a tricyclic antidepressant drug imipramine or amitriptyline. The electric buzzer is effective for the treatment of primary enuresis: the child sleeps on a special pad and the moment wetting occurs the buzzer sounds and the child has to get out of bed to turn it off: it conditions the child to empty the bladder when it is distended. It is successful provided that it awakens the child, and provided the child has to get out of bed to turn it off: he will need to have the buzzer for about three months. The drugs mentioned have possible side effects: they are moderately effective and should be discontinued as soon as possible.

Reference

MILLER F.J.W. (1966) Childhood morbidity and mortality in Newcastle-upon-Tyne. *New Engl. J. Med.* **275**, 683.
For a comprehensive review, see KOLVIN I., MACKEITH R.C., & MEADOW S.R. (1974) Bladder control and enuresis. Clinics in Dev. Med. Nos 48–49. London, Heinemann.

FEARS AND SHYNESS

All children experience fear, except idiots, who are at risk because they have no appreciation of danger. Some have more fears than others. It is normal for the 12-month-old child to be afraid of being left by his mother; for the one to two year old to be afraid of noise, of falling, of motor traffic; for the two to five year old to be afraid of animals, being left alone, or to be afraid of the dark, of imaginary persons, of drowning, of fire. It is normal for the adolescent to be afraid of failure, of making a fool of himself, of losing face, of imaginary sex problems, of death. Excessive fear is partly a personality problem, and is partly based on insecurity. Fear of the dark is a common symptom of nervous children. Fear of desertion is suggested by a mother's unwise threats to the child that if he does not obey, she will leave him. Fears may be suggested by gruesome stories. A child may be afraid of the dark or of thunder or of water because he has seen his mother afraid. He may be afraid of illness or death because he has seen it at home.

Excessive fear should be investigated by a paediatrician, in order that the cause may be sought.

Excessive shyness is a common but troublesome personality trait. It is partly inherited and partly environmental. It is normal for a 12-month-old baby to be shy—to hide behind his mother's apron. It is normal for the three- or four-year-old boy to be shy with other children. One almost always finds that an unusually shy child has an unusually shy parent. In addition the child may have had little opportunity to meet other children and adults, partly because of the parent's shyness and difficulty in establishing friendships.

In all cases the child's fears or shyness must be respected. It is never right to ridicule a child for his fear or shyness. It is unwise to make him face the object of his fear, if the fear is marked.

HEAD BANGING

This is mainly a problem of the toddler, and rarely continues into school age. The toddler repeatedly bangs his head on hard objects, a wooden chair, a table, the wall or the floor. A favourite place for rhythmical head banging is the end of the bed. A mother told me that her boy 'seemed to find a peculiar solace' in banging his head. One sees head bangers with severe bruises on the forehead.

Head banging is nearly always a manifestation of insecurity. It has been produced in experimental animals by rearing them with social and visual deprivation.

I have twice been asked to supply a steel helmet for head bangers. They do little harm to themselves, however, though if it continues well into school age there is a small risk of cataract formation in the eye.

IRRITABILITY AND DIFFICULT BEHAVIOUR

Irritability and difficult behaviour may be merely a feature of a child's personality: it may be due to insecurity—worries at home, worries at school, teasing or bullying. It is an important feature of a low blood sugar, especially in diabetic children, but also occurs in normal children when they are hungry.

An important cause of the symptoms is phenobarbitone—used particularly in the treatment of epilepsy. Phenobarbitone makes some children drowsy and reduces their powers of concentration. Other children are affected differently; they sleep badly, become aggressive, bad tempered and irritable, responding dramatically to discontinuing the drug.

JEALOUSY

All children and most adults are jealous. It is important not to blame or scold a child for it, but rather to try to treat the cause— trying to make him feel more important, more wanted. In the home a wise parent never punishes a child for a jealous act, but goes out of her way to make the child feel more loved, wanted and important.

Jealousy is partly an inherited personality trait. An excessively jealous child usually has an unduly jealous parent. In addition jealousy is occasioned by environmental factors. The jealous child feels that he is not sufficiently loved and wanted now that a new baby has come; or he is disturbed because his older sibling is allowed treats denied to him. Troublesome jealousy is almost inevitable if there is favouritism at home. The closer the gap between births the greater the likelihood of jealousy. As stated in Chapter 2, twins are particularly likely to be jealous.

Some teachers think that allocation of prizes is undesirable, partly because non prize winners are apt to be jealous of those who do win prizes.

Jealousy is a feature of everyday life; wise management in school may prevent it being troublesome.

THE MALADJUSTED CHILD

I have always disliked the term 'maladjusted child'—and the term 'child guidance clinic'. The child is not maladjusted: he is reacting normally and predictably, but perhaps more than other children, to an unsatisfactory home environment. He is apt to be sent to a 'Child Guidance Clinic', but it is not the child who needs guiding, but the parents. The Scottish Education Department in their booklet noted the objections to the term 'maladjusted child', but concluded that no one has thought of a better term. The Department Committee discussed definitions of the term: it covers bad behaviour, restlessness, aggressiveness, timidity, shyness, the child who is unhappy, bad at making friends, consistently late to school, the truant, the underachiever, the bed wetter, the child with nightmares, the daydreamer, the child with poor concentration and many other problems. It covers those who show emotional instability, and other psychological disturbances. As with almost all behaviour problems, the cause lies in a conflict between the child's personality, intelligence and developing mind with the personality, intelligence and attitudes of his parents and his teachers. The neighbourhood and the character of his friends is also a factor. My colleague, Dr Woodmansey, wrote that the main source of emotional damage to children is parental hostility; and that conflict between parent and child is the main cause of psychological illness.

Stott (1962) considered that environmental factors were over stressed. He adduced some evidence that stress during pregnancy might in some way cause a child in later years to respond to an unfavourable environment by developing behaviour problems, including delinquency.

The Education authorities have to ensure that if necessary these children should receive special education. The Scottish Committee considered that about five per cent of school children would fall into the category of 'maladjusted'. The peak age for reference to a child guidance clinic was stated to be six to seven years.

Ascertainment was regarded as a matter for a team, which would include teachers, family doctors, health visitors and social workers.

Whatever the problem, the essential thing is to seek the cause of the symptoms. It is useless to treat the symptoms alone: one has to look for the cause and try to alter the faulty environment (see Chapter 2). As Dr Woodmansey wrote, the principal aim of parent guidance is very simple—it is just to help parents to be nice with their children.

References

SCOTTISH EDUCATION DEPARTMENT (1964) *Ascertainment of Maladjusted Children*. Edinburgh, H.M.S.O.
STOTT D.H. (1962) Evidence for a congenital factor in maladjustment and delinquency. *Am. J. Psychiat.* **118**, 781.
WOODMANSEY C. (1966) *Mental Illness in the Family and its Effect on the Child*. Proceedings of the 22nd Child Guidance Conference. National Association for Mental Health.

Other reading

BURTON L. (1968) *Vulnerable Children: Three Studies of Children in Conflict: Accident Involved Children; Sexually Assaulted Children; Children with Asthma* London, Routledge & Kegan Paul.
CLEGG A. & MEGSON B. (1968) *Children in Distress*. London, Penguin Education Special.

NAIL BITING

Various studies in Britain and America have reached the same conclusion, that slightly more than half of all school children bite their nails (Birch 1955). The subject was reviewed by Billig (1954) in a 90-page monograph. It is rare under the age of three or four. The peak age is 11 to 12 years. It is more common in boys than girls. Only girls bite their toe nails: perhaps only girls can do. Some children suck their wrist or bite their hands as well as their nails. A child or adult is apt to bite the nails when he feels tense. There may be a factor of imitation. It is aggravated by insecurity. There are usually other nervous symptoms. Douglas (1966) found that nail biters, especially if they had other nervous symptoms, tended to do less well at school than children who did not show these habits. Nail biting is a harmless pursuit, but the attitude of parents to it may cause harm. Determined efforts to stop it will cause it to continue.

Nail picking is a similar habit, and gives the same appearance.

References

BILLIG A.L. (1954) Finger nail biting—its incipiency, incidence and amelioration. *Genet. Psychol. Monogr.* **24**, 125.
BIRCH L.B. (1955) Nail biting. *Brit. J. Educ. Psychol.* **25**, 123.
DOUGLAS J.W.B. (1966) The school progress of nervous and troublesome children. *Brit. J. Psychiat.* **112**, 115.

OBSESSIONAL BEHAVIOUR

Mild obsessional behaviour is common and normal. It is normal for the small child to want to walk along the top of a wall, or to jump with one foot on to successive paving stones, or to hop and skip when walking with his mother. Some feel the urge to touch certain objects. Obsessional behaviour is more significant when it causes embarrassment, or takes time, or annoys parents or teachers. The child may realise that his actions are futile, but be unable to resist them. It is never possible to draw the line between the normal and the abnormal. All that one can say is that if the obsessional behaviour is annoying and time consuming or in any way harmful, the opinion of an expert should be sought.

POLYDIPSIA (COMPULSIVE WATER DRINKING)

Polydipsia is usually a habit: it affects children and adults. It is uncertain how it begins. The urge to drink may be extreme, and in class it is a great nuisance. In all cases it should be investigated by a paediatrician in order that he can eliminate organic disease, such as diabetes mellitus, diabetes insipidus (due to pituitary disease or a failure of kidney function) and renal disease.

SLEEP PROBLEMS

Sleep difficulties in children are not a significant problem for the teaching profession. By school age most but not all children have grown out of the common sleep problems of early childhood. The teacher may be faced with the problem of the child who has too little sleep, and falls asleep or nearly does in the classroom. Teachers in residential schools may be concerned with the problem of sleep walking.

The basic problem in the case of the preschool child is the interaction of the child's developing personality with the personality and attitudes of the parents. Children differ widely in their sleep needs: the more active and often the more intelligent child needs less sleep than the more placid inactive child. Efforts to make the child go to sleep inevitably lead to sleep refusal, because of the developing ego and negativism. Parental anxiety leads to efforts to make the child sleep. Habit formation is of the greatest importance. When the 10-month-old child discovers that if he screams when he is put to bed or awakens, he will be picked up, taken downstairs, given a warm drink or taken into his parents' bed, he thinks that this is most desirable and does it every night.

Many older children are said to sleep badly. When a mother complains of this, I always ask her how she knows. There is no reason why she should know unless the child keeps calling out in the night, or the mother keeps going into the child's room to see whether he is still breathing. Many older children call out repeatedly in the evening, because they know that if they do this the mother will take them a warm drink—milk or cocoa. Furthermore, they become aware of the parents' anxiety about sleep and continue to present problems as an attention-seeking device.

If children are put to bed too late, when they are too tired, they are apt to sleep badly. If they are put to bed too soon, before they are reasonably fatigued, the result is the same. Bed time should not be rigid: but once it has been decided that a child should go to bed, there should be no argument about it. I have known parents complain that it takes four hours to get an 11-year-old to bed. If a child can get the whole house revolving about getting him to go to sleep, he will do so. The fuss should be stopped.

Sleep walking is not well understood. It is normal, and does not suggest any disease or emotional disturbance. We do not know why some walk in their sleep and others do not. Some children walk in their sleep only if they go to bed after a recent large meal. It is rare but not unknown for children to hurt themselves in their nocturnal sleep perambulations.

Nightmares are a feature of normal children. If they are frequent —every night—one should look for a cause of insecurity. A nightmare is sometimes a feature of an infection and a rise of temperature. It may also follow a large evening meal.

SMOKING

Because of the health hazard, namely the risk of later development of carcinoma of the bronchus or bladder, chronic bronchitis or cardiovascular disease, paediatricians and others are concerned about the frequency of smoking among school children. In a study of Derbyshire primary school children, it was found that 40 per cent had smoked before the age of nine (Bewley *et al.* 1973). According to *The Times* (1970) 28 per cent of boys aged 15 in this country smoke—many of them 30 or more cigarettes a week. In a Dublin study (1968) of 4,500 school children aged 11 to 18 years, 23 per cent were smokers (31 per cent of the boys, 10 per cent of the girls). In a British study (1959) 8 per cent of 3,500 boys and girls aged 10 to 18, representing 90 per cent of pupils at four secondary modern schools and two grammar schools in an industrial county borough, were regular smokers. One third of the smokers aged 14 to 16 were smoking 20 or more cigarettes a week.

Various studies have shown the greater prevalence of smoking in children in lower grades or streams at school, in the less intelligent children and those with a lower level of academic achievement. Salber *et al.* (1962) in a study of 6,810 high school children, found that in all grades the IQ score and academic achievement was greater in the non smokers. Rogers and Reese (1964) made similar observations. Children who smoked had a higher absence rate than non smokers; there was more smoking in the lower class children (and lower class children had more pocket money (O'Rourke *et al.*)). It was mentioned that the rapidity with which the habit was established was alarming. The younger the age at which the child began to smoke, the greater the risk to his health. There was a high incidence of coughing, wheezing and breathlessness amongst the smokers (Wehrle *et al.* 1969). Teenage boys who smoked were more likely than non smokers to be involved in accidents, to play truant and to have a low grade at school. Tinker (1973) reviewed work which showed that children in families in which smoking occurs suffer more respiratory illnesses, even though they do not smoke themselves, than those in families without smoking.

Brynner (1969) wrote that boys who smoke differ from non-smokers in that they tend to mix more with other boys who smoke: they tend to spend their leisure in more adult activities such as dancing, drinking and chasing girls, rather than in hobbies such as cycling or woodwork: and their parents had a more permissive attitude to smoking.

It is useful to consider the reasons for smoking amongst school children. I suggest that the following are the principal causes or factors:

The example set by parents, siblings, teachers, friends.
The desire to feel grown up, to be 'tough'.
The fact that so many of the other boys and girls do: the desire to conform.
Large amount of pocket money, especially in the lower classes.
Low academic achievement: lower social classes.
A status symbol.
Inferiority complex.
Bravado: children dared to do it.
The fact that it is forbidden by the school.
The fact that the parents object: alternatively—permissiveness on the part of the parents.
Curiosity.
Boredom: something to do.
Worry—examinations, love affair, awaiting a girl.
Advertisements (possibly).

Prevention is difficult because the causes are so varied. It is no use trying to persuade children that they are greatly increasing the risk of certain diseases: they have no idea what it looks like or feels like to die of carcinoma of the lung, and it would not be for many years anyway. To them the pleasures of the moment are more important. It is possible to persuade those interested in athletics that smoking will lower their performance. One thing which one can do is to set the example—and refrain from smoking. It is wise to let children know that if one never starts, one has not the slightest desire to smoke: and that innumerable smokers tell one that they wish that they had never started, but cannot now stop. It is futile to forbid them to smoke. It is more important to teach them that we all have a right to our view and that it is wrong merely to copy others: that if a few smokers criticise them for not smoking, the majority will not. They should do what they think is right and sensible and not be led like sheep. It is doubtful whether advertisements have a significant influence.

References

BEWLEY B.R., DAY I. & IDE L. (1973) *Smoking by Children in Great Britain—a Review of the Literature.* Social Science Research Council and Medical Research Council.

BRYNNER J.M. (1969) *The Young Smoker.* London, H.M.S.O.

O'ROURKE A., O'SULLIVAN N. & WILSON-DAVIS K. (1968) A Dublin schools smoking survey. *Irish J. Med. Sci.* 1, 7th Series 123, 463.

ROGERS K.D., & REESE G. (1964) Smoking and high school performance. *Am. J. Dis. Child.* 108, 117.

SALBER E.J., MACMAHON B. & WELSH B. (1962) Smoking habits of high school students related to intelligence and achievement. *Pediatrics,* 29, 780.

Study Group of the Public Health Department, London School of Tropical Medicine and Hygiene (1959) *Brit. J. Prev. Soc. Med.* 13, 1.

The Times, 21 January 1970.

TINKER J. (1973) Should public smoking be banned? *New Scientist,* 59, 313.

WEHRLE P.F., BRENT R.L., DOYLE J.L., FARR L.E., FAGAN E.L., FINBERG L., NAHMIAS A.J., PICKERING D.E., YAMAZAKI J.M. & HORTON R.J.M. (1969) Smoking and children: a pediatric viewpoint. *Pediatrics,* 44, 757.

See also

British Medical Journal (1969) Leading Article, 4, 6.

STEALING AND LYING

As I have stated elsewhere, that which is normal at one age is not normal at another. The two-year-old cannot seriously be accused of stealing when he helps himself to a sibling's toy without his permission or knowledge, and he is not punished for it. A child of ten gets into serious trouble at school if he helps himself to the property of another without his knowledge or permission. Somewhere in between these ages must be the age at which what was previously normal now becomes abnormal. But no one can draw the line between normal and abnormal.

Stealing is the commonest juvenile crime. Moffatt (1969) studied 500 young thieves. Factors included a family history of stealing, parental unconcern about the child's dishonesty, parental separation, both parents being at work, excessive religious strictness and insecurity. The child was commonly thought by the teacher to be lazy.

Other factors are a bad example set by the parents: tacit approval for the child's dishonesty: overcrowding at home resulting in lack of privacy or any place where the child can keep his own property separated from that of others, resulting in a lack of respect for the property of others at home. The child may feel inferior to others because he has less pocket money. He may steal in order to give money to a friend in order to court popularity.

It is common to hear that a child steals only at home—and often only from his mother. This localises the cause—a faulty child–mother relationship. The stealing may be an act of aggression against his mother. At school it may result from the influence of a gang.

It is normal for a two-year-old to lack understanding of the importance of truthfulness. By the age of ten he should understand the difference between truth and lies. It is normal for a five- or six-year-old to indulge in fantasy thinking and to tell tall stories—but not really with the intention of deceiving anyone: and there is no place for reprimands or punishment for it.

Parents tell lies when they deliberately exaggerate: but they are aiming at impressing their hearers and not deceiving them. The child, however, may not interpret their exaggeration so generously. Example set by the parents is of the greatest importance. If they tell lies to deceive (the mother, for instance, saying in the child's presence that she is out when someone wants to see her or speak to her), it is unreasonable to expect the child to be honest and truthful.

Lies may be due to insecurity: the desire to win praise, gain prestige, win friends, escape punishment or displeasure. When a child lies to get another into trouble, it is essential to try to discover the reason for his behaviour.

In our book *Lessons from Childhood* we recorded a few examples of stealing and lying in children destined for fame. Rousseau, who lost his mother when he was nine days old, was at 13 an expert at pilfering money and vegetables, and nearly embarked on a life of crime. Gandhi stole at 12 so that he could smoke. Charles Darwin wrote that he was much given as a child to inventing deliberate falsehoods.

As a paediatrician I often feel that the punishment for these offences at school is sometimes excessive, though it is easy to see the difficulty in which the teacher is placed. It is important to remember, however, that there must be a good cause for the child's lying or stealing—and the cause is likely to be in the home; yet it is the child who receives the punishment.

References

ILLINGWORTH R.S. & ILLINGWORTH C.M. (1966) *Lessons from Childhood: Some Aspects of the Early Life of Unusual Men and Women.* Edinburgh, Churchill/Livingstone.

MOFFAT J.D. (1969) Stealing: a pattern of behaviour. *South Australian Clinics*, 4, 235.

TEMPER, AGGRESSIVENESS, QUARRELSOMENESS

All normal children display temper, and most have an occasional temper tantrum. All normal young children are aggressive and quarrelsome and want their own way. Most children grow out of these facets of behaviour as they mature, but not all do. It depends on their inherited personality, the home environment, the intelligence and maturation.

By 6 months of age a child may show ire when kept waiting for a feed, or is offered a substance which he does not want or a drink from a cup other than his favourite one, or when he is persuaded or coaxed to eat. By 10 months he may be furious if not allowed to help to feed himself. From 1 to 3 years of age he is in the phase of negativism, and many small children can be little tyrants in this phase—showing their anger and ego in no uncertain way. They hate to be interrupted in their play. They may throw objects in anger and after about 18 months may kick in anger. From 2 to $2\frac{1}{2}$ years of age they are apt to hit other children when there is disagreement about the ownership of a toy. From 3 or 4 they begin to use language for venting their aggressive feelings. At about 6 there is often a recurrence of kicking and hitting. At 8 or 9 children tend to replace physical aggressiveness by arguing, using offensive names, and hurling abuse at their adversaries.

In question time after a lecture I was asked by a parent what she should do about her four-year-old son who was constantly fighting and annoying the neighbours by hitting their children. When I asked what she had done about it, she said 'I have tried absolutely everything.' Therein lay the trouble. If only she had not constantly tried to stop her son fighting, he would have grown out of it: he would have learnt at home that he could not have all his own way. Now the escapades had become an attention-seeking device. He knew that they caused consternation, and that he could get his own way by his annoying behaviour.

Temper tantrums, like many other behaviour problems, represent a conflict between the child's developing personality and ego and his parents' personality and attitudes. If he can get all his own way by having a good tantrum, attracting much attention and causing much parental anxiety, the tantrums will recur. The boy has to put a lot of energy into a really violent tantrum: it would not be worth while if he did not get what he wanted from it.

Tantrums may be due to boredom, restrictions at home because of lack of play space, difficulties in learning new skills, insecurity, overprotection and a bad example set by his parents, who lose their temper when they are tired or worried, and who by nature are irritable, bad tempered and intolerant. Aggressive children have aggressive parents.

It must always be remembered that some children and adults become bad tempered when hungry. This is due to the effect of a low level of blood glucose. When a child is an epileptic the sudden instantaneous onset of an outburst of violence and temper without provocation, without any apparent reason, may be a manifestation itself of epilepsy—a focus in the temporal lobe of the brain. Such attacks may respond well to appropriate treatment.

Quarrelsomeness may be due to similar causes. It is likely to depend in part on the child's personality, but mainly on the management which he has experienced at home. If he is an only child, it must be remembered that he has missed the opportunity of learning from affrays with his siblings that quarrelsomeness does not pay, and that he cannot have all his own way.

Whatever the problem—temper, aggressiveness or quarrelsomeness the essential thing is not to punish the boy and not to blame him for it, but to look for the cause.

THUMBSUCKING

Thumbsucking has largely ceased by school age, but a minority of thumb-suckers continue with the habit after starting school. Provided that it ceases by the age of about six, it does not cause deformity of the front teeth. If it persists after that, it will cause a deformity of the front teeth in about one in eight children.

TICS

Tics, also termed habit-spasms, are an annoying habit. The peak age of onset is seven years (Torup 1962). They consist of sudden movements constantly repeated—blinking of the eyes, twitching of the face, face pulling, shrugging the shoulder, sniffing the nose (when there is nothing to sniff), a cough, tongue clucking or other more complex movements. Fathers are greatly upset by their child's tics: mothers, to a lesser extent, find their child's tics infuriating. Both parents shout at their children, reprimand them and ridicule them. Children do not have tics on purpose, however, and such treatment inevitably makes the tic worse. We do not know why they begin. It is commonly said that insecurity is a factor. Most affected children have other nervous symptoms. They are of a normal intelligence range. In one third there is a family history of tics. They are not easy to treat. No medicine makes any difference. The tic should be ignored as much as possible. Tics generally last several months, and then usually disappear, but some continue into adult life.

References

Torup E. (1962) A follow up of children with tics. *Acta paediat.Uppsala*, 51, 261.

GENERAL REFERENCES

Bakwin H. & Bakwin R.M. (1972) *Clinical Management of Behavior Disorders in Children*, 4th edition. Philadelphia, Saunders.

Illingworth R.S. & Illingworth C.M. (1966) *Lessons from Childhood: Some Aspects of the Early Life of Unusual Men and Women*. Edinburgh, Churchill/ Livingstone.

Verville E. (1967) *Behavior Problems of Children*. Philadelphia, Saunders.

CHAPTER 5
NORMAL DEVELOPMENT AND DEVELOPMENTAL ASSESSMENT

In this section I shall outline briefly the main stages of preschool development in tabular form. I have discussed the normal development of the child in detail in my book *The Development of the Infant and Young Child, Normal and Abnormal* (1972) and in an abbreviated form in a booklet (1973). At the end of the section I have listed useful books on child development written by psychologists. I have tried to cover relevant features of psychological development in the discussion of individual behaviour problems, but have deliberately excluded discussion of theories of learning processes (e.g. those of Piaget), because I have only limited knowledge of them, and they are well covered in textbooks of psychology.

The following (after Gesell) are select 'milestones of development'—mainly after the first year.

5–6 weeks	Smiles at mother in response to social overtures.
3–4 months	Turns head to sound.
5 months	Reaches out and gets object without it being put into the hand.
6 months	Chews. Transfers object from one hand to another. Sits on floor with hands forward for support.
7 months	Sits for seconds on floor, no support.
9 months	Crawls on abdomen.
10 months	Creeps on hands and knees. Walks, holding on to furniture.

Goes for object with index finger.

Picks up pellet between tip of thumb and tip of forefinger.

Plays clap hands (pat-a-cake).

Waves bye-bye.

Helps mother to dress him by holding arm out for coat, foot out for shoe, or transferring object from one hand to another to put hand through sleeve.

Smiles at everyone: behaviour at its best.

12 months   Walks like a bear, on sole of foot and hands.

Walks, one hand held.

Says 2–3 words with meaning.

Has largely stopped taking objects to the mouth.

Beginning to cast objects, one after the other, on to the floor.

Slobbering (drooling) largely stopped.

Understands phrase—where is your shoe?

Beginning to be shy and coy.

13 months   Walks without support.

15 months   Creeps upstairs.

Kneels.

Falls by collapse.

Gets up into standing position without help.

Seats self in chair.

Cannot go round corner or stop suddenly.

Cannot throw ball without falling.

Tower of 2 to 3 one-inch cubes.

Holds two cubes in one hand.

Manages ordinary cup to pick it up, drink from it and put it down.

Feeds self: is apt to rotate spoon just before it reaches the mouth.

Jargon—voluble largely unintelligible speech with odd recognisable words.

Tells mother he has wet himself.

Domestic mimicry—copying mother brushing, washing etc.

18 months   Walks up and down stairs without help.

Pulls wheeled toy.
Throws ball without falling.
Jumps on both feet.
Builds tower of 3 or 4 one-inch cubes.
Jargon—with many intelligible words.
Manages a spoon without rotating it.
Takes off socks, gloves, can unzip fastener.
Dry by day, with a few accidents.
Points on request to 2 or 3 parts of the body.
Turns pages, 2 or 3 at a time.
In picture points to 2 or 3 objects correctly.
Pencil and paper, scribbles. May imitate a stroke.

2 years
Pencil—imitates vertical and horizontal stroke.
Makes 2 or more strokes for a cross, when copying a cross.
Begins to notice sex differences.
Knows sex, full name.
Repeats two digits, in one of three trials.
Names one colour.
Jumps, both feet.
Walks on toes, on request.
Attends to own toilet needs, except wiping.
Tower of 8 one-inch cubes.
Imitates train and includes chimney.

3 years
Jumps off bottom step.
Climbs stairs, one foot per step.
Descends stairs, two feet per step.
Stands on one foot for seconds.
Dresses and undresses fully, except for buttons at back and shoe laces. Unbuttons front and side buttons.
Copies a circle.
Imitates a cross.
May count up to 10.
Tower of 9 to 10 one inch cubes.
Imitates bridge (3 cubes).
Rides tricycle.
Repeats 3 digits, one in three trials.

4 years
Ascends and descends stairs, one foot per step.

Skips on one foot.
Buttons clothes fully.
Copies a cross.
Imitates a gate (5 cubes)
Questioning at its height.
Tells fantasy stories.
Repeats 3 digits, 3 out of 3 trials.

5 years   Skips on both feet.
Ties shoe laces.
Repeats 4 digits, 2 out of 3 trials.
Names 4 colours.
Copies a triangle.

DEVELOPMENTAL TESTING

It is said that Tiedmann in Germany in 1787 was the first to give a detailed account of the development of an individual child. In 1877 Charles Darwin wrote a detailed description of the day to day development of his own child. Bayley (1958) wrote that in 1912 Stern and Kuhlman suggested that a child's status could be shown by the ratio between his mental and chronological age. Binet's original aim was to identify children who were unlikely to benefit from regular school instruction. Arnold Gesell developed his tests because of his interest in mental deficiency, and of the observation that mentally defective children had been slow in development during infancy: he therefore studied the development of normal babies.

THE ROLE OF DEVELOPMENTAL TESTING IN INFANCY

Any parent has a natural desire to know whether his child is developing normally, particularly if there had been some potentially noxious factor operating during pregnancy, or if there had been a difficult delivery. The doctor wants to know whether the baby is normal if there has been an illness, such as a convulsion, which might have damaged the child's brain. His findings of abnormality will alert him to the need to search for one of the known treatable causes of retardation, such as a metabolic defect. He needs to be able to assess a baby's suitability for adoption—a most responsible task, because it is important to prevent foster parents unknowingly adopting a mentally defective or spastic child. The doctor is constantly having to investigate the causes of isolated retardation—backwardness in any of the fields of development, such as walking, talking or bladder control, and he is constantly seeing children who are backward in more than one field. Bad behaviour of a child frequently calls for a developmental assessment in order to determine whether the trouble lies in a low intellectual level: this applies particularly to the older child. For research purposes, such as assessment of the effect of early malnutrition, or a study of the effects of home environment and efforts to improve it, there must be some method of assessing the child's development. For these and other reasons developmental assessment of infants is an essential part of the work of a paediatrician.

ASSESSMENT AND PREDICTION

Infancy

The developmental assessment of infants has become a popular pastime. Large numbers of doctors are attempting it, often, I fear, without knowing how to do it, why they are doing it, or what to do when they have done it. In this section I shall discuss the basis of assessment, the reason for wanting to assess and the action to be taken as a result.

Babies are assessed by determining how far they have developed in relation to the 'norm'—the 'norm' having been determined by studying a large number of apparently well babies. These 'norms' are inevitably composed of developmental items which can be scored: the items are used because they can be scored, but not because they are the most important ones for assessment. At this point I disagree with psychologists in their approach to developmental testing. They give a child a score which depends on whether or not he is able to do certain things which the majority (defined in percentages) can do at that age. I am concerned with *how* a child performs the skills and *when* he first achieved them, rather than *whether* he achieves them. For instance, I am concerned not only with *whether* he turns his head to sound (at six months) but with the *rapidity* with which he responds: the bright child responds instantaneously: the retarded child is apt to be slow in responding.

I am concerned not just with whether he can pick up and hold a one-inch cube, but with the maturity with which he does it—and therefore with the nature of the grasp.

I regard it as essential to take a clinical history, because I must know whether he was born prematurely so that I can make allowance for this. If a child was born two months prematurely, he has missed two months' development in utero, and allowance *must* be made for this. For instance, if he is assessed six months after birth, he must be compared not with an average six months' old baby, but with a four months' old baby. Gross errors would result from failing to make this allowance. The history is essential so that I can determine whether there have been any factors in his management or his past which may have affected his development and yet are unrelated to his intelligence or potential—or whatever one is measuring. For instance, if a mother has deliberately kept a child off his legs because she fears that weight-bearing will give him rickets, knock knees or bow legs, it seems to me to be stupid to give him a low score for weight bearing. If he has had an illness which may have affected his performance, allowance must be made for it. I also want to try to assess his previous rate of development: some babies are slow starters, and are backward at first, and then catch up: others are normal at first but then show signs of mental deterioration, perhaps because of a degenerative disease of the nervous system. By taking a careful history of his previous development, one may determine such unusual features.

For me, as a paediatrician, a clinic examination is essential, because I must know whether there are physical defects which may affect his development. For instance, if he has paralysed legs because of a meningomyelocele, it would seem to me to be foolish to give him a low score for weight bearing: if he is blind, it would be foolish to mark him down on items depending on vision. If he is spastic, it is foolish to mark him down because of his mechanical disability. Yet many psychologists, in their laudable efforts to be scientific, do just this.

Many psychologists, such as Ruth Griffiths, give equal weight to all aspects of development—to his gross motor skills, such as sitting and walking, his fine motor skills, namely manipulation, to his speech and other features. I consider that this is wrong. One cannot reasonably give a score for each of five aspects of development, add them up, divide by five, and say that that is a true picture of his developmental potential or whatever one thinks that one is measuring: for gross motor development is far less important than other fields for assessing his intelligence, and other features are more important. Many mentally subnormal children learn to sit and walk at the usual age (though most are late) and early speech is a certain sign of superior intelligence—though mentally superior children may also be late in speaking.

Psychologists inevitably depend on scorable items of development—on aspects of development which can be translated into figures. But Arnold Gesell pointed out that features which cannot be scored—such as the child's alertness, interest in surroundings, concentration, responsiveness—termed by him 'insurance factors' are far more important. Unfortunately these cannot be converted into figures. The experienced observer notes them and pays due regard to them; but it is uncertain how much his observations are reproducible, depending as they do on clinical impression and experience.

My own feeling is that efforts to be thoroughly objective and scientific, laudable as they are, lead not to accuracy but to unnecessary errors. One must take into account factors which may have affected his development—and factors which will continue to affect it (such as the quality of his home); one must consider the quality of his performance: one must make allowance for prematurity: one must consider his rate of development. One determines how far he has developed in relation to his age, corrected for prematurity, and considers all the factors mentioned and any other relevant ones, weights some of them, puts them all into one's cerebral computer—and makes a judicious guess as to his potential. It may appear to be unscientific: but I believe it to be common sense. I am much in favour of the approach to assessment adopted by Jedrysek *et al.* (1972) following the book by Haeussermann (1958). Their approach is summed up by the following extracts: 'Every moment of contact with the child is important. The very first observations of the child's behaviour are invaluable.' They give no age or grade norms. They add 'We feel strongly committed to the position that classification of a young child is often a deterrent to optimal development. Since the purpose of this manual is to assist the teacher who wants to promote each child's personal growth to maximal capacity, the authors have provided a systematic method for looking at the way a child is functioning, leaving the assignment of a scale score to those professionals who sometimes need to make such a judgment.'

Having assessed him, we must now decide the significance of our findings. To some extent one has assessed his maturity in relation to his age. There is some association between intelligence and maturity. The mentally defective infant is late in all aspects of development (except occasionally gross motor development) and is immature for his age. Arnold Gesell resisted the temptation to convert his findings into a single figure: he sometimes referred to the DQ—developmental quotient—which merely states how far the baby had developed in relation to his age: but in his reports he would hedge this with reservations. For instance, he might record a DQ as 90, but add an important note about the child's 'insurance factors'—his alertness and responsiveness, which could well mean that he would achieve much more than that level in the future. He always recorded separately the development in single fields. It has taken many years since Arnold Gesell's time for psychologists to realise the importance of differential intelligence testing in older children.

Having determined how far a child has developed in relation to his age, and taken all relevant factors into consideration, one has to decide what predictive value this has for the future. Innumerable factors will affect his future development and it is inevitable that there never can be a high correlation between developmental tests in infancy and subsequent development—nor, perhaps to a lesser extent, between IQ tests or examinations in later childhood and subsequent achievement. Anyone assessing infants and children must try to understand what he is testing and the limitations of his tests: and he must know about the variables which will affect the child in the future. He must recognise that the child's performance will be grossly modified by his future environment, his health and many other factors. It has been said that intelligence tests are more of a test of the examiner than of the subject examined.

PERSONAL STUDIES

Some years ago I followed up 137 children who in the first year were thought by me to be backward. Mongols, cretins and hydrocephalics were excluded. Once the opinion was made and

D

entered in the notes, the child had to be included even though further observation a few weeks later had made it obvious that the child had improved and was within normal limits. The original series consisted of 137, but 34 died and 2 had emigrated and could not be traced: otherwise there were no exclusions. Educational psychologists in various parts of the country carried out the follow-up studies with the usual tests, mainly Terman and Merrill. In brief the following were the follow-up scores at the age of five years or later.

IQ score below 50 — 59
50–75 — 24
76–94 — 13
100 or more — 5
Total — 101

With regard to the five who proved to have an IQ score of 100 or more it was realised long before their first birthday that the initial gloomy prognosis was wrong. I described these in detail in the original paper (Illingworth and Birch, 1959).

A second study was that of babies assessed for suitability for adoption on behalf of Nottingham County Council (Illingworth 1971). They were seen by me at the age of six months, and a score of 1 to 5 was written into the notes at the end of the examination. The following were the grades:

1   Superior
2   Possibly above average
3   Average
4   Possibly below average
5   Inferior.

There were no mongols, cretins or hydrocephalics. In several instances when in doubt the babies were seen a second time, at 10 months, for reassessment. The notes were then filed, and at the age of 7 to 8 years the children were tested at school by educational psychologists in various parts of the country. The follow-up was complete. The following were the results:

Original grade	1–2	3	4	5
Total	69	92	54	15
Mean IQ	111·8	108·1	98·6	76

Of the 69 placed in grades 1 to 2, one had an IQ below 80 (1·5 per cent). Of the 69 placed in grades 4 to 5, one had an IQ over 120 (1·4 per cent). Fuller details were given in the original paper.

These studies show that there was some correlation between the modified Gesell tests in infancy and the subsequent IQ scores at school age.

WHAT WE CAN AND CANNOT DO IN DEVELOPMENTAL ASSESSMENT

By developmental assessment in infancy we can determine whether development to date is normal in relation to age. We can detect any but the mildest mental retardation or cerebral palsy. We can recognise moderate or severe visual or auditory defects, and diseases of the central nervous system.

We cannot give an accurate developmental score, because the tests are too crude, and some important developmental items cannot be scored at all, being based entirely on experience and clinical impression. We are particularly liable to underestimate a baby's performance if at the time of the examination he is tired, hungry or not cooperating.

We cannot be sure that a child is not a 'slow starter'—slow in maturing. If he has suffered emotional deprivation, we cannot say how far the effects are reversible, but we know that the longer the emotional deprivation has lasted, the less likely it is that full recovery will be achieved. We cannot diagnose in infancy the mildest forms of cerebral palsy and we may not be able to diagnose mild mental retardation in the first year. We may not be able to diagnose mental superiority in the early months. We certainly cannot predict that a child will or will not suffer mental deterioration. We cannot confidently predict a child's future personality. We may be able to say something about his intellectual potential, but we certainly cannot predict what he will do with his talents and we therefore cannot predict success in life—however we define that. A man may be highly successful in his work but a failure in his domestic relationships and a failure at bringing up his family. Taking the word success in a broad sense, we cannot predict most of the qualities which form a recipe for success. They include a reasonably good level of intelligence, a good personality, determination, concentration, willingness to work hard, creativity, opportunity, the right choice of subjects at school, the right choice of career, a good home, good teaching and good motivation. Of these, the only quality we can predict with some accuracy is a reasonable level of intelligence.

REFERENCES

BAYLEY N. (1958) Value and limitations of infant testing. *Children*, 5, 129.
BRECKENRIDGE M.E. & VINCENT E.L. (1965) *Child Development*. Philadelphia, Saunders.
DARWIN C. (1877) A biographical sketch of an infant. *Mind*, 2, 285.
GESELL A. & AMATRUDA C.S. (1947) *Developmental Diagnosis*. New York, Hoeber.
GRIFFITHS R.C. (1954) *The Abilities of Babies*. London, University of London Press.
HAEUSSERMANN E.C. (1958) *Developmental Potential of Preschool Children*. New York, Grune & Stratton.
HURLOCK E.B. (1964) *Child Development*. New York, McGraw-Hill.
ILLINGWORTH R.S. (1971) The predictive value of developmental assessment in infancy. *Develop. Med. Child. Neurol.* 13, 721.
ILLINGWORTH R.S. (1972) *Development of the Infant and Young Child, Normal and Abnormal*, 5th edition. Edinburgh, Churchill/Livingstone.
ILLINGWORTH R.S. (1973) *Basic Developmental Screening*. Oxford, Blackwell Scientific Publications.
ILLINGWORTH R.S. & BIRCH L.B. (1959) The diagnosis of mental retardation in infancy. A follow-up study. *Arch. Dis. Childh.* 34, 269.
JEDRYSEK E., KLAPPER Z., POPE L. & WORTIS J. (1972) *Psychoeducational Evaluation of the Preschool Child. A Manual utilising the Haeussermann approach*. New York, Grune & Stratton.
SMART M.S. & SMART R.C. (1967) *Children. Development and Relationships*. New York, Macmillan.

CHAPTER 6
PRESCHOOL FACTORS IN THE HOME
AFFECTING DEVELOPMENT

INTRODUCTION

Prenatal factors affecting intellectual development were discussed in Chapter 1. The factors included heredity, the age of the mother, the birth order and the number of children in the family, the parental intelligence (in so far as it would affect the management of the child) and the social class. These factors all overlap with post-natal factors operating in the preschool years. For instance, Nisbet and Entwistle (1967), testing 2,868 Aberdeen school children at the age of 7, 9, 11 and 12, found that there was an inverse relation-ship between family size and IQ test score: but the factors leading to this result are multiple, including the reasons for parents having a large family, the intelligence of the parents of large families as compared with that of small ones, financial matters and the time which parents of families of different size can devote to an indi-vidual child. Others have shown that the more closely births are spaced, the lower is the later IQ score.

Research from many countries (Winick 1969, Cravioto and Delicardie 1970) has indicated that severe growth retardation resulting from malnutrition in the first year retards later mental development, permanently reducing the number of brain cells. The longer the malnutrition lasts, the greater the retardation which occurs.

In any home, rich or poor, insecurity is a serious and important retarding factor. Rejection, parental indifference, inconsistent discipline, intolerance, prolonged absence of a parent, separation from the parents on account of illness, all retard the progress of a preschool child. He may be emotionally disturbed by an experience in hospital, or by attendance at a nursery school, or by bereave-ment—and his ability to learn in the preschool period is adversely

87

affected. His parents may devote so much time to charity, the church and good works that their child suffers—and does not learn.

The reasons for the poor school performance of children of the lowest classes relative to those of the middle and upper classes are not altogether understood, though they have been the subject of several studies. Important factors include the relative lack of conversation and discussion with the child in the poor home: the absence of suitable toys and play material, the lack of books, the lack of interest in the child's learning, the limited visits to places of interest outside the home, the limited interests in the home and punitive discipline.

Parents in low class homes may take no interest in helping the child to learn: or they fear that their efforts may put the child off school and confuse him. They may think that it is soon enough for a child to begin to learn when he starts school, and the whole idea of educational toys, even if they have heard of them, is anathema. Consequently they provide no play material from which he can learn, create or construct. The home lacks puzzles, books, scribbling paper, pencils and toys. The parents converse little, if at all, with their children, except only to criticise them, to remonstrate with them, blame them or accuse them. They do not question their children—and their children's questions are ignored. The only literature which many homes provide consists of 'comics'.

Pavenstedt (1967) described some of the features of slum children. They showed superior gross motor coordination, a good sense of rhythm, but little caution or self protection and failed to learn from accidents. They rarely showed pain. They avoided difficult tasks instead of trying. They became masters at manipulating things for themselves with a minimum of conflict. They distrusted adults, fearing retaliation, punishment or blame. They regarded their surroundings as dangerous and unpredictable. They experienced little back and forth conversation; their vocabulary was poor and their language development was particularly defective.

It would be stupid to suggest that a low social class home necessarily causes underachievement. A low class home may provide love, security and a good learning environment. In our book *Lessons from Childhood* we listed some of the famous men and women who came from homes of the greatest poverty. They included Abel, Bevin, Brahms, Brindley, Bunyan, Burns,

Copernicus, Dickens, Dollfuss, Faraday, Franklin, Keir Hardie, Ben Jonson, Laplace, Lincoln, Luther, Ramsay Macdonald, Mussolini, Anna Pavlova, Rossini, Sexton, Stalin, George Stephenson, Telford and Turner. Martin Luther's father was a miner; John Bunyan's father was a tinker; Gauss's father was a bricklayer; Michael Faraday's a blacksmith; the fathers of Copernicus, Handel and Turner were bakers; those of Thomas Telford, Brindley, Alexander Murray, Rennie, Burns and Bevin were farm labourers.

COMPENSATION SCHEMES

The West Riding of Yorkshire Educational Priority Area Project (at the Red House Education Centre, Denaby Main, near Doncaster) has provided a model to indicate what can be done in a uniformly low class area. The project aimed at providing preschool children with play material of varied types which would arouse and maintain children's interest, provide a basis for learning and teach numbers, colour, shape and sizes at the same time enlisting the help of parents so that they learn the value of toys and play and are guided in their use at home. The project set out particularly to encourage verbal development through toys, books, conversation, singing games and tape recordings. The directors aimed particularly at arousing the mothers' interest in helping their children to learn. The mistake of merely providing a play centre was avoided: children learn in such a centre, but most of their time is spent at home or around home, and it is there that they learn most. Lower class mothers commonly want to do their best for their children, but often have no idea how to help them.

In a report the directors of the study wrote that 'most parents are aware of the importance of their children's early physical development, the need for the care of teeth, hair and skin, adequate diet and injections against sickness and disease. The importance of feeding the child's imagination, helping him to move gradually towards independence in learning, to an increasing interest in thoughts and ideas, and a sense of achievement, is less well understood. By talking to the parents about their importance in the child's learning, they gained an insight into how they could help and take a greater interest in the child's education which they now saw as more relevant'.

When such excellent facilities are not available, children from poor homes can at least benefit from attendance at a good nursery school.

The American 'head-start' scheme did not turn out to be the success expected, for the improvement was only temporary, partly because it may have begun to provide compensatory facilities too late, and partly because the child spends the greater part of his time in and around the home, and it is in the home that the low class children most lack appropriate stimulation.

Karnes *et al.* (1970) over a 15-month period caused 15 mothers of three- to four-year-old children to give extra stimulation at home —and the children were found to achieve much better scores than the control group; but Gray and Klaus (1970) in a similar study of 44 children from low income homes found that the test performance was better only so long as the compensatory help continued: the performance then fell off.

Clarke (1973) in a comprehensive discussion of enrichment programmes, wrote that it is a basic fallacy to assume that disadvantaged children should have the same kinds of experience as privileged ones. He added that if a child is a year retarded, and he is expected to catch up in a year, he must learn at twice the normal rate; it is therefore necessary to focus down the enrichment to central cognitive skills. He also suggested that disadvantaged children may show strong constitutional differences in their vulnerability to adversity and their resilience thereafter.

QUALITIES IN A GOOD HOME

Because of the difficulty of pin-pointing the important harmful factors of the poor home, I have tried to confine this section to positive aspects, namely the desirable qualities of a good home. Many of these are listed in my book *The Development of the Infant and Young Child, Normal and Abnormal* (1972). (See also Chapter 8.)

The qualities of a good home which help a child to achieve his best include the following.

1   Love and security: the avoidance of nagging, criticism, belittling, derogation, disparagement, favouritism. Home atmosphere of love and happiness.

The avoidance of domestic friction.
The avoidance of prolonged separation from the parents.

2 Sensible loving discipline, leading to that degree of independence which is appropriate to his age.
Consistent discipline by both parents, neither parent dominating.
Avoidance of alternating overindulgence and overstrictness.
A minimum of punishment: no punitive discipline, no authoritarianism.

3 Avoidance of overprotection: calculated risks as distinct from thoughtlessness and carelessness.
The chance to make mistakes and learn from them.
Allowing him to practise new skills as soon as he is ready—dressing, feeding himself, helping or doing jobs in the home.

4 The teaching of behaviour acceptable to others.
Thoughtfulness.
Inhibition of cheating.
Good moral values with high standards of conduct suitable for his age.

5 Tolerance and understanding of the child's developing mind, acceptance of the normal negativism, aggressiveness.

6 Parental desire for the child to achieve his best.
Ambition but not overambition—expecting too much of him.
Acceptance however meagre his performance.
Praise for effort, not just for achievement.
Encouragement and reward rather than discouragement.
Expectation of success and of good behaviour.

7 Setting a good example—not only in behaviour, but in reading, television programmes, efforts to find out the causes of things, home interests.

8 Instillation of a tolerant attitude to others—looking for the best in people: avoiding criticism of others.

9 Instillation of a sensible attitude to sex.
Good physical health, abundant exercise, fun and sport.

10 Instillation of a sensible attitude to illness, with no exaggeration of symptoms.

11   Reading to the child (e.g. from 12 months onwards).

12   Provision of suitable play material—which will help him to use his hands, to think, to use his imagination, to construct, to determine how things work.
Scribbling paper, pencils and crayons.
Materials which will help him to find the answer to his questions.

13   Letting him develop his own play rather than directing it or telling him what to do, evaluating his results.
Encouragement of self-initiated learning without providing all the ideas.

14   Encouragement to try to find out, to explore, to observe, to be curious: but it is unwise to allow him to fail. Success breeds success, but failure may lead to failure and refusal to try.
Allowing him to learn from mistakes.

15   Encouragement of accuracy, thoroughness, self confidence, initiative, leadership, persistence.

16   Encouragement of any special interest.

17   Teaching him to discuss, argue, ask the question why, to verbalise, to think round a subject, to question what the parent says, what the radio says, to seek evidence.
To and fro conversation with him—not leaving him out of a conversation (e.g. when friends come).

18   Encouragement to evaluate, to determine what causes what, to seek similarities and dissimilarities.

19   Encouragement of accuracy of speech, avoiding ambiguity.
Teaching clarity of concept: giving opportunity to enlarge the vocabulary.

20   Tolerance of nonconformity.
Respect for unusual and imaginative ideas and play.

21   Providing experiences outside the home—visiting the country-side, seeing natural phenomena, visiting museums and factories.

22   Recognition of the importance of education; when he is at school the acceptance as normal that he should complete his

homework before other pursuits, before watching television
(with, however, some elasticity if there is a special programme
in which he is interested).
The right choice of school.
Contact with the school teachers and discussion where
relevant; guidance with regard to choice of subject.

23 Attention to appearance—yet providing clothes suitable for
uninhibited play.
Avoidance of overweight.
Dental and orthodontic care.

It is hoped that parents will not try to make their child a genius:
but it is hoped that they will succeed in making him a nice child. A
nice child of average IQ may achieve more than a clever child who
is not so nice. The aim should be to help a child to achieve his best
within the limits of his capacity, and to be happy and to be nice.

SOME PLAY MATERIAL

Historical
Rees (1961) and others have traced the history of toys. Balls were
originally of stone, leather, wood, fabric, grass or earth. Throughout the centuries there have been games involving tossing, rolling,
catching or kicking balls. In 2400 BC the Egyptians had a game
called Senet, a gaming board. The oldest toys in European museums
are likely to be Egyptian. In Persia in 1100 BC there were pull toys
of limestone. In Egypt in the same period there was a toy crocodile
with moveable jaws.

The doll was originally a subject of worship or superstition. It
was (and still is) used in the teaching of midwives. Toy soldiers
were made in ancient Egypt, Smyrna and Rome. The yoyo origi-
nated in the ancient East. The kite was used by early armies.

Play material for the preschool child
I shall make this a brief section, because teachers are likely to be
fully conversant with preschool play material. I have discussed the
matter in more detail in my book The Normal Child, 5th Edition,
1972, Churchill Livingstone.

Play material which helps a child to use his new skills, to use his imagination, to create, to think, is more likely to be enjoyed by the child than mechanical toys which do not encourage these skills. The material will be matched to his developmental age, interests and sex. It will include material which helps him to learn eye-hand coordination, to match shapes and colours, to appreciate and match form, texture and weight, to manipulate and to look for detail (e.g. in picture games).

Much useful play material abounds in an ordinary household, and does not have to be purchased from toy shops. It includes bobbins, large curtain rings, boxes, baskets, tins and bricks. In all cases one must ensure as far as possible that the play material is safe, that there are no objects small enough to be inhaled, and that there are no sharp edges.

Probably the best single type of toy is a sack of bricks of different sizes and shapes. Other material includes the posting box, into which blocks of different shapes are posted, the simple form-board, pyramid rings, nesting boxes and barrels, and increasingly difficult jigsaws beginning with the six or eight piece ones. Others are scales and weights, the pegboard, magnetic shapes, pull and push toys, picture lotto, dominoes and picture dominoes, inter-locking building bricks, including stickle bricks with spikes which enable the child to press bricks together, blackboard and chalk, a Bildit, and other construction sets, a painting easel, finger paints, crayons, Plasticine, clay modelling, the gyroscope, animal templates (for the child to trace round plywood forms and paint), stringing coloured beads, picture matching games, flannel-graphs, tracing books, word and picture matching, pile driving, material for domestic mimicry (cookery sets, tea sets, dolls' furniture, sweeping brushes, toy carpet sweepers, baby clothes with suitably large buttons which enable him to dress and undress the dolls), lacing cards, cut out numerals for matching, discarded pieces of cloth, and dressing up clothes. Expensive toys are unnecessary; they can readily be bought secondhand.

A mother begins to read to her child from about the age of 10 months. He begins to enjoy the rhythm of nursery rhymes. She points out objects in pictures—and asks him to do the same. He soon begins to enjoy oft-repeated stories with suitable simple pictures. Gramophone records are appreciated.

Out of doors a sand pit is popular: it is helped by simple wooden implements (rake, shovel and tins). Other material includes a climbing frame, rope ladder, a slide, stilts, a tricycle, pet animals, and later a paddling pool with tins and bits of rubber tubing.

EARLY LEARNING

Some parents (and as a result some private schools) have the erroneous idea that the sooner a child learns, the better. It is uncertain which is the more harmful—trying to teach a child before he is ready to learn, or not giving him the opportunity to learn when he is ready. There is abundant evidence of the existence of a sensitive or critical period in the development of animals, and some evidence that it is important for human beings (Illingworth and Lister 1964). (See p. 25.) For instance, normal babies learn to chew between 6 and 7 months of age: if babies are not given solids to chew within a few weeks of first developing the ability to chew, they will vomit and refuse solids when subsequently given them. If a congenital cataract is not removed early enough, the child will remain blind after its removal. If a squint is not corrected soon enough, the child will be blind in the squinting eye. If deafness is not treated soon enough, it becomes increasingly difficult to get the child to talk. If the cleft palate is not repaired soon enough, normal speech is unlikely to be acquired. Whereas many children learn a foreign language readily at an early age, many highly intelligent adults never learn the idiom and accent of a foreign language after living for years in a country. The predominant theme of Madame Montessori's teaching system was the use of the sensitive period—the provision of suitable facilities for learning and practising a skill as soon as the child is ready—and not before or later. The period three to four years coincides with Piaget's preoperational stage, in which the child is undergoing early socialisation, learning to focus his attention, and to learn the significance of auditory and visual stimuli. Rousseau in Émile (1762) stressed that education should begin while the child is still in the cradle. Bloom (1964) considered that the pattern of learning is established long before the child starts school, and that much harm is done by a bad home in the preschool years by not providing the opportunity to learn. Evidence from studies of the deterioration of the performance of children in underprivileged homes in the early preschool years provides powerful support for that idea.

I do not advocate the intensive early training given to Jeremy

Bentham, John Stuart Mill, Lord Kelvin, Karl Witte, John Wesley, Blaise Pascal and others, as described in our book *Lessons from Childhood*. We found these stories fascinating—particularly the detailed account of Karl Witte's education. Karl's father was a clergyman who believed that the first six years of a child's life were of vital importance from the point of view of education—and he taught Karl in no uncertain way from birth onwards—describing his methods in a 1,000-page book conveniently published in English in an abbreviated form (and summarised in our book). Karl was admitted to the University of Leipzig at the age of nine, was awarded the Ph.D. at 13 and at 16 received the LL.D. and also became professor at the University of Berlin. I shall make no comment on the remarkable methods of early home education used by the parents of these children: but I do suggest that children find great pleasure in learning things which interest them and that suitable play material should be given to them at the time at which they begin to enjoy it and therefore to be ready for it. Kohberg (1968) wrote a good discussion of the place of early preschool teaching and its relation to the critical period. Michael Deakins (1973) has written an instructive 'paper-back' about a highly gifted family brought up in the early years in a remote Welsh house by an intelligent Italian mother and a Jewish father of Polish extraction. The family was the subject of a television documentary programme. The mother gave up her University career and her social life in order to devote her time to the children (who attended the local school when old enough). She used the Montessori methods: she relied on encouragement and praise and avoided all scolding or physical punishment. One boy was a musical prodigy and another was a mathematical genius. The two younger children gave evidence of unusual intelligence.

No-one knows the optimum age for learning. It must be different for each individual child and for individual skills, because it will depend on his intelligence, interests and aptitudes. Piaget emphasised that children have to master one level of intellectual competence before they can assimilate their environment at more advanced levels. The development of cognitive skills follows a definite sequence, but the rate at which the developmental levels succeed each other depends on age and speed of maturation. There is insufficient knowledge to enable us to know precisely when to teach them and in what sequence to present the materials. Wolff and Feinbloom (1969) decried a feeling of urgency with regard to early learning, resulting from overambition. They wrote that 'there is no evidence at present to support the assertion that biologically fixed critical periods control the sequence of cognitive development, no evidence that scientifically designed toys are in any way superior to the ordinary household items available to most infants, no evidence that the systematic application of such toys accelerates intellectual development, and no persuasive evidence that acceleration of specific skills during the sensory motor phase of development, even if possible, has any lasting effects on intellectual competance'. One cannot prove everything, and I feel that this is a rather negative attitude to adopt when there is evidence for a sensitive or critical period for early learning: nevertheless overambition and anxiety about early learning is to be deplored. In a study of 11,000 eleven-year-olds, born in March 1958 (Pringle 1966), it was found that early starters at school (4 years 6 months to 4 years 11 months) were significantly better readers and better at arithmetic than late starters (5 years to 5 years 6 months)—irrespective of social and other factors.

A wise parent is not afraid of 'overstraining' a child, but he must at all costs ensure that early learning is pleasant and enjoyed. If a three- or four-year-old is ready to read, he should be given the necessary material. The essential thing is to provide the right material to help him to learn rather than to attempt to teach him.

Dr Kellmer Pringle, at a meeting in the Royal Society of Medicine, summed up the matter well in the following words:

'Learning to learn does not mean beginning to learn arithmetic or reading at the earliest possible time. It is far more basic and subtle, and includes motivating the child to find pleasure in learning, to develop his ability to pay attention to others, to engage in purposeful activity. It includes developing the child's view of adults as sources of information and ideas, as well as of approval and rewards. Through such learning the child develops his self image, the standards he sets himself for achievement, his attitudes towards others. Evidence is accumulating to show that early failure to stimulate a child's desire to learn may result in a permanent impairment of learning ability or intelligence. The child should learn to learn and decide whether learning is a pleasurable challenge or a disagreeable effort to be resisted. The child must find out early that learning is a pleasure.'

Piaget wrote that the more a child has seen and heard, the more he wants to see and hear.

Many have written to the effect that creativity is learnt at home. Arasteh (1968) reviewed the literature on this subject: play material and factors of management which may encourage creativity have been included in the appropriate sections of this Chapter.

REFERENCES

ARASTEH J.D. (1968) Creativity and related processes in the young child. A review of the literature. *J. Genet. Psychol.* 112, 77.

BLOOM B.J. (1964) *Stability and Change in Human Characteristics.* New York, John Wiley.

CLARKE A.D.B. (1973) The prevention of subcultural subnormality: problems and prospects. *Brit. J. Mental. Subnormality,* 19, 7.

CRAVIOTO J. & DELICARDIE E.R. (1970) Mental performance in school age children. *Am. J. Dis. Child.* 120, 404.

GRAY S.W. & KLAUS R.A. (1970) The early training project—A seventh year report. *Child Development,* 41, 909.

ILLINGWORTH R.S. & LISTER J. (1964) The critical or sensitive period, with special reference to certain feeding patterns in infants and children. *J. Pediatrics,* 65, 839.

ILLINGWORTH R.S. & ILLINGWORTH C.M. (1966) *Lessons from Childhood: Some Aspects of the Early Life of Unusual Men and Women.* Edinburgh, Churchill/ Livingstone.

KARNES M.B., TESKA J.A., HODGINS A.S. & BADGER E.D. (1970) Educational intervention at home by mothers of disadvantaged children. *Child Development,* 41, 925.

KOHBERG L. (1968) Early education. A cognitive developmental view. *Child Development,* 39, 1013.

NISBET J.D. & ENTWISTLE N.J. (1967) Intelligence and family size. *Brit. J. Educ. Psychol.* 37, 188.

PAVENSTEDT E. (1967) *The Drifters. Children of Disorganised Lower Class Families.* London, Churchill/Livingstone.

PRINGLE M.L.K. (1967) Speech, learning and child health. *Proc. Roy. Soc. Med.* 60, 885.

REES E.L. (1961) *A Doctor looks at Toys.* Springfield, Charles Thomas.

WINICK M. (1969) Malnutrition and brain development. *J. Pediat.* 74, 667.

WOLFF P. & FEINBLOOM R. (1969) Critical periods and cognitive development in the first two years. *Pediatrics,* 44, 999.

OTHER READING

The Disadvantaged Child

Cross'd with Adversity (1970) *The Education of Socially Disadvantaged Children in Secondary Schools.* London, Evans Methuen Educational.

DEUTSCH M. (1967) *The Disadvantaged Child*. New York, Basic Books Inc.
DEUTSCH M., KATZ I. & JENSEN A.R. (1967) *Social Class, Race and Psychological Development*. New York, Holt, Rinehart & Winston.
HELLMUTH J. *Disadvantaged Child*: 1967, Vol. 1; 1968, Vol. 2 *Head Start and Early Intervention*; 1970, Vol. 3 *Compensatory Education: A National Debate*. London, Butterworth.

Environment, Creativity, Early Learning

DOUGLAS J.W.B. (1964) *The Home and the School*. London, MacGibbon & Kee.
SLUCKIN W. (1971) *Early Learning and Early Experience*. London, Penguin.
TORRANCE E.P. (1962) *Guiding Creative Talent*. New Jersey, Prentice Hall.
VERNON P.E. (1967) Psychological studies on creativity. *J. Child. Psychol. Psychiat.* 8, 153.
VERNON P.E. (1969) *Intelligence and Cultural Environment*. London, Methuen.

CHAPTER 7
VARIATIONS IN MENTAL ABILITY

DEFINITION OF INTELLIGENCE

Many efforts have been made to define intelligence, but none have been universally accepted (Burt 1969). Shaffer (1965) wrote that it is the product of judgment, reasoning and imagination: and that it includes judgment, integrative ability, comprehension, ability to compare, the power to combine objects into meaningful wholes, the ability to discriminate fine differences, to adjust thinking to new situations, to make appropriate associations between events, to draw inferences from propositions, to solve problems.

Vernon (1969) emphasised that there is no one IQ; a child may excel at verbal, numerical, spatial, perceptual, memory, reasoning, mechanical or imaginative problems, and no-one is good at all of them. Intelligence A is the genetic component, Intelligence B that part of intelligence which is environmental in origin, dependent on prenatal, natal or postnatal factors; while Intelligence C is the IQ score which is based on tests for both A and B.

INTELLIGENCE DISTRIBUTION

Terman and Merrill (1961) gave the intelligence quotient distribution as shown in Table 7.1 overleaf. It should be noted that the mortality of children born mentally defective or spastic is high— probably around 30 per cent before the age of five years. The figures quoted do not give the incidence of mental subnormality in the preschool years.

MENTAL SUPERIORITY

Any paediatrician experienced in developmental assessment is confident that he can recognise a mentally superior infant, but it is difficult to provide proof of his ability—though I have mentioned some evidence in Chapter 5 when discussing the predictive value of developmental tests in infancy. I have discussed the diagnosis of mental superiority in infants in more detail elsewhere (Illingworth 1972).

Briefly the mentally superior infant is not necessarily more advanced in motor development. Gesell and Amatruda (1947) wrote that 'superiority manifests itself in dynamic excellence, in

TABLE 7.1.   Intelligence quotient distribution

IQ	Per cent	Classification
160–169	0·03	Very superior
150–159	0·2	Very superior
140–149	1·1	Very superior
130–139	3·1	Superior
120–129	8·2	Superior
110–119	18·1	High average
90–109	43·5	Average
80–89	14·5	Low Average
70–79	5·6	Borderline
60–69	2·0	Mentally defective
50–59	0·4	Mentally defective
40–49	0·2	Mentally defective
30–39	0·03	Mentally defective

intensification and diversification of behaviour, rather than in conspicuous acceleration. The maturity level is less affected than the vividness and vitality of reaction. The young infant with superior promise is clinically distinguished not so much by an advance in developmental age, as by augmented alertness, perceptiveness and drive. The infant with superior equipment exploits his physical surroundings in a more varied manner, and is more sensitive and responsive to his social environment.' Elsewhere they wrote: 'The acceleration comes into clearer prominence in the second and third years, with the development of speech, comprehension and judgement. However, personal social adaption and attentional characteristics are usually excellent even in the early months. The scorable end products may not be far in advance, but the manner of performance is superior.' They added that the superior infant is emotionally sensitive to his environment, looks alertly, and displays an intelligent acceptance of novel situations. He establishes rapport. He gives anticipatory action to test situations. He shows initiative, independence and imitativeness. He gives a good performance even when sleepy. He is poised, self-contained, discriminating, mature. The total output of behaviour for a day is more abundant, more complex, more subtle than that of a mediocre child.' Hollingworth (1929) and others have noted that most mentally superior children learn to read at about three years of age, and that most learn to talk unusually early. Freehill (1961) noted that the highly intelligent child looks for and sees explanations other than the superficially obvious one. He may say 'Well that depends'. He shows an unusual capacity for reasoning. He develops logical thought at an unusually early age. The early indications of superior intelligence most often noted by parents were quicker understanding, insatiable curiosity, extensive information, retentive memory, large vocabulary (Gemant 1961, Hollingworth 1942), and an unusual interest in number relations, atlases and encyclopedias.

Terman and Oden (1947, 1959) in their study of 1,528 Californian children with an IQ of 135 or more, who were followed up to an average age of 35, found that compared with controls they had tended to walk and talk earlier: they had a better physique and fewer illnesses: they had been less boastful and more honest and they were more stable emotionally: and they tended to have earlier puberty. They had a wide range of interest, and they showed curiosity, sustained attention and creative ability. Nearly half had learned to read before going to school. Their greatest superiority was in reading, language usage, arithmetical reasoning, and information in science, literature and the arts. They were less good in arithmetical computation, spelling and factual information about history. Their main interests were reading and collecting. There was no difference from controls in play interests.

Ogilvie (1973) in his book *Gifted Children in Primary Schools*, noted that children may exhibit general or specific giftedness; they may be gifted for instance, in art, music, maths, science, English, physical education or drama; and he discussed the early features of such giftedness in these subjects. The child gifted in drama was likely to be an extrovert, an exhibitionist, to show sympathy with the experience of others, to have advanced verbal expression and a good memory for words, and to lack self consciousness or at least show a willingness to overcome it. In general the gifted child was an early and avid reader: he showed curiosity, initiative, imaginative forms of expression, an ability to be absorbed in work for long periods, lively conversation, unusual speed of thought, the power to organise material, perception of analogies and relationships, a well developed sense of humour, exceptional energy, a desire to excel, a dislike of failure, a tendency to take the lead and to share ideas with other children. He showed exceptional depth of thought, the ability to organise material, to see the need for many different words to express shades of meaning, to give attention to detail. He would ask innumerable questions: he would be a collector: he would be unusually dependable, alert, observant, a perfectionist, show divergent behaviour and conform less than others, though he would be cooperative and enthusiastic. He would have a good memory: he would tend to need less sleep than others.

The importance of creativity is widely recognised (Getzels and Jackson 1962). Karowe (1965) wrote that the creative child may not score highly on conventional psychometric tests, 'for his special bent is devising ingenious responses, being novel and unconventional and varied in his adaptations to tasks rather than in giving the simple predetermined correct response'. Liam Hudson (1967, 1970) wrote that the academically successful boy is distinguished not by his intellectual apparatus but by the use he makes of it. Hudson thought that in science an IQ of over 125 was of little advantage, for creativity and originality are of much greater importance. Hudson distinguished two kinds of clever schoolboy—the converger and the diverger. The converger excels at the conventional intelligence tests, tends to specialise in physical science or classics, to hold conventional attitudes, to pursue technical or mechanical interests in his spare time, and is emotionally inhibited. The diverger excels at open ended tests—to which there is no single right answer; he specialises in the arts or biology; he holds unconventional attitudes; his interests are connected in one way or another with people; and emotionally he is uninhibited.

Mentally superior children may experience certain difficulties at school, but one feels that Michal-Smith (1957) was going a little too far when he included a chapter on the mentally superior child in his book entitled *Management of the Handicapped Child*. Mentally superior children may be bored, because the work is too easy for them, and become lazy—sometimes doing badly in school work as a result. They may be inattentive and day-dream. They may get into trouble at school because of their originality and creativity, tending to annoy by loquacity and argumentativeness. They are often exasperated by restraint. They may be lonely, because they find it difficult to suffer fools gladly, and may be intolerant towards those less clever than they are. Their physical and emotional development tends to lag behind their intellectual level, so that they are less mature than they are expected to be: as a result, partly as a compensatory measure, they may become boastful.

Terman and Oden (1947, 1959) followed the mentally superior children into adult life. It was found that they suffered less neurosis, insanity and alcoholism than the controls: the suicide rate and incidence of juvenile delinquency was less. The marriage rate was higher, and they tended to marry earlier. They had fewer children than the controls. They tended to choose a partner in marriage of higher intelligence than did the controls. The divorce rate was lower. Their income was greater. Six per cent became doctors. Six per cent became minor clerical workers, policemen, firemen or semi-skilled craftsmen. One became a truck driver. The mean IQ of the 384 offspring was 127·7 and the proportion of children with an IQ of 150 or more was 28 times that of the general population.

Ogilvie (1973) discussed the management of gifted children in the primary school. It was thought that segregation of these children had a bad effect on their social development; that his peers would suffer from his absence; and that parents of children not selected for special schooling would be upset. Nevertheless various possibilities for enrichment were suggested—such as special classes in ordinary school hours, Saturday morning classes, home tuition, early admission to secondary schools, and extramural activities. It was suggested that these children, partly to prevent them becoming bored, should be 'stretched and challenged even to the point of experiencing failure and humbling experiences'; they should be guided and counselled rather than directed; they should be enabled to pass rapidly through the elementary stages; they should be given every opportunity and encouragement to exercise specific talents; they should be made to enjoy the acquisition of knowledge; they should be helped to enquire and investigate; they should be helped to develop powers of concentration, exploration in depth, classification, the development of new interests, enhancement of their verbal and creative abilities; and their needs to talk, to question, to listen and to be listened to, must be encouraged, so that they develop skill in discussion and overcome reticence. Dr Ogilvie's book is a valuable contribution which not only teachers but paediatricians should read and possess.

Mental Superiority references

BARLOW F. (1951) *Mental Prodigies*. London, Hutchinson.

BRANCH M. & CASH A. (1966) *Gifted Children*. London, Souvenir Press.

BURT C. (1969) Review of book by BUTCHER H.J. (1968) *Human Intelligence: Its Nature and Assessment*. London, Methuen. *British J. Educ. Psychol.* 39, 198.

FREEHILL M.F. (1961) *Gifted Children*. New York, Macmillan.

GALTON F. (1962) *Hereditary Genius*. London, Collins-Fontana.

GEMANT A. (1961) *The Nature of the Genius*. Springfield, Charles Thomas.

GESELL A. & AMATRUDA C.S. (1947) *Developmental Diagnosis*. New York, Hoeber.

GETZELS J.W. & JACKSON P.W. (1962) *Creativity and Intelligence*. New York, Wiley.

HOLLINGWORTH L.S. (1929) *Gifted Children*. New York, Macmillan.

HOLLINGWORTH L.S. (1942) *Children above 180 IQ*. New York, World Book Co.

HUDSON L. (1967) *Contrary Imaginations*. London, Penguin.

HUDSON L. (1970) *Frames of Mind*. London, Penguin.

ILLINGWORTH R.S. (1972) *Development of the Infant and Young Child, Normal and Abnormal*, 5th edition. Edinburgh, Churchill/Livingstone.

ILLINGWORTH R.S.& ILLINGWORTH C.M. (1966) *Lessons from Childhood. Some Aspects of the Early Life of Unusual Men and Women*. Edinburgh, Churchill/Livingstone.

KAROWLE H.E. (1965) Creativity. *J. Pediat.* 66, 826.

MICHAL-SMITH H. (1957) *Management of the Handicapped Child*. New York, Grune & Stratton.

OGILVIE E. (1973) *Gifted Children in Primary Schools*. London, Macmillan.

SHAFFER G.W. (1965) The nature of intelligence. In OSLER S.F. & COOKE R.E., *The Biosocial Basis of Mental Retardation*. Maryland, Johns Hopkins Press.

TERMAN L.M. & ODEN M.H. (1947) *The Gifted Child Grows Up*. Stanford, Stanford University Press.

TERMAN L.M. & ODEN M.H. (1959) *The Gifted Group in Midlife*. Stanford, Stanford University Press.

VERNON P.E. (1969) *Intelligence and Cultural Environment*. London, Methuen.

MENTAL SUBNORMALITY

General Comments

The term mental subnormality is loosely used, but it should refer to children with an IQ score of below 70—that is about 2–6 per cent of all school children. Normally those with an IQ of 50 to 70 are referred to a school for educationally subnormal children

(ESN school), and those with an IQ score below 50 to a 'special' school (formerly termed a training centre). It is important to note that there is no hard and fast dividing line between the two groups: other relevant factors which decide the authorities on the choice of school are the child's behaviour and his other handicaps.

The *causes* are of prenatal, natal or postnatal origin. Most of the prenatal factors are not fully known. They include:

(i) *Genetic conditions.* There are scores of genetic conditions associated with mental subnormality. It is not always possible to be certain that a child's subnormality is genetic, because normally there is no family history of mental defect: to some extent the diagnosis is often one of exclusion of other known causes. We know that when a child is born with mental subnormality, and full investigation fails to reveal a cause, the risk of another affected child being born to the mother is about 1 in 30—a much greater risk than that in the whole population. Some of the genetic conditions carry a much greater risk of another being affected, because they are recessives, and then the risk of another being affected is one in four. Others are dominant, with a one in two chance of another child being affected. These include tuberous sclerosis and neurofibromatosis. Severe mental subnormality occurs equally in the social classes: less severe mental subnormality (ESN level) is more common in the lower classes—under 4 per cent of affected children belonging to professional classes, but 25 per cent to social class five.

Chromosomal abnormalities include Turner's syndrome, affecting almost entirely the girl, and Klinefelter's syndrome, affecting the male. Girls with Turner's syndrome usually have only 45 chromosomes instead of 46, and lack the Y chromosome. They are short in stature and at puberty they do not usually experience the normal breast changes, the external genitalia remaining infantile: they do not menstruate and are almost always infertile. They may have some webbing of the neck, a low hairline at the back of the neck, widely separated nipples, and sometimes congenital heart disease. Though by no means always mentally subnormal, their mean IQ is less than the average. Klinefelter's syndrome occurs in 1 in 1,000 live born males, but in 1 in 100 mental defectives. It is due to an abnormality of the sex chromosome. At puberty they have enlargement of the breasts (gynaecomastia) with small testes. A quarter are mentally subnormal.

Mongolism (Down's syndrome) is a chromosomal abnormality, usually trisomy 21. The incidence is 1 in 350 births. The diagnosis is made by an experienced midwife, usually at the moment of birth, but sometimes the diagnosis is delayed. It is made on the basis of the typical face, but there are other non-specific features— a flat occiput, rather small head, incurving little finger, a single palmar crease and spade shaped hands. The finer palmar markings are characteristic in the eyes of the expert with good sight. A quarter have congenital heart disease. After about seven years they develop a fissured tongue, and in later years about 10 per cent develop cataracts. Puberty is delayed, and most are infertile, but if a female mongol produces a child, there is an even chance that the child will be normal. Mongols rarely have fits, unlike other defectives. They are all retarded in development, but they are relatively better in the early months, their development slowing down after the first six to nine months. The average age at which a mongol passes certain milestones is given in Table 7.2. Their

TABLE 7.2.   'Milestone' ages for average and mongol children

Milestone	Age for average child	Usual age for mongol
Sit without help	7 months	1 year
Walks without help	13 months	2 years
Single words	1 year	3 years
Feeds self	15 months	4 years
Controls the bladder	2 years	5 years
Joins words together to make sentence	2 years	6 years

mean IQ is 28; there is some scatter; the majority will go to a 'special' school for SSN children, but a few will get to an ESN school. They hardly ever learn to read or write—or at least to read and write with understanding. There is a common statement, repeated from textbook to textbook, that mongols are placid, easy to manage and musical. This is incorrect. Many studies have shown that they are no different in behaviour from other equally defective children, and they are not musical (Tizard and Grad 1961, Blacketer-Simmonds 1953, Baron 1972). I am aware of only one study which suggested that mongols were less aggressive than other retardates—that of Moore et al. (1968). One has seen many aggressive mongols who are difficult to manage.

Half die by the age of five. The mean expectation of life of survivors is 26 years. They are prone to respiratory tract infections. They tend to become fat because of relative inactivity.

(ii) *Infections in pregnancy.* The most important infections which damage the fetus in utero are syphilis, rubella (German measles) in the first three months of pregnancy, the cytomegalovirus and toxoplasmosis. Syphilis now rarely infects the fetus in Britain, thanks to good preventive measures. Rubella has been discussed in Chapter 1. The cytomegalovirus and toxoplasmosis are ubiquitous, and most adults have been exposed to the infection, as can be shown by examination of their blood. Toxoplasmosis is an infection widespread in domestic animals. If a pregnant woman should be unfortunate enough to acquire the infection for the first time in early pregnancy, the child may have eye defects and hydrocephalus.

(iii) *Prematurity.* The smaller the child at birth the lower the mean IQ. This is due to a variety of factors, including mixed social ones. Toxaemia in pregnancy may cause prematurity and slightly increases the risk of mental subnormality in the fetus.

(iv) *Irradiation and drugs.* Children born of mothers within a certain distance from the centre of the atomic explosions in Hiroshima and Nagasaki were mentally defective. Irradiation of the mother's pelvis in pregnancy may damage the fetal brain (Chapter 1).

(v) *Cretinism.* Cretins are born with thyroid deficiency; they have a characteristic face, and there are other features such as backwardness in development, a dry skin, coarse hair and a gruff voice. As they get older, if untreated, they are found to be severely defective, and they are stunted in growth because of delay in maturation of the skeleton. They are commonly diagnosed at birth or in the first few weeks, but occasionally the diagnosis is delayed. Sometimes the child develops normally, physically and mentally, for some months or years, before thyroid deficiency develops, when the child stops growing and may become sluggish in his responses. The treatment consists of thyroxin. The mean IQ of properly treated children with thyroid deficiency is probably around 90; not many have an IQ much over 100.

(vi) *Birth injury* is a most unlikely cause of mental subnormality, though severe anoxia at birth can certainly damage the brain. McKeown and Record (1971), referring to factors operating during pregnancy, wrote that 'the most convincing evidence that prenatal influences have little effect on measured intelligence is the observation that twins separated from their co-twin at or soon after birth have scores little lower than singletons, in spite of retarded fetal growth, short gestation and increased risks during birth'. They pointed out that the mean intelligence score of twins raised together is five points lower than twins separated at birth: this must be due to differences in postnatal environment. McKeown and Record showed that much of the IQ differences related to birth order are environmental rather than of innate origin. They found little relationship between intelligence and abnormalities of pregnancy or labour. Barker (1966) investigated 607 subnormal children and concluded that 'recognised abnormalities of pregnancy and delivery seemed to play little part in determining subnormality'.

(vii) *Cerebral palsy* is commonly associated with mental subnormality. It is discussed in Chapter 16.

Mental subnormality may develop after birth (see p. 117).

Postnatal Factors
The infant's brain may be damaged in the newborn period by severe jaundice, due to haemolytic disease (rhesus incompatibility) or prematurity; by severe hypoglycaemia (low blood glucose), which is a common cause of neonatal convulsions; and by certain metabolic diseases, most of them associated with abnormal aminoacid metabolism such as phenylketonuria. Severe jaundice of the type mentioned above causes kernicterus—a term meaning that there is yellow staining of nuclei in the brain. Half of the affected babies die in the newborn period. The others survive with a varying picture—some with a form of cerebral palsy (athetosis) and others with mental retardation or deafness. Malnutrition due to any cause (Chapter 1) may damage the developing brain, particularly in the first year. Another serious cause of metabolic brain damage is hypernatraemia—too much sodium in the blood. This occurs in infants mainly with gastroenteritis or respiratory infections, and especially in those who have been given overconcentrated milk feeds made up from milk powder. If these feeds are made up too concentrated, the baby receives too much sodium. The kidney can excrete the excess of sodium as long as he remains well, but if he becomes feverish, or develops a respiratory or alimentary infection, he loses so much fluid by other routes that

the kidney has not enough fluid with which to excrete the sodium, which therefore accumulates, and may cause convulsions and brain damage. The damage done by an unsatisfactory home, with lowering of the IQ, is discussed in Chapter 8.

Brain damage may result from severe head injury, meningitis or encephalitis.

Physical Features

Numerous conditions associated with mental subnormality are associated with a characteristic facies which enables the expert to make an immediate diagnosis. Obvious examples are mongolism and cretinism. There are several large volumes which are devoted to illustrations of syndromes associated with mental deficiency. Nevertheless the majority of mentally subnormal children do not have a specific facial appearance pointing to a particular condition: these are the non-specific mental retardates.

A third of over 1,000 mentally subnormal children seen by me in the outpatient department at the Children's Hospital, Sheffield, excluding mongols, cretins and hydrocephalics, have major congenital abnormalities, such as syndactyly (webbed fingers, fingers joined together), polydactyly (extra digits), cleft palate, congenital heart disease or abnormalities of the eye or other structures. To put it another way, a child with a major congenital abnormality anywhere is more likely than others to have a low IQ: and the mean IQ of children with a major abnormality is less than that of the population as a whole. Obviously this does not imply that no children with a congenital abnormality have a superior IQ.

Most mentally subnormal children have a small head—small in relation to their overall size. Part of the routine assessment of any baby includes measurement of the maximum head circumference and its relation to the baby's weight—for investigation at Sheffield showed that of various measurements, the weight was the best and easiest to which to relate the head size. When in doubt one plots the head circumference and weight on centile charts: the two should more or less correspond in their placement. The baby's head size depends on the growth of the cranial contents: if the brain does not grow properly the head is likely to be small—unless there is obstruction to the cerebrospinal fluid pathways (hydrocephalus), or a rare condition called megalencephaly, which is a big brain of poor quality. Almost all mongols have a small head. If a child suffers a severe head injury, after about the first birthday, resulting in mental deficiency, the head will not be unduly small, because by the first birthday the brain has reached about three quarters of its eventual size. A very small head is sometimes termed microcephaly: as any Greek scholar knows, that simply means a small head: it is not a feature of any one type of mental deficiency.

Doctors are interested not only in the size of the head, but in its shape. Mongols have a flat occiput. Severely defective children have what I term a badly shaped head—the head tapering off to the vertex, often with a sloping forehead. Sometimes one sees a broad head, broad from side to side, but flat, and therefore with a small anteroposterior measurement: this is commonly associated with mental subnormality. Bizarre shapes are found in the rare condition craniostenosis, in which some of the sutures fuse prematurely and so will not permit the normal head growth. There are other abnormalities, often associated with mental subnormality, such as hypertelorism, in which there is an unusually big gap between the orbits, due to an abnormality of the base of the skull.

Convulsions are common amongst mentally retarded persons, and are difficult or impossible to control fully. They take the form of grand mal attacks. They are very rare in mongols.

Cerebral palsy (Chapter 16) is a common additional feature of mental subnormality.

Diagnosis

When a baby is born, certain forms of mental subnormality, such as mongolism and cretinism, can be recognised immediately. It is commonly possible to recognise various chromosome abnormalities at birth, including Turner's syndrome. Even at birth the head may be small and there may be other congenital abnormalities which alert one to the possibility of mental subnormality. Various laboratory investigations may clinch a clinical diagnosis.

The developmental examination is of the utmost importance for the diagnosis of mental subnormality. The mentally retarded infant is backward in all aspects of development, except occasionally in sitting and walking, and rarely in sphincter control. It follows that the newborn retarded infant, being backward in everything, behaves like a prematurely born baby: he sleeps much more than a normal full-term baby, and he may have difficulty in sucking and swallowing. For some months he may sleep excessively so that his mother says that 'he is such a good baby', 'he's not a bit of trouble', 'you wouldn't know you had a baby'. When he reaches the walking stage, usually belatedly, he is apt to show aimless overactivity and to wear his mother out.

Signs of cerebral palsy, except in mild cases, can be detected immediately. The baby, whether he has cerebral palsy or not, will be late in passing all the milestones: he will be late at beginning to smile at his mother, to hold on to a rattle placed in his hand, to turn his head to sound, to reach out and get objects, to chew, to copy his mother (e.g. in making certain sounds), in transferring objects from one hand to the other; he is usually late in sitting, pulling himself to the standing position, creeping and walking: he is late in learning to wave byebye, play pat-a-cake, to help his mother to dress him (by holding his arm out for a coat, his foot out for a shoe), in saying words with meaning, in feeding himself, controlling his bladder, making sentences, domestic mimicry (copying his mother in dusting, sweeping, washing up) and in fact in all aspects of development. Above all he shows less than the usual interest in his surroundings: he does not concentrate as much as he should on play objects: he shows less than the usual rapport, responsiveness, alertness. He may grind his teeth when awake. He is late in stopping taking objects to the mouth—while normal babies largely stop this by about 12 to 14 months: he is late in stopping to cast objects one after the other on the floor—while normal babies stop this by about 14 to 15 months. As he gets older he is late in maturing in his behaviour—late in losing the normal overactivity, late in stopping to cling to his mother, and late in reading. His poor powers of concentration are particularly in evidence.

The diagnosis is confirmed—and always must be confirmed—by developmental tests. I have described the tests in detail elsewhere (Illingworth 1972). Briefly they are the Gesell tests, with the addition of the Goodenough draw-a-man test and the simple and Goddard formboard. It is essential that during the tests one should satisfy oneself that the child can see and hear—remembering that a mentally subnormal child is more likely than others to have a visual or auditory defect. For more formal testing of the older pre-school child, there are the usual Terman and Merrill and other procedures. From the paediatrician's point of view, an accurate figure is not required and the Gesell tests give all the information which one needs.

Prevention

In spite of all modern advances we have only touched the fringe of the problem of the prevention of mental defect. Appropriate genetic advice and contraception may achieve something. By means of thorough biochemical and chromosomal investigation of children found to be mentally subnormal, we can give fairly accurate genetic advice to parents who wish to know the risk of another child being affected. Rubella (German measles) in pregnancy is prevented in Britain by immunisation of girls aged 11 to 13 who have not had the infection. Congenital syphilis is now extremely rare in Britain, thanks to good antenatal care. By examining the amniotic fluid during pregnancy (amniocentesis) certain chromosomal defects, including mongolism, and about 50 metabolic diseases associated with mental deficiency can now be diagnosed, so that pregnancy can be terminated. For about 12 metabolic diseases, of which phenylketonuria is the best known, a special diet is now given, and proper treatment prevents the development of mental deficiency. Haemolytic disease, due to rhesus incompatibility, is now largely prevented by appropriate treatment when a rhesus negative woman has a termination of pregnancy or gives birth to a rhesus positive baby. Haemolytic disease used to be an important cause of severe jaundice in the newborn—and severe jaundice damaged the brain, leading to mental subnormality, deafness or cerebral palsy. The other major cause of severe jaundice in the newborn is prematurity, and the severity of the jaundice due to this cause can now be reduced by appropriate treatment—exposure of the infant to light or a replacement transfusion. Exposure of the pelvis of a pregnant woman to X-rays can usually be avoided. Though drugs taken by a woman in pregnancy rarely affect the fetal brain, there are several drugs which can damage the fetal ear and eye, and therefore indirectly affect his mental development. Now that there is evidence that the fetal brain can be damaged by malnutrition in utero, antenatal supervision of the mother's nutrition is important in particular with regard to dietary measures for maternal overweight. There are a few causes of prematurity which can be avoided. Theoretically improved nutrition would reduce the risk of prematurity. After the birth of the baby, prompt recognition and treatment of a low blood glucose (hypoglycaemia) is important, for hypoglycaemia may permanently damage the baby's brain. Prompt diagnosis and treatment of neonatal meningitis and of infantile cretinism (thyroid deficiency) can do much to prevent mental subnormality. Lead poisoning is an important cause of mental subnormality in other countries, such as the United States, particularly in slum areas, and prevention, diagnosis and treatment are significant steps for its control.

Prognosis
It is difficult to state the prognosis of mental subnormality with any degree of accuracy. The variables include the degree of subnormality, the exact diagnosis, the social class and home environment, and the presence of associated handicaps. As for the degree of subnormality, experience has shown that a child with an IQ of over 50, provided that he has no other handicap, should be able to earn his living. If he has other handicaps, it is much less likely, but it depends on their nature. The diagnosis is important, because one needs to know whether it is one of the degenerative diseases of the nervous system, in which progressive mental deterioration occurs. It is particularly difficult to state the prognosis if a child has epilepsy; as stated elsewhere epilepsy may lead to mental deterioration because of brain damage, psychological factors or the effect of drugs. The quality of the home is bound to have a great effect on the outcome: a good home in which the child has love and security, is taught independence, and is given the opportunity to learn, will help a handicapped child to achieve far more than a child brought up in a poor home or worse still in an institution.

Management
In this section I shall not discuss the education of mentally handicapped children, because I have no experience of it.

The paediatrician's responsibility is to try to understand the problems of the mentally handicapped child in the home, and to try to help the parents in their management of the child. Dr Kenneth Holt (1957) wrote an excellent thesis on the problems of Sheffield families in which there was a mentally defective child, and the Carnegie trust conducted a valuable investigation in Sheffield, Glasgow and an urban area, to determine the problems of the handicapped child. One has to recognise the stresses to which the family is exposed. These are physical stresses—the extra work which the child causes, the fact that he cannot walk and has to be carried, his incontinence, his inability to concentrate on play and therefore his ready boredom; the mother's inability to get out without the defective child: the problem of holidays. There are financial stresses—the extra cost of clothes, the cost of travelling to hospital or special school (or collecting centre), and perhaps the necessity that the mother should give up her professional career to look after the child. There is the emotional stress—of people staring at the child; the difficulty of having friends into the house or of visiting friends: the fatigue and worry.

The siblings are almost bound to suffer. The mother has to devote a large part of her time to the defective child, at the cost of the younger siblings. The siblings have to help more in the house; they are embarrassed by his presence and do not want their friends to see him and therefore to visit the house: they are jealous because of all the time devoted to him, and because of the favouritism which the parents almost inevitably show him. Their holidays suffer from his presence. They suffer from the mother's fatigue and consequent irritability.

According to Farber (1959) in his study of 240 families, a retarded boy, especially after the age of nine, has an increasingly disruptive effect on a marriage, and may adversely affect the relationship of the affected child's siblings to his parents—partly because of favouritism and jealousy. The child's sister suffers because of the many added responsibilities which she is given on behalf of the retarded child. A husband may be jealous because his wife devotes the whole of her time to the defective child.

It is common for a mother of a mentally defective or spastic child to feel a pathological attachment to him. Ounsted at Oxford, child psychiatrist, termed it 'hyperpaedophilia'. The mother devotes her whole life to the seriously defective child, giving up her career, refusing to allow anyone else to look after the child, even for an evening, and doting on his every movement, delighted with every smile which he shows or word which he utters. She shows intense anxiety about his health. Holt (1957) in his study found two families in which a mother of a severely defective child would not allow anyone into the house, not even a relative, in case she gave the child a cold. He found two families in which the mothers, in order to give their whole time to a severely defective child, had had their own normal children adopted. The mother worships her grossly handicapped child; she never goes out with her husband: she neglects her other children—or if she has no others she takes contraceptives to prevent further pregnancies. She may sleep with the defective child, and her husband has to sleep in another room. If she has become pregnant, she asks for an abortion, so that she will not be prevented from giving all her time to the handicapped child.

The paediatrician tries to get the mother to teach the child independence. Unfortunately it is the natural reaction of the parents of a handicapped child to overprotect him—to do everything for him instead of letting him slowly learn to do things for himself. She has to try to teach the child discipline—but that is difficult. She must avoid trying to make him concentrate on lessons, because he cannot concentrate, and her efforts merely add a psychological problem to the intellectual one. One explains the child's need for love and security—and the fact that being backward he will be dependent on her and cling to her longer than a normal child.

Speech therapy is to say the least of doubtful value. It is certain that no amount of speech therapy can make a child talk when he is not talking—unless he is deaf. He cannot talk until his nervous system is ready for it. It is possible, though doubtful, that when he is talking but talking indistinctly a speech therapist can help him.

In the case of a severely retarded child, such as a mongol, one may discuss the question of institutional care—bearing in mind the child's effect on the marriage, on the individual parents and on his siblings. One remembers that the handicapped child does not benefit: the benefit is to the family alone. A good home raises the handicapped child's IQ: an institution will lower it.

Much has been said and written about the desirability of parents keeping a mentally defective child at home instead of placing him in an institution. It has been written by persons who have not experienced the effect of a seriously defective child on the home. No-one can know what it is like to have such a child at home unless he has experienced it. Those of us who have been fortunate enough not to experience it should not be harsh on the parent who wants to have the child looked after in a residential home.

Mental Subnormality references

BARKER D.J.P. (1966) Low intelligence and obstetric complications. *Brit. J. Prev. Soc. Med.* 20, 15.

BARON J. (1972) Temperament profile of children with Down's Syndrome. *Develop. Med. Child. Neurol.* 14, 563.

BERGGREEN S.M. (1971) A study of the mental health of the near relatives of twenty multihandicapped children. *Acta. Paediat. Scand.* Suppl. 215.

BLACKETER-SIMMONDS B.A. (1953) An investigation into the supposed differences existing between Mongols and other mentally defective subjects with regard to certain psychological traits. *J. Ment. Sci.* 99, 702.

Carnegie Trust (1964) *Handicapped Children and their Families.* Dunfermline.

CLARKE A.M. & CLARKE A.D.B. (1965) *Mental Deficiency.* London, Methuen.

FARBER B. (1959) Effects of a severely mentally retarded child on family integration. *Monographs of the Society for Research in Child Development,* 24, No. 2.

FOWLE C.M. (1968) The effect of the severely mentally retarded child on his family. *Am. J. Ment. Def.* 73, 468.

HOLT K.S. (1957) The Impact of Mentally Retarded Children upon their Families. M.D. Thesis, University of Manchester.

ILLINGWORTH R.S. (1962) Some points about the guidance of parents of mentally subnormal children. *J. Mental Subnormality,* 8, 3.

ILLINGWORTH R.S. (1972) *Development of the Infant and Young Child, Normal and Abnormal,* 5th edition. Edinburgh, Churchill/Livingstone.

McKEOWN T. & RECORD R.G. (1971) Early environmental influences on the development of intelligence. *Brit. Med. Bull.* 27, 48.

MILLER L.G. (1968) Toward a greater understanding of the parents of the mentally retarded child. *J. Pediat.* 73, 699.

MOORE B.C., Thuline H.C. & Capes L.V. (1968) Mongoloid and non-mongoloid retardates. *Am. J. Ment. Def.* 73, 433.

National Society for Mentally Handicapped Children (1967) *Stress in Families with a Mentally Handicapped Child. A Report of a Working Party.* Southampton, Millbrook Press.

OUNSTED C. (1963) Psychiatric barriers to learning and emotional maturity. *Spastics Quarterly,* 12, 2.

STERN H., BOOTH J.C., ELEK S.D. & FLECK D.G. (1969) Microbial causes of mental retardation. *Lancet,* 2, 443.

STORES G. (1971) Cognitive function in children with epilepsy. *Develop. Med. Child. Neurol.* 13, 390.

TERMAN L.M. & MERRILL M.A. (1961) *Stanford-Binet Intelligence Scale. Manual for Third Revision. Form L-M.* London, Harrap.

TIZARD J. & GRAD J.C. (1961) *The Mentally Handicapped and their Families.* Oxford, Oxford University Press.

MENTAL DETERIORATION

Deterioration in school work is always a serious problem requiring urgent investigation. Amongst other things, it may be due to serious disease, which can perhaps be treated and cured: but it may be due to psychological problems—equally important to diagnose and treat.

The following are some of the main causes of deterioration.

(1) *Emotional causes and factors at home.* Worries, anxieties and insecurity may cause serious deterioration in work. These difficulties may be due to unhappiness at home, domestic turmoil, worrying about a parent, illness, bereavement, financial problems at home or cruelty. There may be worry at school about work, fear of a teacher, bullying or teasing; there may be worry about health, about the future, about choice of career. An important cause of deterioration is the influence of friends who are themselves young delinquents or future delinquents, or who are against work, discipline and everyone.

Dale and Griffith (1965) in their book *Downstream* studied 39 deteriorators with a good IQ level in a grammar school. It was notable that only one of 78 parents, as compared with 83 per cent of the controls, had themselves been to a grammar school. 36 of 39 'improvers' came from social classes 2 to 5: 37 of 39 deteriorators came from social classes 5 to 7—the other two being from social class 3. Factors included domestic troubles, lack of a place in which to work, parental indifference, and absence of the parents. Other factors included bereavement, illness of a parent, changes of school and excessive outside interests. They remarked that in many cases there was a poor relationship between the staff and the children, and that the school had insufficient knowledge of the home.

(2) *School problems.* Deterioration in work may result from poor teaching, frequent absences from school or moves from one school to another. Deterioration may result from the wrong choice of subjects, causing loss of interest and boredom. Excessive interest in outside pursuits, whether games or other interests, may cause serious deterioration in school work, and pass unrecognised by the teachers. I saw a boy who had to leave a well-known school because it was said by the teachers that his level of intelligence was not sufficiently high to enable him to profit from the type of education which it offered. The boy was devoting too much time to sport, at which he excelled. His IQ score proved to be 145 and he had a distinguished career at another school and later at a University.

(3) *The effect of drugs*—not only drugs of addiction but drugs used for treatment, especially epilepsy. It is most important that teachers should know that drugs used for the treatment of epilepsy all have possible annoying side effects. Barbiturates in

particular may cause impairment of concentration, not just by causing drowsiness; they may cause deterioration of behaviour, in the way of aggressiveness, irritability and insomnia; and they may impair memory. Some of these symptoms are due to a too high blood level—not necessarily because of an overdose. Other drugs used for the treatment of epilepsy may impair school performance.

Some doctors prescribe drugs for the treatment of overactivity, tics and other symptoms. All these drugs have possible side effects which may include deterioration in work.

(4) *Defects of hearing or vision.* Teachers and doctors must remember that the young child cannot make the diagnosis himself: someone else must make it.

(5) *Metabolic diseases.* Severe or repeated attacks of hypoglycaemia (low blood sugar), usually but not always in diabetic children, may damage the brain.

There is commonly some degree of mental deterioration in muscular dystrophy.

(6) *Degenerative diseases of the nervous system.* There are scores of these, but the best known is Friedreich's ataxia, which commonly affects two or three members of a family and gradually reduces a boy to a wheel-chair existence before finally killing him. Other forms are associated with progressive spasticity, blindness or deafness, with associated mental deterioration. They include errors of lipoid and carbohydrate metabolism.

(7) *Lead poisoning.* This is an important cause of mental deterioration in some areas.

(8) *Cerebral tumour* and other intracranial diseases. The first symptom is sometimes deterioration in school work.

(9) *Psychoses.* The development of schizophrenia or other psychosis causes serious deterioration in performance.

(10) *Epilepsy.* The role of epilepsy in a child's mental processes is discussed in Chapter 16.

Mental Deterioration reference

DALE R.R. & GRIFFITHS S. (1965) *Downstream.* London, Routledge & Kegan Paul.

CHAPTER 8
UNDERACHIEVEMENT

HISTORICAL

In our book *Lessons from Childhood* (1966), concerning the childhood of some 450 famous men and women, we devoted a chapter
to 'Unrecognised Ability'—noting the opinions of parents and
teachers about children who they little knew were destined for
world fame. Below is a summary of some of the findings, with
some recent additions.

Amongst artists Sir Joshua Reynolds was regarded as the least
promising of the family in his paintings, and was a poor scholar
otherwise. Gauguin was a day-dreamer and completely indifferent
to his lessons. Turner was said to have a brain which was 'naturally
misty'. Edouard Manet was deplorably inattentive, and caused his
father, a judge, much anxiety. In Latin prose he varied his place
between 42nd and 54th out of sixty-two. Rodin failed three times
to secure admittance to a school of art. His father said 'I have an
idiot for a son.' His uncle said that the boy was ineducable. He was
described as 'the worst pupil in school'.

Of musicians, Beethoven was said by his tutor, Albrechtsberger,
never to have learnt anything. 'As a composer he is hopeless.'
Rossini was a lazy little boy, who preferred to do nothing to any
definite pursuits. Verdi was rejected by the Conservatoire at
Milan. Paderewski showed little early promise in music or other
work. Sibelius was notably inattentive. Delius was an indifferent
scholar.

Many of the greatest scientists showed little promise. James
Watt was described as being 'dull and inept'. Humboldt, Fresnel
and Berzelius showed little promise. Charles Darwin wrote that 'I
was considered by all my masters and by my father as a very
ordinary boy, rather below the common standard in intellect.' It
was said that at 21 he was 'just the nonintellectual pleasant aimless

conforming rather inhibited young man whom we would now view as a disastrous prospect for research'. His father told him 'you care for nothing but shooting, dogs and rat-catching. You will be a disgrace to yourself and to your family'. Edison was always bottom of his class, and was thought to be stupid. Albert Einstein was described by his teacher as being 'mentally slow, unsociable and adrift forever in his foolish dreams'. He failed to secure entrance to the Zurich Polytechnic. Gregor Mendel twice failed the examination in Vienna to qualify as a teacher. Galileo was refused the doctor's diploma at Pisa. John Hunter, physician, was described as being 'impenetrable to anything in the way of book learning'. His teachers finally wrote him off as 'an idle surly dullard, irredeemable by punishment or reward'. Claude Bernard was a mere average student, who regarded reading as a waste of time. Louis Pasteur was only a mediocre pupil; in his Baccalaureat he was 15th out of 22 in chemistry. The famous Spanish neuro-histologist, Ramon y Cajal, was a source of great anxiety to his father, who feared that he would never earn his living. Sir James Mackenzie and Sir Ronald Ross were both poor pupils.

Amongst writers and poets Jean de la Fontaine was described as a hopeless dunce. Jonathan Swift was thought to be dull and inefficient in College. Oliver Goldsmith was described as a 'stupid heavy blockhead, little better than a fool, whom everybody made fun of'. Thomas Chatterton was 'a confirmed dullard' and thought by his mother to be 'an absolute fool'. Wordsworth alone of the four sons caused anxiety about his backwardness. Sheridan was 'by common consent of both parents and preceptor a most impenetrable dunce'. Honoré de Balzac was given up as a failure. John Keats showed no early ability. George Borrow was thought to be 'slow of comprehension and almost dull-witted'. Charles Thackeray was described as an 'idle, profligate, shuffling boy'; he was lazy and would not work. Leo Tolstoy was described as being 'both unable and unwilling to learn'. Émile Zola was a poor student, and secured a 0 in literature at the Lycée. Yeats was thought to be mentally subnormal. Chekhov and G.K. Chesterton were unsatisfactory in their school work.

As for politicians and statesmen, Robert Clive was considered a dunce. Napoleon Bonaparte left school 42nd in place and was undistinguished. He was thought to be the least likely member of the family to achieve success. The Duke of Wellington was thought by his mother to be the dunce of the family; he caused great disappointment when he had to leave school on account of his failure in classics. Gladstone was undistinguished in any way at Eton. Neither Ernest Bevin nor Aneurin Bevan left any impression at school.

Of other famous people, Heinrich Pestalozzi was an awkward clumsy boy with little promise: his spelling, writing and arithmetic were poor: he was expected to be a failure. Lord Beaverbrook was not expected to achieve much because of his inability to concentrate. Nasser was poor at school and failed to secure entry at a law school; he therefore entered the army. Beatrice Webb was said by her mother to be 'the only one of my children who is below the general level of intelligence'. Orde Wingate showed no sign of exceptional gifts or unusual promise. 'He was just an ordinary difficult little boy'.

The following famous persons were in such serious trouble at school or college that they were expelled:

Hernando Cortez—because of poor work in law studies.
Samuel Johnson—from Lichfield Grammar School for truancy.
Edgar Allan Poe and James Whistler from West Point.
Charles Thackeray from Cambridge for poor work.
William Penn from Oxford for holding religious meetings.
Percy Shelley from Oxford for atheism.
William Röntgen from Utrecht, on the grounds that he had drawn a caricature of his teacher.
Guy de Maupassant—for drinking the Father Superior's wine.
Walter Sickert—from University College School, London.
Albert Einstein—for having a disruptive effect on other students.
Benito Mussolini—for aggressiveness.
Sir William Osler—either for unscrewing the desks in the classroom and putting them in the loft: or shouting insults about the headmaster through a keyhole: or letting a flock of geese loose into the school room.
George Gissing—for stealing books.
Brendan Behan.
Salvador Dali—for refusing to allow his teachers to criticise his art.
Negley Farsson—for throwing one of his teachers into a duckpond.
William Randolph Hearst—for sending each of his teachers a potty decorated with the teacher's photograph.

Joseph Stalin.

Benjamin Disraeli.

Field Marshal Gustav Mannerheim—from three schools and a
military academy.

Sarah Bernhardt (expelled three times)—for imitating a bishop,
throwing stones at the Royal Dragoons, and climbing over a
wall at dark to talk to a soldier.

Ignace Paderewski.

INTRODUCTION

In this chapter I am concerned not with backwardness in school
resulting from a low IQ, or, in the case of certain private schools,
an IQ level which though normal is low in relation to the IQ level
required at those schools: I am concerned only with performance
at school below the level to be expected of a child's tested intelligence. Some define underachievement as performance two years
or more below a child's chronological age—not a satisfactory
definition because the backwardness of a five-year-old scoring at
the three-year-level is different from that of a 16-year-old scoring
at the 14-year-old level.

It is impossible to state accurately the frequency of underachievement. Wimberger (1966) suggested that 30 to 50 per cent of school
children were under-achievers. Havighurst (1963) placed the figure
for the United States at about 50 per cent. He wrote that 'It seems
probable that our society actually discover and develop no more
than perhaps half of its potential intellectual talent. Some evidence
for this statement lies in the fact that former immigrant groups,
which at one time did the heavy labor of America, at first produced very few mentally superior children; but after a sojourn in
this country of 2 or 3 generations, they have produced large
numbers of mentally superior people. They did this through
bettering the environment in which they reared their children.'
Wall, Schonell and Olson (1962) suggested a figure of 20 per cent
for Britain. No-one has attempted to give a figure for under-
achievers amongst mentally subnormal children: the figure may be
much higher than that for normal children. Bartlett (1965) studied
715 children in the second year at a grammar or technical school
who were doing badly. He found that

70 (9·6 per cent) had an IQ score of 120 to 135,

65 (9·1 per cent) had an IQ score of 135 to 140 and
73 (10·2 per cent) a score of over 140.

Radin and Masling (1963) described a 10-year-old boy referred for
school failure, apathy, lack of interest in work, and arithmetical
difficulties: his IQ score on the Binet scale was 196. Virginia
Axline (1972) wrote a fascinating account of a boy who was
regarded by his parents as being severely mentally defective. The
boy's IQ score was 168: his backwardness was due to rejection and
other damaging parental attitudes.

    Havighurst (1963) summarised the features of underachievers as
follows: they feel inadequate: they have lower aspirations than
achievers: they do not like school or enjoy learning as much: they
are less popular with their school fellows: they tend to come from
broken or emotionally inadequate homes and homes of low social
class: they have less ambition and work less hard: and they are less
well adjusted. I have included several useful articles and books in
the reference list.

    When a child does badly at school (or when a student does
badly at the University), the child or student is apt to be blamed
by the teacher: the teacher writes in his report 'He could do better
if he tried'. The parent blames the teacher and the school. In fact
underachievement is the end result of a wide variety of causes—
factors

    in the child
    in the home
    in the teaching
    in the method of assessment, including the examination
    in the assessor or examiner.

    When a child or student does badly, it is irrational and un-
scientific to blame the child, on the assumption that it is his fault:
the cause is just as likely to lie in one of the other four groups of
causes.

    It is difficult for a parent to know what to do when he considers
that his child is not doing as well as he should do. The usual
reason for the poor performance is a low IQ, and parents are commonly unwilling to accept the suggestion that that is the cause of
the problem. Sometimes, however, the parents are right: it is not
the fault of the child's intellectual level. I was asked by parents to
see a boy who was said by the headmaster to be 'virtually mentally

defective'—a statement whose truth I checked. The boy's ıǫ score was 124. He did well when moved to another school.

THE CHILD

An overall picture of underachievers was painted by Havighurst (1963), when he compared them with controls. He described them as seeing themselves as inadequate persons: having lower aspirations: not liking school as much as the controls, and not enjoying learning from books: being unpopular and not leaders of their peers: not working as well: having narrower interests: poor personal adjustment: coming from broken and emotionally inadequate homes, especially from a low socioeconomic class: having less clearly defined vocational goals and lacking in ambition.

There is no one type of child who is an underachiever. Some are slow in maturation: like the Darwin family, which produced Fellows of the Royal Society in five generations, they may be later than others in reaching the peak of their ability. Just as some babies are earlier or later than others of the same level of intelligence in passing their milestones of development, so older children are earlier or later than others in showing their true ability.

Some are slow thinkers. Charles Darwin wrote that he was always a slow thinker, lacking the wit of many in conversation, and being slow in comprehension. He wrote 'so poor is my memory that I have never been able to remember for more than a few days a single date or line of poetry'. Only after considerable reflection did he see the weak points of a book. Some are good thinkers but are poor at expressing their ideas. They may write unusually slowly, or take too long to plan their answer and so are unable to complete a written question. Some clever children have sufficient insight and intelligence to realise that there is more than one answer to a multiple choice question—and so rather than put down the obvious answer they do not answer at all—or put down an alternative answer which is in fact a correct one, but not the answer which was expected. Others are equally intelligent but too hasty and inaccurate.

Some are fantasy-thinkers or daydreamers—as were Honoré de Balzac, Hans Christian Andersen and Gauguin. It may be due to boredom with work, to finding it too easy, to poor concentration, or a personality trait. It is commonly associated with insecurity—worry about home or school.

Underachievement may be due to laziness. Laziness is a symptom, but it is the responsibility of the doctor or teacher not merely to name a symptom but to determine its cause. The comment in the end-of-term report that 'He could do better if he tried' is a singularly inadequate statement. He may be lazy because he is bored with the subjects of the curriculum, or the subject chosen by or for him and more interested in other subjects: he may be lazy because the work is too easy for him. He may be in a class which is learning to read, while he was able to read long before he started school. He may have a specific learning disorder, or a visual or auditory defect, so that he cannot keep up with the others in his class. The trouble may lie in poor teaching and lack of motivation. George Bernard Shaw, writing about his school days, said 'I instinctively saved my brains from destruction by resolute idleness, which, moreover, made school meaningless and tedious to me.' G.K. Chesterton referred to, 'The period of what is commonly called education, that is the period during which I was being instructed by somebody I did not know in something I did not want to know.'

Laziness may be a personality trait—an inherited trait or the result of an unsatisfactory home. Laziness may be the result of the influence of a gang, or of friends. A child may be teased because he is working hard or is unusually clever, and is given unpleasant nicknames. He equates achievement with femininity and wants to avoid being teased or bullied for working. Some feel that laziness is encouraged by a Welfare State in which the out-of-work are so well looked after that some see no reason to work.

Overactivity, and poor concentration which is often associated with it, are important causes of underachievement. Their causes are discussed in Chapter 16. They may be hereditary characteristics, emotional problems, or sequelae of prematurity or severe anoxia at birth.

Insecurity in its broadest sense is one of the most important causes of underachievement. It is caused by unhappiness, worries about domestic friction or favouritism or excessive strictness and unkindness at home, or fears with regard to bullying at school—by other children or by a teacher, anxiety about teasing with regard to obesity, unsuitable clothes, a spotty face, imagined sexual abnormalities at puberty or smallness of stature. There may be not only overstrictness at home, but excessive punishment and physical abuse. There may have been serious illness or bereavement at home, or prolonged separation from the parents. Insecurity is a major factor in a wide variety of behaviour problems (Chapter 4); and Douglas (1964) showed that 11-year-olds who bite their nails, wet their beds, have repeated nightmares or recurrent abdominal pain achieve a lower IQ test score than controls without those symptoms, and do less well at school and receive lower marks in examinations. In early adolescence a variety of other emotional problems—anxieties about health, sex or career, depression or other neurotic symptoms may seriously interfere with a child's performance. Psychotic illness, such as schizophrenia, may manifest itself by deterioration in school performance. One often hears about one child in a family of three or four from a good class home who for no discoverable reason, despite excellent home environment and teaching refuses to work and does badly as a result. Fear of failure in an examination, perhaps because of parental overambition or parental anxiety conveyed to the child, is a common reason for a poor performance in an examination. Anxiety inhibits the recall of knowledge, and anxiety, particularly in an oral examination, can cause an emotional block, an inability to think.

Failure is an important cause of failure. Previous failure lowers a child's confidence. He may become convinced that he will be unable to pass a particular examination; he may be expected by his parents or his teachers to fail, and he fails. His expectation of failure is aggravated by his fear of his parents' reaction to his results. Some prefer not to try rather than to risk failing.

Frequent moves from school to school disturb many children. They lose their friends. They may be disturbed at being separated from a teacher whom they like, or take a dislike to the new teacher. They may find that they have not done the work of the new class, and are behind in a subject. For these and undefinable reasons frequent moves from school to school (and from home to home) disturb children and may harm their school work.

Some children deliberately conceal their real ability—partly to avoid being called 'sissy', a 'blue stocking', a 'swot' or other names, partly, sometimes, in revolt against the teacher or education in general. Kornrich (1965) wrote 'the underlying notion is that pupils could do better but won't, so we interpret this as a kind of delinquency on their part, forgetting that it may be as much our fault for putting them in the wrong environment, or teaching them badly, or expecting them to fulfil our needs rather than their own. Moreover, the underachiever has not in fact failed to learn, but he has learnt hostility, inattentiveness, getting by with as little as possible, or perhaps success in athletics or social popularity, instead of what we wanted.'

A variety of physical factors may lead to underachievement. Fatigue from excessively hard work or insufficient sleep may be a factor. Any physical handicap has an adverse effect on performance. Visual and auditory defects, specific learning disorders and cerebral palsy have been discussed elsewhere. Any chronic illness because of fatigue, loss of sleep at night (as in asthma), loss of time because of hospital treatment or school absences or other reasons may be a major cause of underachievement. Anaemia or thyrotoxicosis may pass unrecognised.

Drugs given for the prevention of epileptic fits may cause defective concentration, or impair memory and cerebration. Teachers should know that a variety of drugs which children take on a doctor's prescription (or as an addiction) may impair memory and slow thought. They include not only barbiturates but bromides, chlordiazepoxide, diazepam and nitrazepam. Barbiturates may cause irritability and difficult behaviour (see epilepsy Chapter 16). Trifluoperazine may cause pronounced restlessness and inability to sit still. Drug addiction must be remembered as a possible cause of underachievement.

THE HOME

It was stated in the Crowther report (1959) that 48 per cent of children with an IQ score of 120 or more, and 87 per cent of those with an IQ of 108 to 120, had left school by the age of sixteen. Although in Britain every child, whatever the financial circumstances, can receive a University education if he reaches the required standard, the ratio of children of 'white-collar' fathers to those of unskilled fathers is 62 to one (Furneaux 1961). Douglas (1964) estimated that every year 30,000 children who are bright enough for a professional career leave school prematurely. Eighty per cent of early school leavers belong to the 'working class'. Vance Packard, in his book *The Status Seekers* (1959) wrote that in a New York High School half the children with an IQ score of 135 or more did not proceed to College. He wrote that in Pennsylvania the decision to go to college was related more to the father's occupation than to the child's intelligence. Two thirds of early school leavers are girls.

Douglas (1964) described how children tend to be allocated into a 'stream' at school on the basis of their social background: those placed in a low stream because they come from poor homes stay in a low stream because less is expected of them. At the age of 8 to 11 children from the lower and upper classes grow apart—the working class children's performance deteriorating. 'Neighbourhood' schools are responsible for some under-achievement; children living in a bad area may have to go to the local school where equipment is not so good, the school buildings are poor, and where less is expected of the children; partly as a result, they achieve less. This is not the place to join in the Jensen controversy about the role of innate intelligence of coloured and white children or the reasons for coloured children lagging further and further behind white children at school but Barbara Tizard (1974) in a notable study showed that there was no significant difference in test scores when white and coloured illegitimate children were brought up in the identical environment of a residential nursery, so that the coloured children were not exposed to a home environment less favourable than that of white children. The coloured children fared if anything better than the white children in non-verbal intelligence test scores and tests of language and comprehension.

In the book *Cross'd with Adversity* it was stated that 'it is becoming clear that the educational handicaps of the deprived child derive not so much from the physical factors of poverty, dirt and squalor, as from the intellectual impoverishment of the home and from the parents' attitudes towards education, towards school and towards teachers'. Parents from bad homes have very little contact with the teachers: and they are ignorant of educational opportunities for their children (Jackson and Marsden 1965).

In a bad home there is often little quiet, no privacy, no place for a child to do his homework. The child may sleep badly because he shares a bed with a sibling. The mother may be at work and the house is closed when the child returns from school: he has to await her return to get into the house.

As I have stated elsewhere, parental attitudes are of the greatest importance with regard to a child's performance at school. Some parents equate education with authority and oppose it. Some encourage their children to undertake part time work at the cost of their lessons. There is far more school absence in the lower than the upper social classes, and this is a reflection not on the illness ratio but on parental attitudes. Some parents positively discourage their children against homework and learning: there may be constant derogation and disparagement, so that the child convinces himself that he cannot learn. There may be physical violence in the home, marital discord, bereavement, serious illness in the family, alcoholism, financial problems. The quality of the conversation at home, the home interests, the expectations and ambitions, are all important to the child (Chapter 6): in bad homes there is little conversation with the child, and the only conversation which the child hears concerns dog-racing, betting and the like. The only literature which some parents buy for their child is so-called comics. As Pidgeon wrote (1971) motivation is more important than poverty. A financially poor home may provide excellent motivation if the parental attitudes are positive and stimulating to the child.

Just as underambition, providing too little stimulus to the child, is undesirable, so is overambition. An unsuccessful father may want his son to do better than he; a successful father expects his son to do as well as he has done. In either case it is vital that the parent should not expect more of the child than his intellectual endowment will permit; fear of failure may reduce a child's performance.

The quality of a child's home has the greatest influence on a child's performance—and later on a student's performance at college. Progress and examination results may be profoundly affected by the quality of the home: it would seem regrettable to blame the child for doing badly when it is not his fault and it is the fault of the home.

THE SCHOOL

It has long been known that one factor leading to a child's successful career at school is the expectation of the teachers that he will succeed. Pidgeon (1971) concluded his book by the following:

'The main contention of this monograph is that the level of

performance that children produce in school is governed to no small extent by factors which motivate them to work. It is also maintained that one of the major motivating factors is the expectation that teachers have of the level of performance their pupils are capable of achieving. If a teacher expects his pupils to achieve at a high level, then the pupils will be urged on by this very fact: on the other hand, if the teacher has only low expectations, this will be conveyed to his pupils, albeit subconsciously, and they will have no incentive to perform at higher levels.'

One hears much about the importance of motivation, without finding literature on methods of supplying motivation. In my out-patient clinics I have asked hundreds of school children what they like most and least at school. The most unpopular subjects—apart from work in general—are 'sums', history and geography. The latter two subjects one would have thought should be of great interest to children. One of my own children showed me her English Composition book: she was learning, with difficulty and boredom that 'the future perfect continuous passive first person singular of the verb to teach is "I shall have been being taught" '. She was also learning ten different sorts of pronouns. I found the following, copied down verbatim:

'Mood   This means the mode in which the action is conceived of.
Case   By case of nouns or pronouns is meant the relation in which a noun or pronoun stands to verbs, nouns, pronouns and prepositions.
         Words which have a plural form not ending in S form the plural genitive by adding S, e.g., Mice's holes.'

I pity children who have to learn this sort of thing, and could not feel surprised if they dislike it and are bored.

This is not the place to discuss the pros and cons of comprehensive schools, and the desirability of mixing mentally superior and mentally inferior children. I remember reading that while it may be a good thing to mix sheep with goats, the evidence that this benefits sheep and/or goats is lacking. One has seen many examples of underachievement resulting from the unwise choice of fee-paying schools, particularly for girls: as a result of being sent to a third-rate boarding school for its snob value bright girls as a result of their poor educational standard have lost all chance of getting to a university. Paediatricians commonly see underachievement as a result of handicapped children attending special schools unnecessarily; owing to the wide scatter of age groups and intelligence levels in a class, and the fewer hours of work per week, the standard of work is unlikely to be as high as that of an ordinary school. Handicapped children are apt to start school later than others, and to be absent more, so that underachievement is common.

No one is perfect, and teachers, like all children and all parents, have their behaviour problems. Teachers who use the methods of fear, threats, sarcasm, disparagement, discouragement and ridicule, are unlikely to achieve as much with children as those who avoid these and are liked by the children. Children can become conditioned to equate learning with punishment and unpleasantness—instead of enjoying learning. A good child–teacher relationship is essential if the best is to be achieved.

EXAMINATIONS AND EXAMINERS

'Examinations were a great trial. The subjects which were dearest to the examiners were almost invariably those which I fancied least: I would like to have been examined in history, poetry and writing essays. My examiners, on the other hand, were partial to Latin and Mathematics, and their will prevailed. I should like to have been asked to say what I knew. They always wanted to ask what I did not know. When I would willingly have displayed my knowledge, they sought to expose my ignorance.'

Winston Churchill (1959) My Early Life.

Much has been said against examinations, and it is important that we should question their purpose and their validity. There must be some method of assessing the effect of teaching and of grading children, and faulty as examinations are, no one has thought of anything better. As well as examinations, there must be some form of progressive assessment: but it is questionable whether progressive assessment by itself is any more reliable than examinations. Not all teachers are skilled in assessing the capability of children, and there is always the possibility that a teacher will dislike a child or his parents or be biased by the child's dirty clothes and social class, and give an assessment lower than that deserved. Certainly no assessment should depend on one teacher: it should be the product of a team, and preferably combined with other methods of assessment including essays and terminal tests.

Examinations are necessary to assess a child's comprehension of what he has been taught—and to assess his ability to interpret and apply it. No-one should teach without also examining, so that he can assess the quality of his own teaching. Children have to be graded in some way not only when they are about to leave school but regularly when they are at school so that the level of teaching can be correlated with their ability. In my experience students feel that examinations are valuable as a stimulus to work—but one feels that good teaching of a subject of interest should provide all the stimulus necessary.

Many factors limit the value of examinations. They assess a child's progress in and understanding of lessons which he has received, but not necessarily those in which he is most interested and talented. Examinations measure those things which can be measured, but not necessarily things which are more important. It has been said that not all that counts can be counted: not all that we count counts. The examination, particularly the multiquestion type, tests ability to recall knowledge and the possession of facts— but not necessarily a child's ability or creativity, or the ability to apply the knowledge and facts. Vernon (1967) wrote that the multiple question type of examination gives no chance for the divergent thinker with creativity: they give a child a choice, but do not give him a chance to give a reason for his choice. The really bright child sees other than the obvious answers and may score badly as a result. My own children virtually never asked or re-ceived help in their homework; but my eldest girl when at school once sought my help because she was unable to answer the following questions from an arithmetic textbook:

Three boys eat nine apples in 3 days. How many apples did each boy have each day?
A crew of 4 takes 2 minutes to row x yards: how long would a crew of 8 take?
Three men paint a house in $7\frac{1}{2}$ days. How long would 5 men take?

I told her that I was sorry that I could not answer the questions either.

Good multiple choice questions are extremely difficult to set.

Many such questions are so difficult to understand that they are invalid for the purpose for which they are intended.

Vernon (1964) compared the essay type of question with multiple questions. The objective type of question does not assess fluency, originality or creativity; it is more a test of memory and knowledge of detail, but it can be made to test ability to apply detail. The essay type may be a better test of originality, organisation, principles and application of fact, and the ability to write fluently. The objective type is easier and quicker to mark when there is a large number of papers; and it covers a wider field. There is a greater practice effect in multiple choice questions, and the result depends more on previous coaching than does an essay type.

All who examine children or students should be aware of the lack of validity in the marking of answers. Vernon (1964) noted the frequency with which errors of addition of marks occurred. It is well known that there is more scatter in the marking of the essay type of question than in that of the multiple choice question paper: the degree of scatter varies greatly with the subject: there is much less in arithmetic and certain other branches of science than in other subjects. There have been many studies of the validity of marking of questions. Clegg (1965) spoke of a test at Otley Grammar School in which 28 pupils took English 'O' levels under two boards; none of them were borderline candidates. Under one board 27 passed and one failed; under the other board 3 passed and 25 failed. Under one board the average grade was four; under the other it was eight. Only two of 28 were placed in the same grade by both boards. One was in the top grade under one board and bottom under the other. Professor Graham Bull asked examiners to mark a set of Medicine and Child Health papers twice at an interval of several weeks; one out of four of the medical students received marks which changed from pass to fail or fail to pass.

I have carried out several tests of the validity of marking. In one test three experienced examiners assessed 26 essays. Four were given a fail mark with one examiner and a distinction with another. The marks of 14 essays were different by over 20 per cent and of 5 by over 30 per cent.

Five examiners marked 10 multiquestion papers (not multiple choice questions). Three of the students received a distinction with one and a fail with another. In five cases the variation was 10 to

19 per cent and in three over 20 per cent. In another study seven examiners marked 12 papers; 6 received a fail with one examiner and a distinction with another. One examiner gave a paper 10 per cent and another gave it 73 per cent. The mean difference between the lowest and highest marks for the 12 papers was 43 per cent. In another study of 15 papers, 6 papers were given a fail mark with one examiner and a distinction with another.

Teachers should not only question the validity of the marking of examination questions and the validity of progressive assessment: they should also question the validity of the purpose of the examination—and the purpose of failing a child. We should all question the relevance of our examinations. Perhaps the examination is regarded mainly as a stimulus to work. The difficulty is that material 'swotted up' for an examination is the first forgotten. A medical student is examined in all subjects of the curriculum, and has to pass in all of them. Important requirements for a doctor include caring for the patient, being considerate and sympathetic, taking responsibility, treating patients as he would like to be treated, being dependable, calm in emergency, and keeping up to date with advances in diagnosis and treatment. Is it really likely that examinations in anatomy, physiology, histology, radiotherapy and all the other subjects, involving as they do, mainly ability to recall knowledge, will be valid parameters for those requirements? Are they likely to guide one to decide whether, as senior doctors are apt to say, 'he is safe to let loose on the public?' If we fail a candidate, we should question the reason for failing him. Our marks may show that he has not absorbed as much knowledge as we think he should have done, but tell us nothing about the reasons for that. We may fail him as a punishment, but that assumes that his failure is his fault, whereas it may be no such thing. We may fail him on the supposition that failure will make him better—which is possible but unlikely. We may fail him as a deterrent and a stimulus to others: some would think that that is hardly fair on the victims who fail.

It is well known that examination results at school, though they have some relation to performance at University, have little predictive value for future success. Liam Hudson (1967) remarked that 'it is simply not a fact that we can use school marks or degree class to predict who will do well in mature intellectual work and who will not'. He noted that in one period 23 per cent of Oxbridge graduates obtaining the F.R.S. had had a second or third class degree, as had 43 per cent of those obtaining the D.Sc., and that 54 per cent of High Court judges and 66 per cent of Cabinet Ministers had a second class degree or worse. Lord David Cecil (1966) wrote that 'not more than a third of the really distinguished persons from Oxford—lawyers, statesmen, diplomats, poets, novelists—did outstandingly well at examinations. Their interests were too varied, and they had too much independent initiative to concentrate exclusively on their studies'.

In a University in which progressive assessment is practised, it is obvious that some are good at assessing and that others are poor at it. One fears that an assessor may consciously or subconsciously underrate a student's ability because of dislike of his long hair, unkempt appearance, aggressive behaviour, stuttering, taciturnity or other features which are (largely) irrelevant with regard to his intellectual ability and promise. Studies have shown that there is little correlation between the Head Teacher's report or University interview and a student's subsequent success.

Examiners may give a poor mark because they cannot read a pupil's writing, or because the work is untidy, or because they do not know the correct answer themselves, or because they add the marks wrongly.

In an oral examination a bad examiner may talk too much, and not give the pupil a chance to show his knowledge in the limited time available: he may hurry the pupil and not give him time to answer: he may interrupt him—and so distract his chain of thought: he may frighten him by snapping at him and losing his temper; he may put the questions badly, making them too general and not sufficiently specific: the examiner may deliberately 'lead him up the garden path'—deliberately getting him into deeper and deeper waters, whereas a good examiner will try not to find out what a pupil does not know, but rather what he does know. A bad examiner may distract a pupil by shuffling papers in front of him, or writing down marks as the pupil speaks. He may have a 'bee in his bonnet'—have firm views, not shared by his colleagues, and press for one right answer, ignoring other replies. An examiner may lose his temper because of his personality: because he is tired: because he is hungry: because the pupil cannot recall information which the examiner has repeatedly imparted to him. In the presence of an external examiner or inspector he feels that the pupil has let him down: the examiner's ego suffers. An external examiner may ask difficult questions to show off his knowledge: he may mark a pupil down because he dislikes the internal examiner. One must always remember that the examiner in an oral test is marking on clinical impression: and any doctor knows or should know that clinical impressions are apt to be highly fallacious. It is not surprising that selection of candidates for University by interview has proved unsatisfactory, with little or no correlation with the candidates' later progress.

Children may do badly in an examination because of overanxiety—engendered, perhaps, by over anxiety and overambition on the part of the parents, and unwise promises of rewards for success. They may do badly because of hunger or fatigue. The child may be a slow thinker and write slowly, or organise his answers badly so that some of the paper has not been answered at all. In an oral examination he may suffer an emotional block, so that he just cannot think. This may be the result of nervousness, of being hurried, or of fear of the examiner.

It should not be forgotten that a child's poor performance in an examination may be due to his being unwell at the time. He might, for instance, be suffering from migraine or hay fever. Dalton (1968) studied the relationship of menstruation to examination results. Girls sitting examinations in the pre-menstrual phase secured a lower pass rate in 'O' levels and 'A' levels than controls, secured a lower average mark and obtained fewer distinctions. (In 42 per cent the stress of the examination caused an alteration in the menstrual cycle, usually lengthening it, but sometimes causing amenorrhoea.)

THE ROLE OF IQ TESTS IN THE SCHOOL CHILD

An IQ test is often an essential part of the investigation of a school child's problems. It is often an essential in paediatric practice. The circumstances under which an IQ test are required are mainly the following:

1 Backwardness at school, particularly if the child is thought to be doing less well than expected, or if the parents find it difficult to accept the teacher's opinion that the child is of low intelligence.
2 Deterioration in school performance.

3   Behaviour problems, when it is thought that these could be related to underachievement, learning disorders or difficulty in keeping up with the work.
4   Learning disorders, including reading difficulty.
5   Deafness or other handicap.
6   Any problem which raises the question of whether the child is in the right type of school for his ability or handicap.

Some sort of IQ test is often essential: but it is just as essential that all concerned should be aware of the limitations of tests used. Just as teachers and paediatricians should be thoroughly sceptical of the value of examinations they should be equally sceptical of the value of IQ tests. Teachers reading this section must remember that I am not experienced in psychological testing after infancy and that I am writing as a paediatrician. The limitations as I see them are as follows:

1   The child at the time of testing may be unwell—as in the case of examinations.
2   The child may think that the test is silly and so does not try.
3   He may be a slow writer or thinker, and yet clever, so that the result is a poor estimate of his intellectual status.
4   There may be physical difficulties—illness, visual or auditory handicaps, or specific learning disorders.
5   Many IQ tests are affected by previous practice or coaching.
6   The score is not a static one. The IQ score will change from time to time: it is greatly affected by environment and the quality of teaching, and a test repeated after an interval of a year or two may give a very different result from earlier tests.
7   No satisfactory test has been devised for immigrant children from a different culture. Verbal tests are not suitable. Jensen (1972) wrote that most traditional IQ tests depend on information and skills already acquired—and may not be suitable for immigrant children. He described 'direct learning tests'—to measure the rate of learning, something new in the test situation. Children from some areas (e.g. Central Africa) commonly have certain visuo-spatial problems which make it difficult or even impossible for them to recognise the significance of pictures or shape and form. Some tests depend on the ability to read, and immigrant children may be unable to do this or to understand the language.
8   The tests may fail to reveal a child's ability in a particular

subject. They are not a test for creativity, which is more a matter of personality than of intelligence.

9   The tests reveal nothing about the child's personality, diligence, behaviour and psychological problems, which will have a profound effect on his future performance and his success in life. The test score at school will have only a limited relationship to his performance at University, if he goes there, and still less to what he achieves in late years. It is doubtful whether they indicate his potential ability. They may point to some of his talents; but they do not show what he will do with them.

REFERENCES

AXLINE, VIRGINIA (1972) Dibs: In Search of Self. London, Penguin.
BARTLETT E.M., in HOWELLS J.G. (ed.) (1965) Modern Perspectives in Child Psychiatry. London, Oliver & Boyd.
BULL G. (1956) An examination of the final examination in medicine. Lancet, 2, 368.
CECIL, LORD DAVID (1966) Examinations: the end of education? Weekly Telegraph, 7 October.
CHURCHILL, WINSTON (1959) My Early Life. London, Odhams.
CLEGG A.B. (1965) Dangers ahead. Education, 5 February.
CLEGG A.B. (1965) Presidential address to the Association of Chief Education Officers. Education, 5 February.
Cross'd with Adversity (1970) The Education of Socially Disadvantaged Children in Secondary Schools. London, Evans Methuen Educational.
CROWTHER REPORT: Report of the Central Advisory Council for Education (1959). London, H.M.S.O.
DALE R.R. & GRIFFITHS S. (1965) Downstream. London, Routledge & Kegan Paul.
DALTON K. (1968) Menstruation and examinations. Lancet, 2, 1386.
DOUGLAS J.W.B. (1964) The Home and the School. London, MacGibbon & Kee.
FURNEAUX W.D. (1961) The Chosen Few. Oxford, Oxford University Press.
HAVIGHURST R.J. (1963) Conditions productive of superior children. In GRINDER R.E. (1963) Studies in Adolescence. New York, Macmillan.
HUDSON L. (1967) Contrary Imaginations. A Psychological Study of the English Schoolboy. London, Penguin.
ILLINGWORTH R.S. & ILLINGWORTH C.M. (1966) Lessons from Childhood: Some Aspects of the Life of Unusual Men and Women. Edinburgh, Churchill/Livingstone.
JACKSON B. & MARSDEN D. (1965) Education and the Working Class. London, Routledge & Kegan Paul.
JENSEN A.R. (1972) Genetics and Education. London, Methuen.
KORNRICH M. (1965) Underachievement. Springfield, Charles Thomas.
PACKARD V. (1959) The Status Seekers. London, Penguin.
PIDGEON D.A. (1971) Expectation and Pupil Performance. National Foundation for Educational Research in England and Wales.
RADIN S.S. & MASLING J. (1963) Tom, a gifted underachieving child. J. Child. Psychol. Psychiat. 4, 183.

Tizard, Barbara (1974) I.Q. and Race. *Nature.* **247**, 316.

Vernon P.E. (1964) *The Certificate of Secondary Education. An Introduction to Objective Type Examinations.* London, H.M.S.O.

Vernon P.E. (1967) Psychological studies on creativity. *J. Child. Psychol. Psychiat.* **8**, 153.

Wall W.D., Schonell F.J. & Olson W.C. (1962) *Failure in School.* Institute for Education, Hamburg. Unesco.

Wimberger H.C. (1966) Conceptional system for classification of psychogenic school underachievement. *J. Pediat.*, **69**, 1092.

OTHER READING

Brodie R.D. & Winterbottom M.R. (1967) Failure in elementary school days as a function of trauma, secrecy and derogation. *Child Development*, **38**, 701.

Deisher R.W., Cressey C.O. & Tjossem T.D. (1963) Adolescent school failure. G.P. **89**, 27 February.

Floud J.E., Halsey A.H. & Martin F.M. (1956) *Social Class and Educational Opportunity.* London, Heinemann.

Glaser K. & Clemens R.L. (1965) School failure. *Pediatrics,* **35**, 128.

Hammar S.L. (1967) School underachievement in the adolescent. *Pediatrics,* **40**, 373.

Pringle M.L.K. (1967) Speech, learning and child health. *Proc. Roy. Soc. Med.* **60**, 885.

Steisel I.M. (1969) Some pitfalls in the interpretation of the I.Q. *J. Pediat.* **75**, 969.

CHAPTER 9
SCHOOL PHOBIA, TRUANCY AND
SCHOOL ABSENCE

School phobia and truancy are not synonymous. Nevertheless they both involve absence from school and I shall discuss them both in this section, though separately.

There have been many publications on the subject of school phobia. By far the best discussion of the problem seen by me is the book by Kahn and Nursten (1968) entitled *Unwillingly to School*. The term school phobia means that the child is afraid of going to school: but the experts appear to agree that the basic problem is not fear of going to school but fear of leaving home—a separation anxiety. It would be idle to suggest, however, that factors at school are irrelevant. The symptoms cover a wide spectrum from tears to a complaint of slight headache, abdominal discomfort on getting ready for school, to vomiting or to absolute refusal to go to school. There are many somatic symptoms: they include loss of appetite, nausea, vomiting, headache, abdominal pain, malaise, diarrhoea and limb pains (Hersov 1972). They characteristically occur in the early morning, they subside when school is avoided, they do not occur on holiday or in the early weekend. It is difficult for a suspicious parent when her child complains of a symptom when getting ready to go: she does not want to insist on his going if he is starting with measles or appendicitis: but she does not want him to succeed in evading school if there is no organic disease. The wise parent if in doubt takes the child's temperature, and if it is normal and he looks normal sends him to school, hoping that she is right. The symptom is slightly more common in girls than boys. Though common in the older child, it is particularly common between the ages of five and eight, and again at eleven.

There have been many studies of the home background of children with school phobia. The mother tends to be a perfectionist, domineering, overprotective and overindulgent; the father to be ineffective and disinterested. The parents are apt to have an inadequate idea of the importance of education. There is a high incidence of neurotic or psychotic traits and instability. The grandmother may be a factor. The mother is lonely when the last of the children goes to school, and likes to have the children at home. There may be friction between her and her husband, and she particularly wants the love and company of her children. When I took one of my own children to school on her first day, at the age of five, I saw some mothers in tears. Eisenberg (1959) remarked that the mother clings to the child more than the child does to her. She has an ambivalent attitude—knowing that the children have to attend school, but wanting them at home. She lets it be known by subtle ways that she would not be sorry if the child stayed at home, and yet tells him unconvincingly that he must go. When her child starts school she makes unnecessary remarks and tells him, 'You'll be OK', 'It's not so bad'—and immediately suggests to him that he will not like it. The mother may have disliked school herself, and manages to convey her real feelings to the child. There is a high incidence of neurosis in the family. The homes of children with school phobia are likely to be 'good' homes with no rejection or cruelty—unlike the homes of truants.

The child with school phobia usually has a good IQ and is likely to be doing well at school and to behave well there. He is apt to be timid, immature, passive, withdrawn, to avoid fighting, strenuous sport or social activities (Davidson 1961). He has had less than the usual experience of separation from the parents in early childhood. He is overdependent on his mother and clings to her; he cannot make decisions without consulting her. Though all children are jealous, sibling rivalry may be a factor: the child is reluctant to leave his sibling at home with his mother.

Factors in the school which contribute to school phobia include bullying by other children or by a teacher, teasing, nicknames, fear of failure, examination stresses, specific learning disorders, a move to higher forms or to a different school, dropping behind as the result of an illness and therefore anxiety about returning to school or fear of punishment for some misdemeanor. The final refusal may occur as the culmination of days or weeks of somatic symptoms or tears on getting ready for school: or it may occur suddenly when return to school is due after an illness, when there is to be a move to another class, when there has been a move from one home to another, or death or illness or other new stress at home.

It would be naive to accept the child's explanations for his refusal at face value. As Hersov wrote (1972) the child fixes for his excuse on a teacher, punishment, bullying, school meals, fear of failing an examination, PE or showers with other children. In fact the school refusal is the product of a combination of instability and unwise management at home, the child's personality (which is partly inherited and partly the product of his environment) and perhaps factors in the school. It is a much more complex problem than the child's explanations would suggest.

Dibden (1968) suggested that school phobia was often a repressed mutual hostility between a girl and her mother, projected by the girl on to the school. Refusal to go to school may be an attention-seeking device—an attempt to exert her right. 'Perhaps the real problem is aggression, the wish to conquer the adversary. One may speculate whether the child who refuses to attend school is really playing a game whose theme can be expressed as follows: "I pretend I am very afraid of going to school, and I beg you not to make me go because I feel so sick, but see how I am driving you up the wall by my illness and my refusal." School phobia represents an inability to use aggression properly. The hostile urges are repressed and anxiety is the manifest symptom.'

The treatment is difficult, especially in the case of the older child. A mother or father cannot make a strong 10 stone 14 year-old-boy go to school if he resolutely refuses to leave his home. One must feel sympathy for the parents in their dilemma. The mother cannot be blamed for her personality problems: she inherited much of her personality: she may have herself been brought up in a neurotic household. The parents have made mistakes in their management, but they did their best. We all make mistakes, though the results are not necessarily so dramatic. Above all, one must feel sympathy for the child. He cannot help it. He cannot control his feelings. An eleven-year-old boy, to whom I was talking about his school phobia, impressed me by saying, 'You can't possibly know what it feels like.' Neither teacher nor doctor should ridicule a child for his phobia. Sympathy and understanding on everyone's part are essential.

The approach should be that of a team, consisting of the teachers, the family doctor, the paediatrician and often the child psychiatrist. All are agreed that the sooner the child gets back to school, the better: but it is not right to compel him to go when it is causing him great stress: he may have to be away for a short time (deliberately undefined). There is no one rule applicable to all. A change to a new school is rarely helpful. The provision of a home tutor is not likely to help. Drugs and sedatives are of very little use, if any: I have never had to prescribe them myself for the purpose. A mother must be brought to understand the effect of her attitudes. The child must be brought to understand that he is required by law to attend school: sometimes one can suggest to the child, if mature enough to understand, that as he has to attend school, and refuses to attend his own school, the only other possibility is some other school (which one knows that he would regard as a most unpleasant alternative).

TRUANCY

Whereas the child with school phobia is usually doing well at school, and has a good if not superior IQ, the mean IQ of truants is less than the average. The child with school phobia stays with his mother: the truant roams the streets (Tyerman 1968). Half the truants are unpopular with their fellows: half commit other offences. Factors at home include rejection, excessive strictness, inconsistent discipline, beatings, dirt, disinterested parents, a bad neighbourhood, unhappiness at home or school, and large families (Tyerman 1968, Hersov 1960). There is a greater than usual incidence of separation from the mother in early childhood, and from the father after the age of five (as in the case of juvenile delinquency). The school work is commonly poor, but the problem is not that of dislike of school or teacher.

Punishment will only aggravate the problem, which is a complex one. Psychiatric help should be sought, because there are likely to be many problems in the home and in the child's and parents' personalities. It is essential to seek and try to treat the cause.

References

DAVIDSON S. (1961) School phobia. *J. Child. Psychol. Psychiat.* **1**, 270.
DIBDEN W.A. (1968) School refusal. *South Australian Clinics*, **3**, 120.

EISENBERG L. (1959) The pediatric management of school phobia. *J. Pediat.* **55**, 758.

HERSOV L.A. (1960) Persistent non-attendance at school. *J. Child. Psychol. Psychiat.* **1**, 130.

HERSOV L.A. (1972) School refusal. *Brit. Med. J.* **3**, 102.

KAHN J.H. & NURSTEN J.P. (1968) *Unwillingly to School*, 2nd edition. London, Pergamon.

TYERMAN M.J. (1968) *Truancy*. London, University of London Press.

SCHOOL ABSENCE

There is a remarkable dearth of literature on school absence. Attempts to conduct research on this important problem are difficult, because one is apt to find that no records of school absences are kept. Yet it would be interesting to compare school absences in different social classes, different neighbourhoods, different towns or different general practices—and the duration of absence in different areas for the same illness, such as measles. There are many factors to which one would like to relate school absences. Probably 10 per cent of school children are absent from school at any one time (Tyerman 1968). It is said that children in Britain have lost, on the average, a year's attendance at school by the age of fifteen.

An early study was that of Bransby (1951), who studied school absences in two urban areas, Birmingham and Sheffield, and two rural areas, Kesteven (Lincs.) and Worcestershire. There was no difference between absences of boys and girls from the age of 8 to 11, but thereafter girls were absent much more than boys. There was more absence in poor districts, more in large families, and more in homes in which parents took little interest in education. Under the age of 7 a third of the absences were due to infectious diseases. Over the age of 12, a third of the absences were for non-medical reasons—such as looking after a younger child. Half of the absences of young children were due to holidays with the parents. Cook (1959) wrote about the high absence rate among children starting school—as a result of the common respiratory infections. Sandon (1961) found that there were 25 per cent more absences at the end of a week; the worst period for absences was the Lent term; the worst month was February. There were more absences from the primary school than the grammar school.

Rogers and Reese (1965) in America found that there was a

significant association between absences and employment in evenings and weekends. There was a tendency to add a Friday to the day of absence if the child were absent on a Thursday, and to commence a period of absence on a Monday. They found that absences correlated with general social maladaptation; those with higher absence rates had a poorer academic performance, took less part in school activities and had a high drop out rate. Douglas and Ross (1965) showed that repeated short absences were more harmful to progress than an occasional long one. Children in the upper middle class who were repeatedly absent tended to maintain their place; but those in the lower classes dropped back (Douglas 1968). A survey of 6,000 Buckinghamshire school children showed that the average number of absences was as follows:

Average number of half days lost per term

Age	Boys	Girls
5	18·9	17·2
7	11·8	12·9
9	7·9	10·2
11	8·0	8·8
13	8·3	10·4
15	9·5	11·9
All ages	10·4	11·1

No doubt the figures would be very different in a low class industrial or slum area.

There can be little doubt that many children are kept away from school without good reason. Some mothers keep their child away for a trivial cold or cough or wheeze. It is not clear why they should think that a child with a cough following a cold would be better away from school, travelling in a bus to accompany his mother when shopping or taking the younger child to a welfare clinic, than he would be going to school. It is a common practice to keep an asthmatic child away from school when he has the slightest wheeze. There is an important psychological factor in asthma, and when an asthmatic child is kept away from school he may worry about work missed and drop behind his fellows, so that he wheezes more—and a difficult vicious circle is set up. Children are kept away from school far too long for common infections, such as chickenpox. Mothers often like to have their child at home, and are in no hurry to send him back to school.

Children with the common recurrent abdominal pain or trivial headaches are kept away from school—thus encouraging them to magnify their symptoms. There are still doctors who believe in quarantine for childhood infectious diseases, though its lack of value has been thoroughly proved.

The children of unskilled workers are absent almost twice as much as those from professional classes; absences from secondary modern schools are almost twice as frequent as those from grammar schools (Tyerman 1968).

It is regrettable that children miss school so much for hospital attendances. Sometimes this cannot be avoided: but it is undesirable to keep children off school on account of the uncertain value of physiotherapy or speech therapy.

References

BRANSBY E.R. (1951) A study of absence from school. *Medical Officer*, **86**, 223, 237.

COOK N.J. (1959) Starting school: a sociomedical problem. *Medical Officer*, 19 June, 337.

DOUGLAS J.W.B. (1968) *All Our Future*. London, Peter Davis.

DOUGLAS J.W.B. & ROSS J.M. (1965) The effects of absence on primary school performance. *Brit. J. Educ. Psychol.* **35**, 28.

HERSOV L.A. (1960) Persistent non-attendance at school. *J. Child. Psychol. Psychiat.* **1**, 130.

ROGERS K.D. & REESE G. (1965) Health studies of presumably normal high school students. *Am. J. Dis. Child.* **109**, 9.

SANDON F. (1961) Attendance through the school year. *Educational Research*, **3**, 153.

SHEPHERD M., OPPENHEIM B. & MITCHELL S. (1971) *Child Behaviour and Mental Health*. London, University of London Press.

F

CHAPTER 10
LEARNING DISORDERS

INTRODUCTION

In a review of dyslexia, Westman *et al.* (1965) wrote that there have been 20,000 articles and books on the subject. In the reference list I have listed several of the books and papers which I have read, and which I think are valuable contributions. I would particularly refer the reader to papers by Ingram and the book by Myklebust (1971).

It is impossible to state the incidence of specific learning disorders because of inaccuracy of definition: but the incidence of severe delay in reading has been given by various authors. According to Ingram (1971) the Ministry of Education in Britain estimated that 4·2 per cent of eleven-year-olds had a reading age of less than seven. Rutter *et al.* (1970) found that 3·9 per cent of 2,299 neurologically normal children aged 9 to 12 were two or more years behind in reading age.

The Council for Exceptional Children in America suggested the following definition: 'A child with learning disabilities is one with adequate mental ability, sensory processes and emotional stability who has specific disabilities in perceptual, integrative or expressive processes which severely impair learning efficiency.' Others have referred to reading disability as a difference between mental age and reading age of two years or more.

HISTORICAL

Reading difficulty
There are not many mentions of reading difficulties in the biographies of famous persons. The famous British physician, Dr John Hunter, despite all efforts to teach him, could not read until he was seventeen. Jan Smuts could not read until he was twelve.

William Yeats was a late reader, despite the efforts of his aunts to teach him. He fared especially badly at school. His father tried to teach him but ended up by flinging the book at his head. Woodrow Wilson could not read until he was eleven. Friedrich Froebel had great difficulty in learning to read.

Spelling difficulty

Many children destined for fame experienced difficulty in spelling, and in almost all of them it persisted throughout life. They included Hans Christian Andersen, Harvey Cushing (neurosurgeon), Thomas Edison, Paul Ehrlich, Henry Ford, Napoleon Bonaparte, William James (psychologist), General Patton, George Bernard Shaw, Joshua Reynolds, Pablo Picasso, Auguste Rodin and William Yeats. Henry Ford never learned to spell, write well, read easily or express himself in a simple sentence.

Mathematics

Mathematics baffled numerous children destined for fame. They included Schubert, Epstein, Picasso, Rodin, Emerson, Lord Lytton, Yeats, Henry James and Benjamin Franklin. Lord Northcliffe was 'defeated by the simplest exercises'. Gandhi 'had more difficulty in mastering multiplication tables than in learning naughty words for his teachers'. Adler nearly had to become a cobbler because of his weakness in mathematics. Jung wrote that 'mathematics classes become sheer terror and torture to me'. Charles Darwin was 'hopeless' in algebra at the university, despite all efforts, including those of a private tutor. Paul Nash wrote that 'I was extremely deficient in mathematics calculation. The answers were fantastically wrong. It was as if, instinctively, I argued that 2 and 2 make 5, or on other occasions, no more than three. My unfortunate masters were in despair. I think almost from the first, all those who attempted to teach me mathematics were baffled. I think, sometimes, I must have been given marks for sheer perverse ingenuity. I have seen mathematics teachers reduced to a sort of awe by my imbecility'.

Languages baffled many others, including Corolus Linnaeus, Thomas Carlyle, Nikolai Gogol, Charles Thackeray, Sir Oliver Lodge, Hogarth and Lord Balfour. Winston Churchill was unable to go to the university because of his difficulty with languages. Richard Wagner played truant for six months because of his trouble with Latin declensions. Charles Darwin wrote that 'during my whole life I have been singularly incapable of mastering any language'. The Duke of Wellington had to leave Eton because of his failure in classics and went to a military academy.

Without more knowledge of the facts, and in the absence of psychological testing, one cannot say that the above were all examples of a specific learning disorder. Some probably were—particularly those concerned with reading difficulties.

CAUSES

Non Specific Causes
The factors behind learning disorders can be summarised as follows:

1 Low IQ.
2 Prenatal circumstances.
3 Poor environment.
4 Emotional problems.
5 Visual defects.
   Auditory defects.
6 Speech defects.
7 Delayed maturation.
8 Postnatal brain damage.
9 Problems of handedness and laterality.
10 Deficient teaching.

By far the commonest factor in learning disorders is a low level of intelligence. Hence in order to establish the diagnosis of a specific learning disorder psychological testing is essential. One may guess the diagnosis, but before one can be certain expert testing must be done.

There is a suggestion that prenatal factors, particularly maternal toxaemia, prematurity, multiple pregnancy and natal factors, notable anoxia, may be a factor; but it is difficult to prove this because of the necessity of equating the variables, such as social class, for there is a higher incidence of toxaemia and other pregnancy complications in the poor than in the well-to-do, and learning disorders are more prevalent in the lower social classes. Denhoff and Hainsworth (1972) wrote that children were 'at risk' of learning disorders if they were 'small for dates' at birth and if in the newborn period they had the respiratory distress syndrome (itself usually occurring in low-birthweight babies), anoxia, haemolytic disease or severe jaundice.

Learning disorders of postnatal origin may be a sequel of a serious traumatic brain injury.

The home environment is an important factor. Learning disorders are not only more common amongst the lower classes, but they are more common in large families. Social factors include lack of books in the home, lack of interest in reading at home, lack of pre-reading play material, paucity of conversation with the child and poor speech 'models'. Emotional deprivation may by various subtle means retard a child's progress in learning (see Chapter 8). Emotional problems, such as unhappiness at home or school, and any form of insecurity, impairs learning.

Visual and auditory defects and delay in speech for any cause delay reading. If speech is significantly delayed, the child is late in learning to read. Delayed maturation for any cause is an important factor. The relationship of problems of handedness and laterality to the development of speech and other skills is discussed in Chapter 11.

Deficient teaching, including absence from school, moves from school to school, large classes and teaching methods may be relevant factors. I have read about the relative value of the flash method and the phonemic methods of teaching children to read, but have no personal knowledge of the matter. Poor child–teacher relationship may be a factor; unkindness or lack of patience with a child who is slow to read will still further slow his progress.

Makita (1969) writing from Tokyo, discussed the remarkable fact that reading disability is 10 times more common in Western countries than in Japan, in which the incidence in school children is 0·98 per cent. He wrote that, 'Theories which ascribe the etiology of reading disability to local cerebral abnormalities, to lateral conflict, or to emotional pressure may be valid for some instances, but the specificity of used languages, the very object of reading behaviour, is the most contributory factor in the formation of reading disability. Reading disability is more of a philological than a neuro-psychiatric problem.' 'It is unthinkable that the Americans and the Europeans have ten times the population with maldevelopment or malformation of cerebral gyri than do the Japanese. It is hardly believable that the prevalence of hemispheral dominance conflict or split laterality is ten times less in the Japanese than in Westerners. It is equally absurd to suggest that children with emotional distress are ten times less frequent in Japan.' 'The impression I myself gathered in Europe was that the largest numbers of reading disability were from English-speaking countries, next from German-speaking countries and least from Latin-speaking countries such as Italy or Spain. Perhaps English by far exceeds German or any other Western language in the number of words in which irregular or unstable relationships exist between spelling and pronunciation.'

FEATURES

In the case of specific learning disorders, there is almost invariably a family history of the same complaint—though often of different aspects of the complaint. I should strongly suspect the accuracy of the diagnosis if there were not such a history. When a child has specific dyslexia the family history may be mainly that of a spelling difficulty, or delay in the establishment of handedness or delayed speech, with only trivial delay in reading: or the family history may be one of delay closely similar to that of the child. Inheritance is by an autosomal Mendelian dominant gene. The condition is five times more common in boys than in girls. The genetic aspect of these disorders is further shown by the fact that if one of uniovular twins has the disability, the co-twin will have it; if one of dissimilar twins has it, the likelihood that the co-twin will have it is only small. Emotional problems are not a cause of specific learning disorders, but they aggravate them and make their treatment more difficult.

The features of specific learning disorders involving principally dyslexia are as follows. The child confuses letters in reading and writing. He may read from right to left; he mistakes one letter for another; he reads letters in the wrong order, interpreting, for instance, WAS as SAW, CALM as CLAM, or omits letters, interpreting, for example, PLUCK as LUCK. He may interpret ; as ?, or *h* as *y*, *d* as *b*. He may sound letters and produce correct spoken syllables from a book but be unable to synthesise the syllables into words: or he may be unable to sound the letters or to recognise them. He may misread short words and yet read longer ones correctly. He may be unable to understand the meaning of a word even though he reads it correctly. He may be unable to break down a word into syllables. Many affected children can read figures correctly, but not words.

When writing he may misplace letters, omit letters or reverse them, and confuse letters of similar shape. He may separate the letters by too great a distance, or too small a distance, or fail to join them properly. He may speak a word correctly but be unable to write it. He may omit small words or put them into the wrong place in a sentence. He may write words in their mirror image. He writes slowly, often with the paper at a peculiar angle, sometimes with facial contortions and protruding tongue. He fails to correlate the sound of the word with the written word, and therefore spells badly.

There is nearly always an abnormality of handedness—usually ambidexterity, and sometimes crossed laterality. Ingram (1963) found that of 78 cases, only 29 per cent were firmly right or left handed, and 18 per cent were truly ambidextrous. There is commonly difficulty with right-left discrimination and this presents problems in subjects like geography and geometry. For instance, he may interpret the River Severn as being on the East coast of Britain and the Thames on the West. Poincaré, possibly the greatest mathematician whom France has produced, presumably had the problem to some extent, because he was unable to do any geometry.

Other difficulties experienced by these children are spelling, and sometimes difficulty in arithmetic and music note blindness. The exercise book of one of my patients had a page of calculations like the following:

$$16 + 1 = 71$$
$$14 + 1 = 51$$

These children are usually late in acquiring speech. They are commonly bad writers and in general clumsy and therefore often bad at games. They are often overactive and distractable, concentrating badly.

Boder (1971) has analysed the problem. Boder wrote that 'reading requires visual perception and discrimination, visual sequential memory and recall, directional orientation, visual auditory integration—that is the translation of visual letter symbols into meaningful auditory equivalents, which includes the synthesis of letter sounds into syllables and syllables into words. Spelling requires the reverse translation of speech sounds into their visual letter symbol equivalents. In addition to the visual function prerequisite to reading, this auditory visual integration requires auditory perception and discrimination and auditory sequential memory. Writing requires in addition fine motor and visual motor coordination and tactile kinaesthetic memory and constant correlation between reading and spelling.' Chalfont and Flathouse (1971) wrote that 'reading requires auditory and visual learning, the reception of visual and auditory information, the analysis and synthesis, storage and retrieval, and resultant response (output)'. But affected children lack the necessary visuospatial sense and auditory discrimination.

Diagnosis

The diagnosis must be made only after full psychological testing with such tests as the Wechsler, Bender visual-motor Gestalt and the Goodenough draw a man test. All other causes of the learning disorder, environmental and emotional, should be excluded: and there must be positive features which should include a family history of the complaint, laterality problems and visuomotor confusion.

The diagnosis may be suspected on the basis of preschool features. As Denhoff *et al.* (1971) remarked, learning problems do not begin suddenly when children start school: they were there before, but may have been unrecognised. Efforts are now being made to screen preschool children so that those with learning disorders can be detected. This may not lead to their alleviation before they start school, for they probably depend largely on delayed maturation: but early detection may prevent psychological trauma when they start school. If it is not known that there is a specific problem, the child may be blamed for carelessness and bad writing, when he deserves no blame because he cannot help it. He needs encouragement and not discouragement.

Denhoff *et al.* discussed possible early features; undue activity and irritability in the young infant, or undue drowsiness and lack of responsiveness. Later, after six months there may be delayed motor development and ataxia. After the first year delayed speech may be a prominent feature. Simple tests with formboards may reveal difficulties with spatial appreciation. Motor incoordination and clumsiness may be detected by hopping, skipping and hand-clapping patterns. Dykman and colleagues (1971) used tests for matching, visual memory, block patterns, copying geometric forms and drawing. De Hirsch *et al.* attempted to forecast learning disorders in preschool children by various visual-perception and auditory perception tests, tests for manual control, pegboard speed, tying a knot, word recognition, language comprehension and auditory memory span.

Results

The results of specific learning disorders can be severe. Emotional problems of various kinds are usual, and show themselves in a variety of behaviour problems, such as temper tantrums, bed wetting, tics, truancy, withdrawal or depression. There is a loss of self-esteem. Rutter *et al.* (1970) showed that there is a strong association between reading disability and antisocial behaviour. The child drops behind in his class work and may be regarded as generally backward and unintelligent, when in reality he is highly intelligent. The inevitable consequence is that he is thwarted and disturbed: this in turn interferes with efforts to teach him. When any school child is referred to me in the Outpatient department I always make sure that the problem is not related to learning disorders. I ask him what he likes most in school and what he likes least. I make sure that the problem is not one of reading, spelling and writing.

Prognosis

This is uncertain. Specific learning disorders are of all degrees of severity: some are relatively trivial, and cause little trouble at school, while others are severe and greatly retard a child's performance. The problem is that one has no means of telling whether the difficulty is one of delayed maturation, which will resolve itself in time, or whether there will always be a problem throughout life—as in the case of the children destined for fame, named in the historical section. Most of these children learn to read, but many continue to be bad at spelling. If there is a residual problem it may be only a trivial one.

It is not possible to predict the effect of treatment. If a child improves after treatment, it is usually impossible to determine whether he has improved because of the treatment or because of maturation. Remedial treatment may help the child while he is receiving it, but when it is discontinued, he may drop behind again. The psychological aspects of management are of the utmost importance. It is vital that all concerned should be aware of the problem and not think that he is being naughty and not trying.

Treatment

This is largely an educational matter, and I am not competent to discuss it. When an affected child is to sit a competitive or other school examination, those marking the papers ought to be made aware of the problem so that an unfair low mark is not given (e.g. for bad writing or bad spelling). It has been my practice to inform examination boards, with the parents' permission, so that if there is doubt about the examination results the specific disability can be borne in mind.

REFERENCES

BODER E. (1971) Developmental dyslexia: prevailing diagnostic concepts and a new diagnostic approach. In MYKLEBUST H.R. (1971) *Progress in Learning Disabilities*, Vol. 2. New York, Grune & Stratton.

CHALFONT J.C. & FLATHOUSE V.E. (1971) Auditory and visual learning. In MYKLEBUST H.R. (1971) *Progress in Learning Disabilities*, Vol. 2. New York, Grune & Stratton.

DENHOFF E., HAINSWORTH P. & HAINSWORTH M. (1971) Learning disabilities and early childhood education. In Mykelbust H.R. (1971) *Progress in Learning Disabilities*, Vol. 2. New York, Grune & Stratton.

DENHOFF E., HAINSWORTH P.K. & HAINSWORTH M.S. (1972) The child at risk for learning disorders. *Clinical Pediatrics*, 11, 164.

DYKMAN R.A., ACKERMAN P.T., CLEMENTS S.D. & PETERS J.E. (1971) Specific learning disabilities: an attentional deficit syndrome. In MYKLEBUST H.R. (1971) *Progress in Learning Disabilities*, Vol. 2. New York, Grune & Stratton.

DE HIRSCH K., JANSKY J.J. & LANGFORD W.S. (1966) *Predicting Reading Failure.* New York, Harper & Row.

INGRAM T.T.S. (1963) Dyslexia. *Proc. Roy. Soc. Med.* 56, 199.

INGRAM T.T.S. (1971) Specific learning difficulties in child: a medical point of view. *Brit. J. Educ. Psychol.* 41, 1 et seq.

MAKITA K. (1969) The rarity of reading disability in Japanese children. In CHESS S. & THOMAS A., *Annual Progress in Child Psychiatry and Child Development.* New York, Brunner Mazel.

MYKLEBUST H.R. (1971) *Progress in Learning Disabilities*, Vol. 2. New York, Grune & Stratton.

RUTTER M., TIZARD J. & WHITMORE K. (1970) *Education, Health and Behaviour.* London, Longman.

WESTMAN J.C., ARTHUR B. & SCHEIDLER E.P. (1965) Reading retardation: an overview. *Am. J. Dis. Child.* 109, 359.

Other Reading

COHN R. (1971) Arithmetic and learning disabilities. In MYKLEBUST H.R. (1971) *Progress in Learning Disabilities*, Vol. 2. New York, Grune & Stratton.

HERMANN K. (1959) *Reading Disability*. Copenhagen, Munksgaard.

HUGHES J.R. (1971) Electroencephalography and learning disabilities. In MYKLEBUST H.R. (1971) *Progress in Learning Disabilities*, Vol. 2. New York, Grune & Stratton.

ILLINGWORTH R.S. & ILLINGWORTH C.M. (1966) *Lessons from Childhood. Some Aspects of the Early Life of Unusual Men and Women*. Edinburgh, Churchill/ Livingstone.

INGRAM T.T.S. & MASON A.W. (1965) Reading and writing difficulties in childhood. *Brit. Med. J.* 2, 463.

INGRAM T.T.S., MASON A.W. & BLACKBURN I. (1970) A retrospective study of 82 children who suffered from difficulty in learning to read. *Develop. Med. Child. Neurol.* 12, 271.

KEENEY A.H. & KEENEY V.D. (1968) *Dyslexia, Diagnosis and Treatment of Reading Disorders*. St. Louis, C. V. Mosby.

MASON A.W. (1967) Specific (developmental) dyslexia. *Develop. Med. Child. Neurol.* 9, 183.

NATCHEZ J. (ed.) (1968) *Children with Reading Disorders*. New York, Basic Books Inc.

SCHECHTER M.D. (1971) Dyslexia. *Australian Paediat. J.* 7, 123.

THOMPSON L.J. (1968) *Language Disabilities in Men of Eminence*. The Orton Society Reprint Series. Connecticut, The Orton Society.

VERNON D. (1962) Specific dyslexia. *Brit. J. Educ. Psychol.* 32, 143.

VERNON D. (1971) *Reading and its Difficulties*. Cambridge, Cambridge University Press.

CHAPTER 11
SPEECH PROBLEMS

Children pass through an orderly sequence of stages of speech development. All children are different, and there are wide variations in the rate at which speech matures. The development of speech is greatly affected by the child's intelligence: speech is always delayed in mentally subnormal children.

Babies have non-verbal methods of communication—crying, smiling, clinging to the mother, putting the arms round the mother's neck, holding the arms out to be picked up, pushing a mother's hand away (when offering unwanted food), making noises to attract attention, pulling the mother to see something, pointing, laughing, screaming and throwing temper tantrums. They show their feelings by their facial expression and total body movement.

The average full-term baby begins to smile at the mother when she is talking to him at four to six weeks, and about a week later begins to vocalise as well as smile. Vowels precede consonants in the vocalisations. At three to four months the baby holds long conversations with the mother, and uses consonants *b*, *g*, *k*, *m*, *p*. At four to five months the baby says *ah*, *goo*, *ka*, and razzes (making 'rude noises' with the lips). He talks to his toys and himself. At six months he says *da*, *ba*, *ka*, *ma* and at seven or eight months he combines syllables, saying *mumum*, *babab*, *dada*, without meaning.

By 10 months the baby varies the pitch and inflection of his vocalisations; he understands many words said to him including *No*, *Byebye* and *Pat-a-cake*. By the end of the first year about three-quarters of the vowels and a third of the consonants are recognisable. He says two or three words with meaning. If he is deaf his vocalisations decrease between nine months and a year, and he cannot imitate sounds. At this stage, 12 to 18 months, the normal child 'jargons', talking incessantly with apparently meaningful inflections and sounds, with an occasional intelligible word interspersed. He often pronounces only the beginning or end of a word (e.g. g for dog)—tending more to omit the end of a word. It is common for a child at this stage to enter a lull in speech development, making no progress at all, and worrying the parents: then suddenly he makes rapid progress. I have known babies who were a long way below the average at 15 months and a long way above the average a month later. At 18 months the child knows nursery rhymes and can point on request to parts of his body. At 21 to 24 months he reaches an important milestone, joining words spontaneously—as distinct from repeating phrases like 'Oh dear' in imitation. At 2½ years he uses pronouns I, me, you, and says practically all vowels and two thirds of the consonants intelligibly. He repeats a few nursery rhymes. At three years he uses pronouns, prepositions and plurals, and can be understood in part by strangers. He pronounces vowels intelligibly—but some consonants much later.

At three or four years he often has difficulty in thinking of the right word and repeats words, so that a mother might think that he is beginning to stutter. It is normal for children at this stage, three to four, to go through a stage of non-fluency: provided that his attention is not drawn to it and it is ignored, a child is likely to pass through the stage in 6 to 12 months. By five years his articulation, except for certain consonants (e.g. S, Z, SH, CH, J) is largely correct: these consonants are usually pronounced correctly by about seven.

On the average, girls learn to speak sooner than boys.

DELAYED DEVELOPMENT OF SPEECH

Historical

Delay in the development of speech caused anxiety to the parents of Albert Einstein: at four his level of intelligence was questioned and even at eight he was not speaking well. Alessandro Volta (of voltage fame) was a late speaker, despite all efforts to get him to talk: he did not say any words until he was four.

Causes of Delayed Speech
They can be summarised as follows:

Mental subnormality.
Familial factor.
Lack of opportunity.
Multiple pregnancy.
Emotional deprivation.
Deafness.
Delayed maturation.
Cerebral palsy.
Psychoses.
Unknown.

By far the commonest cause of delayed speech is mental sub-normality. All mentally subnormal children are late in learning to speak. Delayed speech is commonly a familial feature: there is a history of similar delay in a parent or other members of the family. Sometimes speech delay is due to lack of opportunity—there being little or no conversation with him. Twins are commonly late in learning, and the reasons for this are uncertain. It is likely that one factor is the mother's lack of time to talk to the twins: a mother of a singleton has more time. It is argued by some that twins are late in learning to talk because they understand each other's language and have no need to learn properly. I do not believe this. The first of a family on the average speaks earlier than subsequent children. The idea that children learn mainly from other children is untrue. Emotional deprivation is an important cause of delayed speech. Severe deafness will make speech impossible unless special methods are used by the expert to teach the child to speak. The older the child before special teaching begins, the more difficult will it be to teach him. The less severely deaf child may see the letters b, f, w made, but not g, l and r, and so he substitutes for these. The child with high-tone deafness may hear the door bang, aeroplanes overhead and other sounds, so that his parents do not realise that he is deaf; but he is apt to omit high-pitched sounds such as s and f, and final consonants. Speech may be greatly delayed. Children with cerebral palsy are usually late in learning to speak—partly because of a lower than average IQ, partly because of deafness (in some), partly because of the defect in the cerebral cortex and partly because of spasticity and inco-ordination of the relevant muscles concerned with speech production. Children with infantile autism are almost invariably late in speaking.

The cause of delayed speech is often unknown. One tends to ascribe it to delayed maturation—just as some children are later than others in learning to sit, walk or control the bladder. There may be delayed auditory maturation—the child appearing to be deaf in the early months, only gradually learning to distinguish noises, localise them and understand them. As delayed maturation is such an important factor, it follows that speech therapy for delayed speech is useless.

There is some association with delay in the establishment of handedness. Bilingualism in the home is probably not a factor.

It is important to note that understanding of speech precedes the ability to articulate: a child of 15 or 18 months may understand the meaning of numerous words—pointing to objects in books on request—and yet he cannot articulate them. A child with delayed speech (or deafness) is in danger of being regarded as mentally backward. Late speech is *not* due to laziness, it is *not* due to 'everything being done for him', it is *not* due to tongue tie.

Ingram (1960, 1963) analysed delay in speech as follows:

Mild—only delayed acquisition of speech sounds, and delay in articulating them.
They know words but cannot say them.
There may be some dyslalia.

Moderate—delay in acquisition of articulation, with normal comprehension. They have difficulty in finding the words which they want. Some have termed this developmental motor aphasia.

Severe—impaired ability to comprehend speech, with some difficulty in expression.

Most severe—true auditory imperception. Not only a defect of comprehension, but also a failure to perceive the significance of other sounds.
Some have termed this congenital word deafness or developmental receptive aphasia.

The majority of these children have intelligible speech by six or seven years: but if a child says no words at all by the age of five, the outlook for the later development of speech is poor. Delayed speech is often followed by delayed reading.

Mentally subnormal children often learn to say a few words and then appear to forget them, so that they can no longer say words which they could say only a few weeks or months before.

INDISTINCT SPEECH

Emile Zola had a severe lisp. Michael Faraday had to leave school because of his severe dyslalia.

In a follow-up study of a cohort of children born in one week of 1958, 10 to 13 per cent of British 7-year-olds had significant speech impairment (Butler *et al.* 1973). Morley (1972) found that 14 per cent of 5-year-olds had serious articulatory defects and that 4 per cent were unintelligible to teachers. Faults of articulation (dyslalia) are the commonest deviation. They consist especially of difficulty with consonants—notably R, Z, SCH, TH, CH, ST, T, SK, KS, RS. Children may omit sounds which they cannot pronounce or substitute sounds. The commonest substitution is TH for s, the lisp, due to protrusion of the tongue between the teeth when attempting to pronounce the s. A child may be able to imitate an isolated s, or pronounce it at the beginning of a word, and yet be unable to say it at the end of a word.

The cause of dyslalia is unknown. It is more common in children who learn to speak late than in early speakers. It is largely a problem of delayed maturation, and with the exception of the lisp, which can readily be corrected by a speech therapist, most of these errors of articulation correct themselves. In other words, if they improve after speech therapy, the improvement is due to maturation and not to the treatment.

Malocclusion of the teeth may cause distortion of the sibilants s and SH. A cleft palate causes difficulty with consonants—P, B, T, D. K. G, but does not delay the onset of speech. A cleft in the soft palate gives speech a nasal quality. Dental malformation may be a factor in some. Large adenoids sometimes cause speech to be nasal —and they may interfere with speech by causing deafness. Tongue tie, if severe, is thought by some to interfere with the pronunciation of some consonants, but others do not think that it interferes with speech at all.

Defective articulation may be due to imitation of a parent or sibling. Emotional factors may play a part: worry, anxiety or teasing may delay maturation of speech.

The term dysarthria means difficulty in articulation due to organic disease, such as cerebral palsy or other defects of the brain.

Abnormalities of the voice affect speech. One of my patients spoke always in a whisper as a result of hysteria.

STUTTERING

The words stuttering and stammering should be regarded as synonymous.

Historical

Many famous persons stuttered in childhood and mostly later as well. They included Moses, Aristotle, Aesop, Demosthenes, Virgil, Robert Boyle, Charles Lamb, Charles Darwin, Charles I, Aneurin Bevan and Somerset Maugham. Lewis Caroll (Rev. Dodgson), who was also left handed, stuttered so badly that he could not preach. The causes of stuttering were discussed by Aristotle, Galen, Hippocrates and Celsus. According to Jenks (1953) the New York Institution for Correcting Impediments of Speech was opened in 1830. 'The stammerer is to press the tip of his tongue as hard as he can against the upper row of teeth: he is to draw a deep breath every 6 minutes, and is to keep perfect silence for 3 days, during which the pressing of the tongue and the deep inspirations are to be continued without interruption. During the night, small rolls of linen are placed under the tongue in order to give it the right direction even during sleep. When three days have expired, the patient is to read aloud slowly to the physician for an hour.' Other treatment included cauterising the tongue, dividing some of the muscles of the tongue, and speaking with the mouth full of pebbles.

There have been many interesting and often surprising and far-fetched explanations of stuttering. Moses Mendelssohn, logician, thought that stuttering was due to a collision between many ideas flowing simultaneously from the brain. Stein and Mason wrote about stuttering as follows:

'the rhythmical reiteration as an oral-erotic archaic linguistic pattern indicates dissolution and also points to a further essential factor: the stammerer's intense desire for oral gratification. The stammerer is compelled to pour out words (gifts) quickly and abundantly to others in compensation for this feeling of deprivation. In essence, the stammerer, as a deprived and exploited person, is thus, symbolically speaking, both the infant who needs to be fed and the all-giving Mother.'

Bluenel (1960) described stammering as a 'narcissistic neurosis' and a 'pregenital conversion neurosis'. Coriat wrote that

'stammering is a psychoneurosis caused by the persistence into later life of early pregenital oral nursing, oral sadistic and oral sadistic components. In the speech of stammerers the illusion is maintained and the oral gratification continues the illusory substitution for the maternal nipple, the stammerer thus retaining his mother into adult life.'

Features
Stuttering is more common in boys than girls. It commonly begins at the age of three to five years with the normal stage of non-fluency, when a parent, mother-in-law or neighbour suggests that the child is beginning to stutter. His mother listens carefully, agrees, and tries to stop it by saying 'Take a big breath before you speak.' 'Speak slowly and distinctly.' 'Say it again slowly.' The child becomes worried and self conscious, and true stuttering begins. One is reminded of the story of the centipede with its hundred legs:

> The Centipede was contented, quite,
> Until the toad one day, in spite,
> Said say, which foot comes after which?
> This so wrought upon her mind
> She lay distracted in a ditch
> Considering which came after which.

Stuttering rarely begins after the age of seven. The majority, but not all, acquire continuity of speech without treatment. About one per cent of school children stutter. About three per 1,000 of the whole population has a persistent stutter (Morley 1957).

The mean IQ of stutterers is slightly less than the average. The condition is relatively more frequent in twins. There is often a family history of the same complaint: this may be due partly to imitation, and partly to an inherited unstable family background. Stuttering is more common in children who were late in learning to speak. It occurs only in civilised peoples, in which reading and writing is taught, but it is said to be unknown in the Chinese.

The association with abnormalities of handedness is uncertain, but there is a high incidence of left handedness in families having a high incidence of stuttering. On the other hand Andrews and Harris (1964) found no relationship to handedness, ambidexterity or change of handedness; of 80 stutterers 56 were right handed, 21 were ambidextrous and 3 were left handed: of 80 controls 52 were right handed, 23 ambidextrous and 5 left handed. There was no crossed laterality in the stutterers. Stuttering is certainly not due to a teacher changing a child from left handedness to right. Insecurity resulting from unpleasantness and unkindness in trying to make a child use his right hand might be a factor.

There have been many studies of the family background of stutterers. The usual description of the family is one of domination, excessive discipline, overprotection, oversupervision, perfectionism, and often constant disapproval by the parents.

It is notable that stutterers usually have little difficulty in group speaking, singing, talking when alone, talking to animals, or talking to their friends. When trying to talk otherwise they may contort the face, clench the fist and close the eyes. Stuttering causes anxiety and self consciousness.

Treatment

The first essential is to persuade the parents to try to ignore the child's speech. They have to stop trying to get him to speak clearly and distinctly: they should not help him to speak by guessing what he is going to say and saying it for him. As far as possible stress and insecurity should be reduced. A speech therapist then sets about trying to help the child to stop stuttering. A successful method is 'timed syllabic speech' in which the child is taught to separate all syllables equidistantly as he speaks.

REFERENCES

ANDREWS G. & HARRIS M. (1964) Syndrome of stuttering. *Clinics in Developmental Medicine* No. 17.
BLUENEL C.S. (1960) Concepts of stammering. *J. Speech. Hearing. Dis.* **25**, 24.
BUTLER N.R., PECKHAM C. & SHERIDAN M. (1973) Speech defects in children aged 7 years. A national study. *Brit. Med. J.* **1**, 253.

INGRAM T.T.S. (1960) Paediatric aspects of specific developmental dysphasia, dyslexia and dysgraphia. *Cerebral Palsy Bulletin* **2**, 254.

INGRAM T.T.S. (1963) Delayed development of speech with special reference to dyslexia. *Proc. Roy. Soc. Med.* **56**, 199.

JENKS W.F. (1953) *The Exceptional Child.* Washington, The Catholic University of America Press.

MORLEY M.E. (1972) *The Development and Disorders of Speech in Childhood.* Edinburgh, Churchill/Livingstone.

STEIN L. & MASON L.E. (1968) in MILLER E., *Foundations of Child Psychiatry.* London, Pergamon.

OTHER READING

BLOCH E.L. & GOODSTEIN L.D. (1972) Functional speech disorders and personality: a decade of research. In CHESS S. & THOMAS A., *Annual Progress in Child Psychiatry and Child Development.* New York, Brunner Mazel.

BURGI E.J. & MATTHEWS J. (1963) Disorders of speech. *J. Pediat.* **62**, 15.

LILLYWHITE H. (1958) Doctor's manual of speech disorders. *J. Am. Med. Ass.* **167**, 850

RENFREW C. & MURPHY K. (1964) The child who does not talk. *Clinics in Developmental Medicine* No. 13. London, Heinemann.

ZANGWILL O.L. (1968) Language and language disorders. In DORFMAN A., *Child Care in Health and Disease.* Chicago, Year Book Publishers.

CHAPTER 12
TWINS

INTRODUCTION

The incidence of twins in this country is 1 in 87 births: that of triplets is 1 in 87^2: that of quadruplets 1 in 87^3. In Britain about 10,000 twins (5,000 pairs) are born each year. In Western Nigeria the incidence of twins is 10·1 per cent of births: there is a higher incidence of twins amongst American negroes than others, and a lower incidence in Japan. These differences concern non-identical twins only: the incidence of identical twins is constant—3 per 1,000 pregnancies. A Moscow woman had 69 children in 27 confinements—4 sets of quadruplets, 7 sets of triplets and 16 pairs of twins. The biggest live born twins weighed 4,075 and 5,180g—a total of 9,255g (20·4lb).

There is probably a genetic factor for the birth of non-identical twins: it is probably a recessive, inherited through the mother. If a mother has twins, there is a three to ten times greater likelihood of her having more twins than there is for the normal population. The incidence of non-identical twins rises with the age of the mother and her parity, and is greater in the lower classes. A woman of 35 to 40 is three times more likely to have twins than a woman under twenty; after the fifth birth, a woman is five times more likely to have twins. In Finland the incidence of twin conceptions is greatest in July and least in January. It is said that there are fewer twin births in time of war; and that the incidence of twinning is greater when conception occurs in the first three months after marriage.

The administration of gonadotrophins for certain forms of sterility, particularly in an overdose, may cause multiple pregnancy.

HISTORICAL

Twins were viewed with superstition, and still are amongst

primitive peoples. Twins were thought to have power over the weather, fertility and survival in battle. In some cultures it is thought that no man can father more than one child at a time, so that the mother must have been unfaithful. The aborigenes of Japan (the Ainus) and Australia, and primitive peoples among the Eskimos, Africans and North and South American Indians killed one or both twins. In New Guinea, when one twin dies the survivor is given a wooden image of his sibling.

Famous twins included Castor and Pollux, Romulus and Remus, Jacob and Esau, Viola and Sebastian, and Tweedledum and Tweedledee. For a fascinating account of the life of the famous Siamese twins, Chang and Eng, see the book by Hunter (1964), and a summary in our book *Lessons from Childhood* (1966).

ZYGOSITY

Identical twins (monozygos, uniovular) are the product of the fertilisation of a single ovum. Non-identical twins (dizygos, fraternal) are binovular. Triplets are uniovular, binovular or triovular. The zygosity cannot be diagnosed satisfactorily by examination of the placenta and membranes. It is best diagnosed by a detailed determination of the blood groups. Other methods, none so satisfactory, include inspection of the palm prints, the iris pattern, the eye colour, the hair colour and texture, the hair whorls, the dental morphology, the shape of the nose, ears, lips and fingers. Identical twins are closely similar in these features and are almost invariably the same sex.

FEATURES

The mean birth weight of twins is 2,395g, of triplets 1,818g and of quadruplets 1,395g. About half of all twins are born prematurely. The first born tends to be the heavier at birth and to be larger at school age. Identical twins tend to weigh less than non-identical ones. The smaller of twins is liable to have a low blood sugar in the newborn period, and unless this is adequately treated, the brain may suffer. Sometimes, as in the case of Jacob and Esau, one twin bleeds into the other in utero, so that one is born plethoric and the other is born anaemic. Twins present feeding problems, sleeping problems and financial problems to the parents and perhaps are more likely than singletons to be the object of jealousy on the part of other siblings because of the time which their mother has to devote to them and the interest which they arouse. Twins are extremely likely to be jealous of each other, and sibling rivalry is increased when one of non-identical twins is more clever than the other, or there are differences in appearance, performance in sport or other skills. Jealousy is increased by favouritism—shown perhaps, to one because he is of the desired sex. Jealousy may have a deleterious effect on school work, sometimes to such an extent that the twins have had to be sent to different schools. Further psychological problems are presented by the fact that twins are so much an object of curiosity and interest.

The incidence of cerebral palsy is eight times that in singletons. If one twin is spastic there is a one in two chance that the co-twin will be stillborn; if he survives, he is more delicate than usual in the first three or four years. The birth weight of the twin with cerebral palsy is usually less than that of the surviving twin. Delay in the development of speech in twins is common (Chapter 11) and stuttering is slightly more common than in singletons. According to Benirschke and Kim (1973) in their review (with 220 references) there is a much higher incidence of congenital anomalies in twins; these include congenital heart disease and cleft palate.

There is rather more left-handedness amongst identical twins than amongst non-identical ones. The identical twin is more likely to be born by a younger mother, to be smaller at birth, more prematurely born and more delicate in the early months. According to Very and Hine (1969) the first born is more likely to be a leader, to be more responsible and more aggressive than the second born, who tends to be more easy-going, cheerful, stubborn, gentle and light hearted. According to Koch (1966) identical males tend to be less gregarious, less aggressive, less jealous and to show less initiative than singletons. Non-identical males tend to be more aggressive than identical males. Identical twins tend to be closer to each other than non-identical ones. There is possibly a slightly greater tendency to homosexuality among twins.

Newman and his colleagues (1938) in their well-known study compared 50 pairs of identical twins with 50 pairs of non-identical ones. They found that they differed most in physical traits, next in intelligence, less in achievement tests and least in tests of personality and temperament. In arithmetic, nature study, history and literature, and in neurosis, the identical twins were little different from non-identical ones. They suggested that the role of heredity was greater for some traits than others, for which environment was more important. Non-identical twins may be more influenced by environment than identical ones; and physical traits were least affected by environment, intelligence more, education achievement still more, and personality or temperament the most. They thought that much of the difference in the intelligence of non-identical twins was of environmental origin. Identical twins tend to retain their likeness in mental traits, while non-identical ones, being more affected by the environment, grow less alike.

Mittler (1971) wrote that the mean IQ of twins is around 95. McKeown and Record (1952) studied the mean verbal scores in the 11-plus examination in Birmingham multiple births. The mean scores were as follows:

48,913 singletons   100·1
 2,164 twins   95·7
    33 triplets   91·6

These differences were not related to the age of the mother, birth order, birth weight or the duration of gestation. They showed that the mean score for 148 twins whose co-twins had been stillborn or had died in the first four weeks was 98·8—indicating that the difference between twins and singletons was largely environmental. The IQ of the smaller of twins tends to be lower than that of the co-twin, and the score achieved by non-identical twins was worse in verbal than performance tests (Willerman and Churchill 1967). This may have been due to a low blood sugar at birth or to the smaller of the twins having a smaller placenta or smaller part of a placenta. Other complications of pregnancy, more common in multiple pregnancy, may have been relevant: they include hydramnios, toxaemia and antepartum haemorrhage and abnormal delivery.

It is said that middle class twins tend to be more retarded than twins in the 'working classes'. It is also said that an identical co-twin may do badly in IQ tests unless his co-twin is in the same room with him at the time of the test; presumably cheating is excluded as the relevant factor.

Mittler quoted work describing an 'overall poverty and reduction of vocabulary, more immature and primitive sentence construction, more limited range of those parts of speech which contribute to cognitive operations involving classification, abstraction and conceptualisation.' Possible factors responsible for the lower scores of twins were low birth weight and greater family size.

Studies of twins reared apart have not been entirely satisfactory, partly because the environment of twins reared together is not necessarily the same for both twins, and partly because if twins are to be reared apart, similar environment may be chosen for both of them—or the environment might be very different. Allen and Pollin (1972) found personality differences in identical twins even in the first year: responsible factors were the size and feeding behaviour—which affected the mother's attitude to the twins: and their responsiveness, rate of development, and illnesses.

Erlenmeyer-Kimling and Jarvih (1963) reviewed genetic studies over 50 years in eight countries, covering 1,082 identical and 2,052 non-identical twins. The mean correlation in the scores were as follows:

Non-identical	0·53
Identical reared together	0·87
Identical reared apart	0·75
Unrelated children living together	0·23

Newman and his colleagues (1938) studied 19 pairs of identical twins separated in infancy. In some of the physical characteristics, especially weight and head measurements, separated twins were more alike than non-identical twins and approximately as much alike as unseparated identical twins. In weight, intelligence and educational achievement, separated identical twins were as different as non-identical twins. Others have shown that separated identical twins show considerable disparity in educational achievement, even though the IQ is equated.

MANAGEMENT

Twins should be treated as individuals, and encouraged to develop apart. Failure to do this, and encouragement of the normal tendency of identical twins to be dependent on each other, may lead to unpleasant psychological problems later, when separation becomes inevitable. It is unwise to dress them alike or to give them the same toys. Determined efforts should be made to reduce jealousy of one twin towards the other.

REFERENCES

ALLEN M.G., POLLIN W. & HOFFER A. (1972) Parental, birth and infancy factors in infant twin development. In CHESS S. & THOMAS A., *Annual Progress in Child Psychiatry and Child Development*. New York, Brunner Mazel.

BENIRSCHKE K. & KIM C. (1973) Multiple pregnancy. *New Engl. J. Med.* **288**, 1276.

ERLENMEYER-KIMLING L. & JARVIH L.F. (1963) Genetics and intelligence. *Science* **142**, 1477.

HUNTER L. (1964) *Duet for a Lifetime*. London, Michael Joseph.

ILLINGWORTH R.S. & ILLINGWORTH C.M. (1966) *Lessons from Childhood: Some Aspects of the Early Life of Unusual Men and Women*. Edinburgh, Churchill/Livingstone.

KOCH H.L. (1966) *Twins and Twin Relations*. Chicago, University of Chicago Press.

McKEOWN T. (1970) Prenatal and early postnatal influences on measured intelligence. *Brit. Med. J.* **3**, 63.

McKEOWN T. & RECORD R.G. (1952) Observations on foetal growth in multiple pregnancy in man. *J. Endocrinol.* **8**, 386.

MITTLER P. (1971) *The Study of Twins*. London, Penguin.

NEWMAN H.O., FREEMAN F.N. & HOLZINGER K.J. (1938) *Twins: a Study of Heredity and Environment*. Chicago, University of Chicago Press.

VERY P.S. & HINE N.P.V. (1969) The effect of birth order upon personality development of twins. *J. Genet. Psychol.* **114**, 93.

WILLERMAN L. & CHURCHILL J.A. (1967) Intelligence and birth weight in identical twins. *Child Development*, **38**, 623.

OTHER READING

GEDDA L. (1961) *Twins in History and Science*. Springfield, Charles Thomas.

SCHEINFELD A. (1968) *Twins and Supertwins*. London, Chatto & Windus.

ZAZZO R. (1960) *Les Jumeaux. Le Couple et La Personne*. Paris, Presses Universitaires de France.

CHAPTER 13
PHYSICAL GROWTH

INTRODUCTION

All children are different. Some are thin and some are fat, some are small and some are tall. There is a wide difference between the average and the normal. A child may be pounds below the average in weight and inches below the average in height, and yet be perfectly normal. It is more healthy to be below the average weight than above it. Of greater importance than the weight and height is the child's abundant energy, *joie de vivre*, freedom from infection and freedom from lassitude. It is wrong to suppose that the bigger the baby or child is, the better he is. Maximum growth is not optimum growth: maximum growth shortens life.

Table 13.1 shows the average weight and height of children up

TABLE 13.1. Average height and weight, 0–10 years (Tanner *et al.* 1966)

Age in years	Boys				Girls			
	In	Cm	Lb	Kg	In	Cm	Lb	Kg
0	21·5	54	7·7	3·5	21·2	53	7·5	3·4
0·25			13·1	5·93			12·3	5·6
0·5			17·4	7·9			15·2	6·9
0·75			20·3	9·2			19·2	8·7
1	30·4	76	22·5	10·2	29·5	74	21·4	9·7
2	34·8	87	28·0	12·7	34·2	86	26·9	12·2
3	39·5	94	32·4	14·7	37·2	93	31·5	14·3
4	40·5	102	36·6	16·6	40·0	100	35·9	16·3
5	43·3	108	40·7	18·5	42·8	107	40·3	18·3
6	45·8	115	45·2	20·5	45·2	113	45·0	20·4
7	48·2	121	49·8	22·6	47·7	119	49·8	22·6
8	50·4	126	55·1	25·0	50·0	125	55·3	25·1
9	52·6	132	60·6	27·5	52·2	131	61·1	27·7
10	54·9	137	66·8	30·3	54·4	136	68·6	31·1
11	56·8	142	73·9	33·6	57·2	143	77·4	35·2
12	58·8	147	82·9	37·7	59·5	149	89·1	40·5
13	61·2	153	93·7	42·6	62·4	156	100·8	45·8
14	64·4	161	107·3	48·8	64·0	160	112·2	51·0
15	66·8	167	120·3	54·7	64·8	162	119·7	54·4
16	68·8	172	131·1	59·6	64·8	162	122·8	55·8

to the age of ten. After that age the onset of puberty has such a great effect on the rate of increase in weight and height that it would not be useful to tabulate the average.

Table 13.2 from my book *The Normal Child* (1972) shows the

TABLE 13.2.   Height in childhood in relation to expected adult height (R. S. Illingworth 1972)

	\multicolumn{6}{c}{Expected adult height}					
Age in years	5ft	150cm	5ft 6in	165cm	6ft	180cm
Boys	In	Cm	In	Cm	In	Cm
1	25·8	65·5	28·3	72·0	30·9	78·6
2	29·4	74·7	32·1	81·7	35·3	89·6
3	31·8	80·8	35·1	89·2	38·1	97·0
4	34·4	87·3	37·8	96·1	41·2	104·7
5	36·6	93·0	40·3	102·3	43·9	111·6
6	38·7	98·4	42·7	108·4	46·6	118·4
7	40·7	103·5	44·8	113·9	48·9	124·2
8	42·6	108·2	46·9	119·0	51·1	129·9
9	44·6	113·2	49·0	124·4	53·4	135·7
10	46·2	117·4	50·8	129·1	55·5	140·9
Girls	In	Cm	In	Cm	In	Cm
1	27·0	68·5	28·3	72·0	32·4	82·2
2	31·1	79·2	34·3	87·1	37·4	95·0
3	33·9	86·0	37·2	94·5	40·6	103·1
4	36·5	92·8	40·2	102·1	43·9	111·4
5	39·0	99·1	43·0	109·1	46·9	119·0
6	41·3	104·8	45·4	115·3	49·6	125·9
7	43·5	110·4	47·8	121·5	52·2	132·6
8	45·6	115·7	50·1	127·3	54·6	138·8
9	47·6	120·9	52·4	133·0	57·1	145·1
10	49·5	125·7	54·4	138·3	59·4	150·9

height of boys and girls from one to ten, in relation to the final adult expected height. For example, if a boy is to reach a final height of 5ft 6 in, it is likely that at the age of 5 years he will be approximately 40·3 inches.

It will be noted that the average increase in height from the age of two to five years is about 3 inches per year, and from six to puberty about 2½ inches a year. The earliest sign of impending puberty is then a growth spurt—a rapid increase in weight and height.

CATCH UP GROWTH

When children acquire an infection, such as measles, they stop gaining weight or lose weight, but in convalescence they have a compensatory increase of appetite so that the weight is soon what it would have been if no infection had occurred. As Tanner *et al.* (1963) put it, it seems as if in the brain there is some record of the size which the body ought to have achieved after a given period of time and some signal which informs the central nervous system of the difference between the actual size of the body and its expected size. This phenomenon is termed 'catch-up growth'; its mechanism is not understood. It only occurs if the illness is of relatively short duration: a long illness may cause a permanent reduction in weight.

FACTORS

The main factors relevant to differences in physical growth are as follows:

Hereditary factors.
Size at birth.
Social factors.
Nutrition.
Emotional deprivation.
Disease.

When a child is unusually small or unusually tall, the common explanation is the fact that he takes after one or both of his parents. One frequently sees children who are well but small, and whose parents are worried about their small size. It has not occurred to the mother that as she herself is small, it would not be surprising if her son took after her.

Studies in Sheffield showed that there is a strong correlation between the size at birth and the size in later childhood. There are exceptions, and exceptions are common, but on the average the smaller the child at birth, especially if he were small in relation to the duration of gestation, the smaller he is likely to be in later years, and the bigger he is at birth, the bigger he is likely to be in later childhood. The difference is in both weight and height. The child who was very small at birth is likely to be small in build, 'petite', while the child who was a big baby usually has a big build in later years. In Sheffield we found the same difference throughout childhood. In Scandinavia it was found that there was the same correlation between birth weight and the weight and height of recruits for the army. In Newcastle (1972) it was shown that there was the same correlation at the age of twenty-two.

Social factors are relevant. Children in large families tend to mature late, and children in small families tend to mature early. Tanner *et al.* (1966) showed that there is a constant difference in height between social classes—from two to at least twenty years of age. At the age of seven, the child from social class 5 is on the average 3·3cm smaller in height than the child of social class 1 and 2. Malnutrition is presumably the main cause for the smaller height of children in the lower classes, and of children in the developing countries as compared with others. Numerous studies on animals have shown that there is a critical period for growth; if rats or pigs are malnourished in the early part of their life, and then given as much to eat as they want, they remain small, never catching up to their fellows. The same applies to other animals. Work in Sheffield and elsewhere (Eid 1970) has shown that when a child is small in the early months, as a result of malabsorption or other disease, if the cause of the failure to thrive is not removed by about the second year, he is likely to remain small in later years.

Malnutrition in the early months after birth in addition to preventing normal physical growth damages the brain, reducing the number of brain cells. The human brain grows principally during the last three months of pregnancy and the 18 to 24 months after birth; in that period the number of brain cells is determined, and correction of malnutrition after that date will not alter that number; in other words, the damage will be permanent. There are corresponding chemical changes in the composition of the brain.

Growth is retarded by emotional deprivation. This applies not only to the child's weight but to his height. The mechanism is not clear: it is not just a matter of malnutrition.

Various famous people were unusually small: they included Alexander the Great, Napoleon, Nelson, d'Annunzio, Christopher Wren, Chancellor Dollfuss and Lawrence of Arabia. Alexander Pope was a mere 4 feet 6 inches in height.

A wide variety of diseases may cause smallness of stature and weight. Smallness of stature may be due to hereditary disease, such as achondroplasia—a form of dwarfism seen in the circus. The dwarfism is due to a defect in cartilage at the end of long bones, causing shortness of the humerus and femur. Affected children have a relatively large head with a depressed bridge of the nose. The mean IQ level of children with achondroplasia is slightly below the average.

Mentally defective children tend to be smaller in height than others. Children with severe chronic chest disease, such as severe asthma or bronchiectasis, severe congenital heart disease, chronic renal insufficiency or fibrocystic disease of the pancreas tend to be smaller than others. In fibrocystic disease and coeliac disease there is defective absorption of fat, and growth may be defective, though children with coeliac disease, if properly treated, should reach a normal height. Children with chronic vomiting or chronic diarrhoea (as in ulcerative colitis) are apt to be stunted in growth. Stunting of growth is caused by thyroid deficiency, if improperly treated, or rarely by pituitary disease.

Undue tallness is usually genetic, but certain rare diseases are associated with excessive height. Obese children are usually tall until puberty, but growth ceases earlier than usual, so that they may ultimately be rather small.

Undue tallness leads to psychological difficulties, including the fact that too much may be expected of an unduly tall child, in the way of behaviour, sports ability and other achievement. Douglas showed, however, that except in the upper middle class, tall children are usually more clever than small ones. Terman and Oden, in their study of 1,528 mentally superior children, found that compared with controls these children were tall for their age.

An unusually small child is apt to feel inferior to his fellows. A true dwarf, such as a child with achondroplasia, is apt to be treated as a baby, at least in the early years after infancy. He feels conspicuous. He has to inhibit his normal aggressiveness because he cannot fight, and is apt to withdraw from company. Dorner and Elton (1973) wrote about some of the results of undue smallness of stature: there is commonly parental anxiety with consequent food-forcing and overprotection. The child may be teased. Less may be expected of him and he may react by reduced achievement.

THE HEAD SIZE

The growth of the head in infancy depends largely on the growth of the cranial contents. If the brain does not grow normally, the child being mentally defective, the head is usually small (micro-cephaly), unless there is obstruction to the flow of cerebrospinal fluid (hydrocephalus). There is a rare condition termed megalen-cephaly, in which the brain is large, so that the head is big, but the brain is of poor quality, and the child is mentally subnormal. In infancy one must relate the head size to the size of the child, for a big child is likely to have a bigger head than a small child, and a small child a smaller head than a big child.

Familial factors are important: in some families there is a tendency for the head to be unusually large or unusually small.

Various famous people as children had a notably large or small head. Thomas Hardy was described as 'the littlest fellow with the biggest head in his class'. Swinburne was said to have the largest hat at Eton, and to resemble a pumpkin balanced on a forked radish. Thackeray was taken to the doctor because of his large head. Thomas Edison had a notably large head. Napoleon on account of his ill shapen head was the member of the family of whom greatness was least expected; his large head was said to balance itself with difficulty on his shoulders. Mirabeau and Swinburne had notably large heads. Lord Byron had a notably small head.

TEETHING

As a milestone of development the age of eruption of teeth is useless.

The average age at which the second or permanent set of teeth erupt is as follows:

First molars	6–7 years
Lower central incisors	6–7 years
Upper central incisors	7–8 years
Lateral incisors	7–9 years
Lower canines	10–11 years
First bicuspids	10–12 years
Second bicuspids	10–12 years
Upper canines	11–12 years
Second molar	12–14 years
Third molar	17–30 years

About 5 per cent of children in ordinary schools and 12 per cent in special schools are left-handed. Left-handedness is more common in social class 5 than in the middle and upper classes, and more common in mental defectives. It is three times more common in uniovular twins than in the whole population. It is probably partly genetic and partly environmental. There may also be intrauterine factors: it is said that the presentation at birth is related to handedness.

Handedness is not usually established until the age of two or three years, or even four. Most left-handers are not purely left-handers but ambidextrous, favouring the use of the left hand. I have discussed the relationship to speech patterns on p. 165 and learning disorders on p. 153. I have no experience concerning the effect of left-handedness on handwriting and fatigue when writing.

Handedness can be tested by getting the child to pick up an object, to draw, cut paper, rub with a duster, comb the hair, wind a clock or hammer nails.

I have discussed the problem in more detail in my book on development (Illingworth, 1972).

REFERENCES

DORNER S. & ELTON A. (1973) Short, taught and vulnerable. *Special Education*, 62, 12.

EID E.E. (1970) A follow-up study of physical growth following failure to thrive with special reference to a critical period in the first year of life. *Acta. Paediat. Scandinav.* 60, 39.

ILLINGWORTH R.S. (1972) *The Normal Child: Some Problems of the Early Years and their Treatment*, 5th edition. London, Churchill/Livingstone.

ILLINGWORTH R.S. (1972) *The Development of the Infant and Young Child, Normal and Abnormal*. Edinburgh, Livingstone.

MILLER F.J.W., BILLEWICZ W.Z. & THOMSON A.M. (1972) Growth from birth to adult life of 442 Newcastle-upon-Tyne children. *Brit. J. Prev. Soc. Med.* 26, 224.

PRADER A., TANNER J.M. & VON HARNACK G.A. (1963) Catch up growth following illness or starvation. *J. Pediat.* 62, 646.

TANNER J.M., WHITEHOUSE R.H. & TAKAISHI M. (1966) Standard from birth to maturity for height, weight, height velocity and weight velocity. *Arch. Dis. Childh.* 41, 613.

TERMAN L.M. & ODEN M.H. (1926 to 1959: 5 vols) *Genetic Studies of Genius*. Stanford, Stanford University Press.

CHAPTER 14
OBESITY

There is no satisfactory definition of obesity; hence a simple way of avoiding a scientific definition which would be open to criticism is to say that if a child looks fat, he is fat. A definition based on weight is unsatisfactory, because the body is made up of different components of which fat is the lightest (Brook 1973). It is unsatisfactory to base a definition on weight in relation to height, because children become tall as a result of being obese (through a secondary effect on the adrenal gland). The skin fold calipers are a good way of recording the amount of fat.

Obesity has been described as the commonest form of malnutrition—though most would regard the word malnutrition as synonymous with undernutrition. Paradoxically obesity is more a problem of the poor than the well-to-do. This is because in the lower social classes less attention is paid to the figure, the diet tends to be more starchy, and adults drink more beer. In an Australian study of six-year-old girls it was found that the incidence of obesity was nine times greater in the lower classes than in the upper classes. Obesity is now extremely common in infants and in older children.

The causes of obesity can be summarised as being heredity, increased intake, decreased output and metabolic or hormonal factors. Heredity plays an important part. There are genetic strains of mice, rats and sheep dogs, and these are used for experimental purposes. Most fat children have a fat parent, but the explanation is not necessarily a genetic factor: it could be a familial liking for good food and plenty of it.

The most important of all factors is increased intake. It is virtually impossible for anyone to become fat without eating more than he needs. Nevertheless it is obvious to all that some eat large amounts of rich foods and remain thin, while others put on weight if they have the slightest lapse from their good intentions. In other words there are additional metabolic factors, and these are little understood. One factor is the number of fat cells in the body. The number of these is determined in the first one or two years, and after that modifications of diet do not affect their number. It is therefore likely that wrong feeding in infancy may cause an increase in fat cells which will make it difficult for the rest of his life to keep the weight down. It follows that early overfeeding and wrong feeding (e.g. with excess of cereal) may cause the baby to become fat, and thereafter he remains fat even though the food intake is reduced. Apart from the effect of early overfeeding on the number of fat cells, there is a hormonal factor (to be explained below) which has the same effect—the development of obesity and its maintenance despite reduced food intake.

It is useful to consider why children should have an excessive intake. Mothers are apt to think that the bigger the child is, the better he is. When I reassured a mother, anxious about her child's weight, that his weight was exactly average, she said, 'That's pretty poor, isn't it, to be just average?' When I explained to another mother that her ten-year-old daughter was 58lb above the average weight, the mother exclaimed, 'That's all very well, but are all children average?' In Sheffield mothers apply the adjective 'bonny' to their fat children. Mothers are delighted when their child has a big appetite: one mother in replying to my question about her grossly fat child, said, 'Oh yes, she has a marvellous appetite. She never stops eating.' One constantly sees fat children eating in the street—eating sweets, potato crisps, peanut and icecreams. Mothers argue that 'he's so big that he takes a lot of filling'. In fact he has become big as a result of overeating.

Habit is a major cause of overeating. Mothers introduce their children to the sweet-eating habit. They think that they are being kind to their children or show them love by giving them sweets, not realising how unkind they are in making their children fat and giving them dental caries. The amount of food which children and particularly adults take is governed much more by habit than by hunger. The number of pieces of bread or toast and the amount of potato at dinner is decided much more by habit. The first thought of many when they go to a cinema, music hall, theatre or concert, as soon as they sit down, is to eat. Some mothers, regarding their child as delicate, give him rich food and make him fat.

Food intake and appetite are considerably affected by emotions

—jealousy, love, grief, excitement, fear, disgust, worry, boredom, tenseness, anxiety, depression or bereavement. Jealousy or sibling rivalry causes a child to ask for more pudding because his sibling has asked for more: the second child asks for more partly so that his sibling cannot have it all, and partly because he does not want to be outdone. It is well known that people nibble at food when they are feeling bored, tense, worried or waiting for something to happen. Bereavement may cause overeating. Disgust and excitement may take the appetite away. An emotion may have one effect in one person and the opposite effect in another.

By the term decreased output I mean decreased exercise. Lack of exercise, laziness, sedentary habits or TV watching instead of outdoor games all reduce the need for food. Certain diseases immobilise a child; such a child has a greatly reduced need for calories, and if the food intake is not adjusted accordingly he becomes fat.

It is the metabolic aspects of obesity which are least understood. Much is known, but not enough, and a great deal of research is being done on this subject. Many have the incorrect idea that obesity is due to 'glandular trouble'. As I shall explain below, the endocrine glands are involved, but no child can become fat unless he eats more than he needs: this is the basic fact: but the exact mechanisms involved in overweight are less clear. We know that there are two centres in the hypothalamus in the brain which are concerned with appetite, and that they are affected by impulses from other parts, such as the nose (a pleasant smell of food making one hungry), the eyes and other centres. They are particularly affected by the blood sugar and by the amount of body fat. There are several methods of damaging these centres in experimental animals: the destruction of one of the centres causes the animal to overeat and overdrink and simultaneously to become less active: he becomes fat, and later his appetite falls off, but he remains fat on a normal intake. The destruction of the other centre causes the animal to eat and drink much less—to lose its appetite. The weight of a human being must be controlled by a delicate balance between these centres. It is remarkable that one's weight is so static. A gain of one ounce a week will in 10 years mean a weight gain of 32lb. A weight gain of one ounce a day—a very small amount in relation to the normal food intake—would mean a gain of 22lbs 12oz in a year.

The results of obesity are almost uniformly unpleasant. The child looks unsightly. He is teased, given annoying nicknames and may become worried, depressed or withdrawn as a result. He may try to reduce weight and repeatedly fail—and worry all the more. The effect on the physical build is striking; almost all fat children are tall, because of a secondary action on the adrenal cortex, and they tend to reach puberty early: but as a result of the action on the adrenal they prematurely stop growing, so that ultimately they are smaller than usual. Fat children commonly develop striae—linear scars on the abdomen and other parts of the body, the same as the striae following pregnancy. The penis looks small, but this appearance is due to it being buried in fat.

There is a strong correlation between excessive weight in early childhood and obesity in adult life. We have long known that most fat two-year-olds will be fat adults. We showed in Sheffield (Eid 1970) that excessive weight gain at six weeks of age is statistically significantly correlated with overweight at the age of seven or eight. A fat child is still more likely to be a fat adult if he has a fat mother or father—particularly if both his parents are fat.

A variety of diseases in adult life are associated with obesity. They include cardiovascular disease, high blood pressure, kidney disease, toxaemia in pregnancy, cirrhosis of the liver, gallbladder disease, diabetes, hernia and osteoarthritis. When an adult is 20lb overweight, the death rate for his age is 10 per cent greater than average; when he is 50lb overweight it is 75 per cent greater than average. The incidence of diabetes and of cardiovascular disorders in adults is highest in those who were fat in childhood.

The treatment of obesity is unsatisfactory. It is far better to prevent it than to wait for it to develop fully and then belatedly to take action. It should be prevented by proper supervision of the diet in infancy (and in particular breast feeding instead of bottle feeding), avoidance of the premature introduction of cereals, and weighing at intervals so that a tendency to gain weight excessively can be immediately checked. The early diagnosis and management of obesity is an important function of the school medical officer. In schools in which children are weighed at the beginning of each term, overweight children should be referred to the school medical officer. Once the child has become fat, it is very difficult to treat. It is difficult to persuade a child to adhere to a rigid diet—and difficult from the psychological point of view. It is not possible by reducing his weight to remove fat without removing his protein. We aim at stopping him putting more weight on, without getting him to lose weight, while he is still growing. It is unwise to attempt to make a growing child reduce weight. One tries to stop him eating sweets, icecreams, lollipops, fish and chips, peanuts, potato crisps and other high calorie foodstuffs: to stop putting sugar into his tea, to stop taking fruit squash, because of its carbohydrate content, and to reduce the amount of bread and potatoes which he takes. He should cut down the intake of milk to not more than half a pint a day. Those responsible for serving school meals should help to reduce the food intake. There is evidence that large infrequent meals are more harmful with regard to weight-gain than small frequent snacks, which assuage the appetite. One encourages him to take more exercise. Drugs are of little value. On rational grounds they are unlikely to help, because the cause is not often an excessive appetite. It is habit, and drugs designed to reduce appetite are unlikely to assist. They may help for the first two or three months, but then they usually lose their effect. They have untoward side effects, they may cause unpleasant symptoms when they are discontinued, and they may lead to addiction. I feel that they have little place in the treatment of obesity.

CONCLUDING NOTE

In the Leicester City Art Gallery there is a painting of Daniel Lambert, the son of the warden of the gaol; Daniel died at the age of 39 years weighing 52st 11lb. Ruth Pontico of Florida died weighing 58 stones. Robert Hughes of Illinois died at 32 years, weighing 74st 5lb: his waist circumference was 10 feet 2 inches.

REFERENCES

BROOK C.G.D. (1973) Fat children. *Brit. J. Hosp. Med.* **10**, 30.
EID E.E. (1970) Studies on the subsequent growth of children who had excessive weight gain in the first six months of life. *Brit. Med. J.* **2**, 74.

ADDITIONAL REFERENCES ON OBESITY

BÖRJESON M. (1962) Overweight children. *Acta. Paediat. Uppsala.* **51**, Suppl.132.
BRUCH H. (1974) *Eating Disorders.* London, Routledge and Kegan Paul.
HIRSCH J., KNITTLE J.E. & SALANS L.B. (1967) Cell lipid content and cell number in obese and non-obese human adipose tissue. *J. Clin. Invest.* **46**, 1112.
Journal of the American Medical Association (1970) Obesity, a continuing enigma. Leading Article, **211**, 492.

CHAPTER 15

PUBERTY AND SEX

At 15 to 18 months, children commonly show interest in the excreta, and between two and three they notice differences between boys and girls. At three the child knows whether he is a boy or a girl. Boys openly handle their genitals and proudly display them. From about five to twelve sex play is almost universal; when there is a boy and a girl in the family they are bathed together when young, and it is normal for the girl to make remarks about her brother's penis and to handle it. The wise parent completely ignores this. Modesty begins usually at about seven, and soon the children want to be bathed separately. Most children begin to ask questions about sex by the age of four or five. Girls begin to show their maternal instinct by about five. By about seven boys begin to enjoy only boy's games. Masturbation is almost invariable in boys and it is practised by the majority of girls: it can begin at any age, and is often seen in infancy: the girl sits astride the arm of a chair and rocks backwards and forwards. The peak age for masturbation is 14 to 16 years.

By about nine children enter the homosexual phase, wanting friends of the same sex, and teasing children of the opposite sex. At the age of puberty they commonly develop an intense friendship with someone of the same sex—so intense, sometimes, that it may guide a child in the choice of career: he wants to take up the same work as his hero so that he can be with him—and enjoy sex play with him. There is then a gradual change to heterosexuality so that in early adolescence a crush for someone in the opposite sex may develop—with hero worship of some male 'pop star' or other personality. At puberty and early adolescence sex interest reaches its peak.

THE MANAGEMENT OF SEX INTEREST

Before children start school they should have acquired basic sex knowledge from their parents. Questions should be answered honestly and never with amusement or embarrassment. The correct names for the genital organs and for eliminations should be used. Children should know where babies come from, and the anatomical differences between the sexes. It is essential that the parents should never show shock or disgust at anything said or done by the children. Nothing should ever be said to embarrass them about sex matters. Children should learn that sex interest is normal and that there is nothing nasty about it. Before puberty the parents must explain menstruation to the girl and erections and nocturnal emissions to the boy. Boys and girls should know the normality of the homosexual stage preceding heterosexual interests. Of great importance is the behaviour of the parents to each other, with mutual love and respect and the absence of domestic discord.

Children will discuss sexual matters with their friends at school, and it is important that they should be properly informed and have a sensible attitude to sex imparted at home. They should be provided with suitable books to supplement information given by the parents. There are many to choose from: the following are useful.

Recommended Books for Children on Sex

ALLEN A. (1963) *The Way You Are*. London, Robert Hale.
BRITISH MEDICAL ASSOCIATION FAMILY DOCTOR BOOKLETS: (i) *The Facts of Life for Children* (PILKINGTON R.). (ii) *15 + Facts of Life*.
GUTTMACHER A.F. (1971) *Understanding Sex—a Young Person's Guide*. London, Allen & Unwin.
HACKER R. (1966) *Telling the Teenagers*. London, Deutsch.
SHULTZ G.D. (1969) *It's Time you Knew*. London, Darwen-Finlayson.
TAME H.W. (1969) *Peter and Pamela Grow Up*. London. Darwen-Finlayson. (Suitable for the 11-year-old.)

MASTURBATION

Historical

According to Levine and Bell (1956) Vogel in 1890 wrote that boys who masturbate 'become visibly emaciated and anemic, remain backward in their body and mental development, the integument of the lower eyelids turns to a brownish or bluish colour: they have an apathetic expression of the countenance and flaccid muscles. They become indifferent to amusements which they once enjoyed and withdraw from all society, preferring to be alone, in order to indulge in their passion. The gait becomes unsteady and cumbersome and the knees fall inward. The emaciation is most strikingly seen on the lower extremities and lumbar region, while the penis increases proportionately in length and thickness. Tabes dorsalis and paralysis of the lower extremities are occasional though rare effects of this practice.'

In Holt's *Diseases of Infancy and Childhood* (1906–25) it is suggested that the child's legs should be tied to the crib; or that the clitoris should be cauterised; the thighs, vulva or prepuce should be cauterised: horseback riding should be avoided.

Other methods recommended have been sewing the labia together or castration. In some cultures masturbation was a major crime punishable by death. In the Talmud, masturbation was considered a greater sin than non-marital intercourse and punishable by death.

Discussion

Masturbation is almost universal in children, certainly in boys, reaching a peak around puberty. It is harmless in itself, but the attitude of others, parents or teachers, may be harmful. It should be ignored except when it is carried out in public, in which case the undesirability of this should be explained to the child in a matter-of-fact and non-punitive manner. It is only harmful to the child if he is made to feel guilty or to feel that there is something wrong about it.

Unfortunately there are still parents who were made to feel guilty in childhood about doing it themselves, and repress all memory of it, and then proceed to make their own children feel guilty about it.

HOMOSEXUALITY

It is usually held that homosexuality is for the most part a product of the environment: but there is probably an inherited personality trait which causes a child to react in a particular way to the home, management, attitudes and atmosphere. The typical background is that of a weak, hostile, punitive ineffective father with a dominating mother who establishes an abnormally strong relationship with the boy. She may bath him long after he ought to be able to bath himself, handling his genitalia unnecessarily: she may even sleep with the boy. She establishes an intense mother fixation in him, making it difficult for him to decide anything himself without consulting her. Several workers came to the same conclusion— namely that the most important factor in male homosexuality was a hostile relationship with the father: and in female homosexuality a hostile relationship with the mother.

Another factor is prolonged separation of the sexes. One would think that an only child would be more at risk than a child with siblings of the opposite sex, provided that there is a normal non-puritanical attitude to sex. In some homes however, particularly in the lower classes, extraordinary efforts are made to prevent the children of opposite sexes seeing each other undressed (Newson 1968), and punishment is meted out for genital play. The Newsons in Nottingham found that amongst the managerial and professional classes 5 per cent of the children were punished for this, as compared with 48 per cent in the unskilled classes. They wrote that 'it is in the strategies chosen for the child's sexual naïveté that the social classes differ so markedly'.

Other factors mentioned include specific exciting and gratifying homosexual experiences in childhood, seduction by an adult homosexual, or threatening and painful experiences in connection with sex play or relations with the opposite sex—for example reprimands to or ridicule of a small boy for entirely normal sexual curiosity with a small girl, mutual inspection of genitalia or merely kissing the girl (Brown 1963).

In a study of 24 female homosexuals (Kaye et al.) factors found included a significant history of threats and punishment for sex play with boys: a tendency to like guns and boys' games more than dolls: a tomboy personality: dominant, puritanical mothers who were contemptuous of their daughters, and overpossessive puritanical fathers who were interested physically in their daughters, exploiting them and feared by them. There is commonly a poor relationship between the daughter and the mother (British Medical Journal 1971) and with the father, an unhappy childhood, and a repressive family attitude to sex. In the case of both boys and girls education at a boarding school was irrelevant.

The early childhood of John Ruskin illustrated some of the points above. He was grossly overprotected by a domineering mother and was prevented from mixing with boys and girls. He grew up unable to enjoy sex. It is said that Oscar Wilde was dressed on occasions as a girl: his mother had particularly wanted a girl, and was disappointed when a boy was born. Alfred Nobel shared a bedroom with his mother, while his brothers slept in another room. When an adult he felt a deep revulsion against normal sexual relationships with the opposite sex. Marcel Proust was grossly overprotected by his mother: the seeds of an unhappy sex life were sown by his mother—as they were in the case of Dostoevsky.

There have been studies of possible biochemical and endocrine differences between homosexuals and heterosexuals (Margolese and Janiger 1973); several workers have claimed that there are biochemical and endocrinological differences between homosexuals and heterosexuals. (Kolodny and Masters (1973).)

PUBERTY

The age of onset of puberty varies from country to country. Malnutrition delays the onset of puberty, and it has even been suggested that a good parameter for the health of a country is the age of the onset of menstruation. It is earlier in the 'developed countries' than in the developing countries. Puberty occurs on the average two years earlier in girls than boys. It is earlier in children of big build—but the changes of puberty occur more quickly so that they stop growing sooner. Children of small build tend to reach puberty later, but the changes continue longer so that they cease growing later—and to some extent catch up to early maturers. Obese children usually reach puberty early. There are important genetic factors: early or late puberty is commonly a familial feature. Puberty tends to occur earlier in small families, and later in large families. It is delayed by malnutrition or by chronic illness.

The child who reaches puberty early tends to be superior at school in measured ability and to do better in examinations. This may be due to the fact that children from small families tend to do better than those from big families, and children from small families tend to mature earlier.

The remarkable secular changes in the age of onset of puberty are unexplained. The age of the onset of menstruation (menarche) has been about four months earlier each decade. In Norway in 1840 the age of the menarche averaged 17 years, and it is now thirteen. Children in Europe, North America and Japan amongst other places, are maturing progressively earlier. There is now evidence that in Norway and Britain the trend to earlier puberty has ceased.

Children are now much taller than they used to be. In Glasgow children are now on the average 5cm taller than children in 1906: at 9 years they are 8cm taller. In Europe and North America since 1900 there has been an average increase in height of 2–3cm per decade at 10 to 14 years. Fifty years ago men reached their maximum height at 26: now they reach it at 19.

Physical Changes
The changes of puberty are initiated by the pituitary gland in the brain: this emits hormones which stimulate the adrenal glands and the gonads (the ovaries and testes). The adrenal gland then causes the increase in height, the development of sexual hair and acne: the gonads cause enlargement of the breast and the changes in the vagina.

The Girl. The early signs of puberty commonly appear at the age of ten, with a spurt in weight and height, enlargement of the nipple (commencing about two years before the first period), pigmentation around the nipple and increase of tissue around the nipple. The whole breast tissue then enlarges. Pelvic girth then increases and pubic hair appears—straight at first and then curly. The sweat glands in the axilla (armpit) become activated and axillary hair appears. The usual age for the onset of menstruation is 13 years, but the range is a wide one—from 9 years (or even sooner) to 16 or 17 years. The main growth in height occurs a year before the first menstrual period; after the first period there is an abrupt slowing in the rate of increase of height, ceasing at about seventeen. During the changes there may be a mucoid discharge from the vagina. There is commonly acne—spots on the face and trunk, due to overactivity of the sebaceous glands around the hair follicles; the thick material may block the orifices in the skin, causing 'blackheads' and infection. There may be striae—linear scars on the abdomen or buttocks, such as occur after pregnancy. There are simultaneous changes in the larynx, affecting the voice.

There is commonly a feeling of lassitude, in contrast to the abundant energy of pre-pubertal days.

The Boy. The early signs of puberty are the spurt in weight and height, usually about two years later than that of the girl. There is then enlargement of the penis and testicles, the appearance of pubic hair, followed by hair in the axilla, on the upper lip, in the groin, on the thigh and between the pubis and umbilicus. There are changes in the larynx, affecting the voice, and commonly acne. As in the girl, there may be lassitude. At the age of about 14 years, nocturnal emissions of seminal fluid occur with erection of the penis in association with erotic dreams. There is then an abrupt slowing of the growth of weight and height, ceasing at about eighteen or nineteen. Enlargement of the breasts of a boy in early adolescence is normal, though it may cause some embarrassment: it occurs in about half of all boys. It lasts up to a year or two and then subsides.

Variations

One in about 500 boys has an abnormality of the chromosomes causing Klinefelter's syndrome. In adolescence the testes are small and enlargement of the breasts is common. Pubertal development is commonly delayed and sterility is usual. One in four is mentally retarded.

One in 2,500 live born females has Turner's syndrome, in which there is an abnormality of chromosomes. The normal sex changes at puberty do not occur; the breasts do not develop, and menstruation does not occur. The diagnosis may have been made long before puberty on account of oedema of the legs in the new-born period, webbing of the neck, a low posterior hair line and unusually small stature, with widely spaced nipples, heart defect and many other abnormalities. Doctors may prescribe hormone treatment so that the girl develops breast changes and has monthly vaginal bleeding: but the girl is sterile.

Unusually early puberty can occur in girls without disease. Menstruation and breast enlargement may occur in infancy. There is a well authenticated case of Lina Medina in Peru who at the age of 5 years gave birth to a child by caesarian section. The child and her mother were at school together. It is embarrassing for a girl to commence school at the age of five with fully developed breasts. Sometimes after one or two menstrual periods there may be no further period until the usual age. Very early puberty in a girl is commonly a normal variation, but it may be due to disease of the pituitary, adrenal or ovary; in a boy it is usually due to disease of the pituitary, adrenal or testis.

Other variations consist of the development of pubic hair with-out enlargement of the breast or other sign of puberty, or of the breast without pubic hair or other signs. Vaginal bleeding may occur without the appearance of pubic hair, and then cease, to be followed at the usual age by normal menstruation. Breast enlarge-ment may be asymmetrical.

The absence of breast changes and of menstruation in a teenage girl may be due to Turner's syndrome, a chromosome anomaly, and should be investigated.

PSYCHOLOGICAL FEATURES OF PUBERTY AND ADOLESCENCE

Though one should not generalise, one can outline the common psychological features of puberty and adolescence—recognising, however, that all children are different, and that some find puberty and adolescence a difficult time, while to others it presents no problem.

Common features at puberty are a recurrence of the normal negativism of the one- to three-year-old: rudeness, moodiness, sulkiness, withdrawal, a desire for isolation and privacy in contrast to the fondness of gangs of a year or two previously. There is often fatigue, in contrast to the abundant energy of a year before, day-dreaming, restlessness and boredom, with a disinclination to work. There is often a loss of self confidence—whereas a year or two before the boy thought that he knew everything. In girls there is the development of sensitiveness about appearance—a desire to be like others—and for the parents to dress like the parents of others. Hence there is an interest in powder and paint, make up and hair styles, though the urge to wash the face comes later—and to wash the neck and ears later still. Boys may grow long hair, because others do: boys and girls who are emotionally immature feel that they should smoke and take alcohol, because others do. There is anxiety about possible sex variations—especially if puberty is delayed: there is anxiety about acne, obesity and lanky legs. Boys may be worried because girls reach maturity so much sooner.

In early adolescence worries and anxieties are common—worries about attainment, popularity, career, finance, social position and health. Adolescents are often afraid of appearing to 'show off'; they are concerned about what others think of them: they are afraid of seeming foolish. They are particularly concerned about sexual matters; the boy is worried because of his breast enlargement, the girl about the irregularity of her menstrual periods (which are normal) and especially amenorrhoea: boys and often girls are worried about masturbation—particularly if they have been told that it causes insanity and all manner of ailments. Both boys and girls are worried about acne or obesity. Boys worry about their nocturnal emissions, their short stature or athletic ability: girls about being too tall or unattractive.

Adolescents are often gauche: they blush readily, are awkward and shy, and have unpleasant mannerisms. They rapidly change from tears to laughter, from giggling to weeping. They continue to be interested in their appearance, and strive for approval, so that they may smoke or drink beer, though they secretly hate both; but they have the great urge to conform to the practices and attitudes of their peers. They tend to take part in group activities—social groups, religious, political, debating groups, CND—and if their home background has been unsatisfactory in delinquent groups.

FRICTION WITH THE ADOLESCENT

In many homes puberty and adolescence present troublesome problems to the family, and these problems are carried through into school life. Fortunately for parents adolescence is not a permanent condition: teenagers grow out of it.

In a brilliant and valuable article, which should be read *in toto*, Gibson (1971) cited four quotations, which I have permission to reproduce here: they were given in the introduction to a lecture.

'Firstly:
"Our youth loves luxury, has bad manners, disregards authority and has no respect whatsoever for age; our today's children are tyrants; they do not get up when an elderly man enters the room— they talk back to their parents—they are just very bad."
'Secondly:
"I have no longer any hope for the future of our country if today's

youth should ever become the leaders of tomorrow, because this youth is unbearable, reckless—just terrible.''

'Thirdly:

"Our world has reached a critical stage; children no longer listen to their parents; the end of the world cannot be far away.''

'Finally:

"This youth is rotten from the very bottom of their hearts; the young people are malicious and lazy; they will never be as youth happened to be before; our today's youth will not be able to maintain our culture.'' '

The first came from Socrates, 470–399 BC; the second from Hesiod, *circa* 720 BC; the third from an Egyptian priest about 2,000 years BC; and the last was discovered recently on clay pots in the ruins of Old Babylon, and these were more than 3,000 years old.

It is important to understand the reasons for such attitudes, as common today as they evidently have been for many generations.

Behaviour problems are basically dependent on the interaction between the child's developing mind and personality and the personality and attitudes of the parents (and teachers) (Chapter 4). By the time adolescence is reached, the child's mind has been largely moulded by the experiences of early childhood: if the child has had his psychological needs satisfied (Chapter 2)—particularly his need for love, security, wise discipline, acceptance and a good example of honesty, unselfishness, kindness to others and avoidance of criticism, then adolescence, though it may still be difficult, is likely to be easier. Much depends on the child's personality, which is partly inherited and partly the product of his environment. Old favouritisms are an important cause of difficulty: if the parents have shown favouritism to the adolescent's siblings in earlier years, the adolescent when he acquires independence can be expected to grow apart from his parents. If he has been subject to much unkindness, nattering, criticism and lack of understanding, the adolescent is much more likely to rebel. He is no longer willing to tolerate his parents rudeness, intolerance, or their irrational demands and prohibitions. He wants to know the reason why: he questions authority—at home and at school: he is now able to think for himself, and will no longer accept the words 'because I say so'. He resents their criticism of his clothes or

behaviour—and particularly their criticism of his friends. The
parents, in turn, fail to appreciate the sensitiveness of the adolescent. They may have some justification for failing to understand
his choice of girl-friend—but it is unwise to say so. The adolescent
no longer accepts what his parents say as gospel—and his parents
resent having their authority questioned.

The normal psychological features of puberty and adolescence
lead to friction. These features include jealousy, sibling rivalry,
sarcasm, criticism, moodiness, shyness, obstinacy, seclusiveness,
and withdrawal from the family circle. His parents object to his
totally unavailing efforts to reform them.

A major cause of conflict is the transition of the adolescent from
dependence to independence. The more the parent tries to keep
control, the firmer the adolescent's resolve to be free: the more he
feels that his maturity is being underestimated, the more rebellious
will he become. Tolerance is essential. He must be allowed to grow
up, to make his own decisions. He needs guidance, but the fact
that he is being guided must be concealed: if he feels that he is
being pushed, he will adopt the opposite course because of the
normal negativism of this age period. This applies in particular to
choice of career; the adolescent needs and appreciates guidance,
given in a subtle way, but will not be pushed. Efforts to do so will
lead to much friction—and the opposite of the effect desired.
Parents must take calculated risks: they must not pry into his
affairs: they must give him a latch key and not stay up so that they
know when he comes in. But risks must be calculated, and calculated with judgment. It would be sheer folly to allow teenagers to
have a mixed party at home without the presence of an adult.
Adolescents do not seriously object to firmness on the part of
parents provided that the reason for the firmness is rational and
is properly explained.

Parental possessiveness and exploitation is a fruitful source of
friction. Some parents feel that they have a right to expect their
children to look after them when they are old, and to renounce
any intention of taking up a career which would make this impossible—or to renounce a suitable post which would separate
them at an inconvenient distance. Parents are apt to demand that
their children should give their whole life to looking after them in
their old age. It is commonly the girl who suffers in this way: it is
particularly difficult for her if she is conscientious and has a strong

sense of right and wrong. When a mother demands this behaviour from her son, the son is likely to resist unless there is serious mother-fixation resulting from her previous attitudes. Over-possessiveness on the part of the parents is disastrous, and must be avoided at all costs. Decent parents should know that their children have their own life to live.

Parents find it difficult to realise that what was wrong in one generation is accepted in another. The irrational attitudes of one generation are often discarded by the next generation. They do not stop to think that sexual behaviour which is wrong in one country is accepted as normal in another. There was a time when a bikini was accepted on the Spanish beaches, while the wearing of a bikini on the promenade above the beach led to imprisonment. It is difficult for parents to accept current fashions in clothes and hair styles for men.

Parents often have difficulty in accepting imperfection. Before their children are born, and after, they expect their children to be perfect: as their children grow up, imperfections appear, and parents are apt to show their disapproval in no uncertain way. Parents expect their children always to be even tempered, always to be unselfish, honest, polite and kind—despite the fact that they themselves are very far from perfect in these respects. Parents have great difficulty in keeping their mouths shut. When the adolescent is spoiling for a fight, he invites his parents to join in. He knows that he is feeling irritable—and he tries to put his parents in the wrong so that he can satisfy his mind that it is not his fault at all. Adolescents appreciate tolerance above all times when they are feeling tired, irritable, bored or worried. In Chapter 2 I wrote that children need loving most when they are being most unlov-able. This applies equally forcefully to the adolescent. Unfortu-nately it is just then that the parent is unable to repress his ire, to keep his mouth shut: he joins in the fray and expresses his fury and disgust—making the adolescent's irritability all the worse. Parents should never retaliate: if the adolescent is unhelpful, nothing could be worse than for the parent deliberately to show that he can be unhelpful too. In this and in many other problems, the difficulty is that each finds it hard to put himself into the position of the other.

In many homes there are many stock phrases, almost clichés, which are constantly uttered by parent or adolescent. They include the following:

When I was your age—
You're too old to understand.
You're too old fashioned.
Can't you hear me?
I don't know what's got into you. What's the matter with you?
How many times have I told you?
I could wring her neck.
When will you learn?
Don't just sit there.
Why? Because I say so.
I don't know what they're coming to.
Why pick on me?
It's my life: I can do what I like with it.
Why should I?
This is a fine time of night to come in.
You treat me as a child.
After all I've done for you.

MEDICAL ETHICS AND THE ADOLESCENT

There has at times been conflict between the medical officer of a
school and the head teacher concerning matters of confidentiality
affecting school children. When a doctor has examined a teenage
pupil, the headmistress may expect to be told about the outcome.
The earlier sexual maturation of girls and increasing permissiveness
on sexual matters has focussed attention on the problem. The
Medical Defence Union in 1972 published a booklet entitled *The
Child, The Doctor and The Law*, to guide doctors. It recommended
that after the 16th birthday confidentiality must be observed, and
that the doctor had no legal right to talk to teachers about the
patient, even though the doctor felt that he had a special duty to
the school for which he is medical officer. When his patient is
below the age of 16 there may well be occasions on which the
doctor does not feel ethically justified in talking to the head
teacher about a child's problem, but the law in this case is not
precise.

The situation may arise when the doctor wants information
from the teacher, but having obtained it and examined the patient
he is not able to reciprocate and tell the teacher about his findings.
For instance, a pupil may develop certain symptoms which should

be investigated and which therefore demand the doctor's attention. If a teacher notices in a teenager the symptoms of withdrawal, a falling off in school work or other psychological symptoms, the doctor should look into it.

MENSTRUAL DISORDERS

It is normal for menstruation to be irregular at first: there may be many months after the first period before subsequent periods occur. Amenorrhoea is particularly common when girls start at a new school or at the University, especially if they are dieting for obesity or overweight. When a period is missed unexpectedly, pregnancy must be eliminated.

Gibson (1971) wrote that a wise school doctor knows that most menstrual disorders can be ignored, provided anxious parents allow them to be ignored. The vital point is to know an irregularity exists, to judge the occasional one which needs investigation, to follow up others unobtrusively, and to leave the rest alone.

Dysmenorrhoea is said by Sloan (1972) to be the biggest single cause of absenteeism from work or play in the United States: in the younger patient it is the main cause of absenteeism. Almost 100 per cent in teenage girls is psychogenic, and without disease.

VAGINAL DISCHARGE

A clear muccid discharge from the vagina, especially around puberty, is of no significance. A discharge should be ignored unless it is offensive or purulent. It may be due to lack of cleanliness, rubbing because of itch, threadworms, a thrush (monilia) infection, or a foreign body.

A wide variety of foreign bodies have been found in the vagina—toilet paper, safety pins, coins, hairpins, crayons, sand, twigs, splinters of wood, cherries, paper clips, beads, pencil erasers, stones, marbles, sea-shells, nuts, corks and insects.

After the age of 12, gonorrhoea has to be considered if there is a purulent vaginal discharge.

REFERENCES

British Medical Journal (1969) Female homosexuality. Leading Article, **1**, 330.
BROWN D.C. (1963) Homosexuality and family dynamics. *Bull. Menninger Clinic*, **27**, 227.

GIBSON R. (1971) The satchel and the shining morning face. *Brit. Med. J.* **2**, 549.

KAYE H.E., BERL L., CLARE L., ELLSTON M.R., GERSHWIN B.S., GERSHWIN P., KOGAN L.S., TORDA C. & WILBUR C.B. (1967) Homosexuality in women. *Arch. Gen. Psychiat.* **17**, 626.

KOLODNY R.C. & MASTERS W.H. (1973) Hormones and Homosexuality. *Ann. Int. Med.* **79**, 897.

MARGOLESE M.S. & JANIGER O. (1973) Androsterone/etiocholanalone ratios in male homosexuals. *Brit. Med. J.* **3**, 207.

NEWSON J. & NEWSON E. (1968) *Four Years Old in an Urban Community.* London, Allen & Unwin.

SHEARER M. (1966) Homosexuality and the pediatrician. *Clinical Pediatrics,* **5**, 514.

SLOAN D. (1972) Dysmenorrhoea and pelvic pain. *Pediatric Clinics of North America,* **19**, 669.

OTHER REFERENCES

BURTON, LINDY (1968) *Vulnerable Children.* London, Routledge & Kegan Paul.

DEWHURST C.J. (1965) *Gynaecological Disorders of Infants and Children.* London, Cassell.

DOUGLAS J.W.B. (1964) *The Home and the School.* London, MacGibbon & Kee.

LEVINE M.I. & BELL A.I. (1956) The psychological aspects of pediatric practice. *Pediatrics,* **18**, 803.

WHO TECHNICAL REPORT SERIES NO. 308 (1965) *Health Problems of Adolescence.* Geneva, WHO.

CHAPTER 16
THE HANDICAPPED CHILD

HISTORICAL

Famous persons with physical handicaps included Socrates, Plato, Alexander Pope, Lord Byron, Sir Walter Scott, Karl Weber, Sir Patric Manson, Steinmetz, Toulouse Lautrec, Nietzsche, Conrad, Dickens, Heine, Handel, Chopin, Wagner, Strauss, Schubert, Schopenhauer, Beethoven and Rudyard Kipling.

THE NUMBER OF HANDICAPPED CHILDREN

The Department of Education and Science lists ten official categories of handicapped pupils. They are

Blind.
Partially sighted.
Deaf.
Partially hearing.
Physically handicapped.
Delicate.
Mentally subnormal.
Epileptic.
Maladjusted.
Speech defect.

Physically handicapped children include those with cerebral palsy, spina bifida, orthopaedic conditions, congenital heart disease, asthma, diabetes (Not an 'official' cause of handicap) and haemophilia.

The Seebohm report estimated that the number of handicapped school children in Britain was as follows:

	Per 1,000 children
Asthma	23·2
Educationally subnormal	20

Eczema	10·4
Epilepsy	7·2
Seriously subnormal	3·5
Cerebral palsy	3·1
Heart disease	2·4
Diabetes	1·2
Hearing defect	1·2
Visual defect	1·2

According to the publication *Statistics of Education* (1972) the following are the numbers of children in special schools in England and Wales.

Visual defect	2,865
Hearing defect	5,039
Deaf and partially sighted	173
Physical handicaps	5,310
Delicate	4,588
Delicate and physically handicapped	6,210
Delicate and maladjusted	375
Maladjusted	4,482
ESN	56,924
SSN	10,000
Epilepsy	590
Speech defect	103
Multiple handicaps	165
Hospital school	3,537

Each year approximately 20,000 are ascertained as needing special education.

The figures include about 3,000 children with cerebral palsy, 2,000 with spina bifida, 500 with muscle disease, 200 with haemophilia and 100 with diabetes.

Peckham (1973) in an analysis of 17,000 children born in England, Scotland and Wales in one week of March 1958, found that by the age of 11 years 407 children (3 per cent) had been ascertained by the Local Authority as needing special education. The figures were as follows:

	Rate per 1,000
ESN	16·2
SSN	3·2

Maladjusted   3·1
Physically handicapped   1·7
Delicate   1·2
Partially hearing   1·2
Epilepsy   0·5
Partially sighted   0·4
Speech defect   0·3
Deaf   0·2
Blind   0·1

It is estimated that for a school population of 10,000, special schools are needed in the following proportions:

ESN   74·6
Physically handicapped   16·4
Delicate   15·0
Maladjusted   11·0
Auditory defect   8·9
Visual defect   5·1
Epilepsy   1·2

About 1,000 handicapped children are born in Britain each week. 1,500 children are born each year with spina bifida. 6,000 are born with congenital heart disease—but half of them die before school age. There are about 200,000 school children in Britain suffering from asthma. Thanks to preventive measures poliomyelitis, blindness due to retrolental fibroplasia, and kernicterus due to rhesus blood group incompatibility or prematurity are now diseases of the past. Many handicaps are multiple.

The number of handicapped children is increasing. This is due to better medical care in infancy. For instance, mongols are more likely than others to have alimentary tract obstruction in the newborn period, or Hirschsprung's disease (a cause of extreme constipation) and to suffer infections of the respiratory tract: all these are now treated and the survival rate has increased. Whereas a few years ago 90 per cent of children with hydrocephalus and spina bifida died in the first year, many more now survive as a result of surgical methods. More children survive with congenital heart disease, because of surgery, and more survive with cystic fibrosis of the pancreas, phenylketonuria and haemophilia as a result of medical treatment. Far more small premature babies now survive, but they are at special risk of handicap, especially cerebral palsy. Babies born of diabetic mothers had a high mortality a few years ago: there is a much higher survival rate now. Drugs taken during pregnancy, notably thalidomide, have led to handicaps in children. It is said that after artificial abortion there is a greatly increased risk of prematurity and therefore of handicaps in children. In the case of many genetic diseases, such as diabetes, children who would previously have died now live, have children and so propagate the disease.

THE EFFECT OF A HANDICAP ON THE CHILD AND HIS FAMILY

A variety of reactions to handicaps occurs—dependent on such factors as the child's sex, the severity and nature of his handicap, the age of onset, the parental and sibling attitudes, the nature of his education and the type of treatment, medical and surgical, which he has to receive. If he has been in a residential home from an early age, he has experienced emotional deprivation, and missed normal family life: he is apt to feel unloved and unwanted. He may become depressed or even apathetic because he feels isolated, lonely, restricted and different from others, and feels jealousy of other normal children. He sees family discord, and may have sufficient insight to see that he is the cause of it. His siblings may be jealous of him, because he is the subject of favouritism. He may be overprotected by his parents who are anxious for his safety, and as a result he becomes overdependent on them. His experience of life and normal day-to-day experiences may be restricted. He may even be rejected by his parents, but that is unusual. His parents may bring him up without discipline because of his handicap and he suffers as a result. Perhaps in the case of epilepsy his parents fear that punishment might cause him to have a fit. He learns to use his handicap to get his own way. He may become aggressive and antisocial. As an adolescent he has sexual difficulties, because although he has normal sexual desire, he may not be able to satisfy his impulses. He is afraid of being unattractive, he is ashamed of being different from others, and finds it difficult to make friends. He is worried about future employment prospects. In the case of some handicaps, he may have had several surgical operations, and be seriously worried about the prospect of more. He is upset by the obvious anxiety shown by his parents.

Siblings

Other children in the family may have been neglected on account of the presence of the handicapped child. They have had more than the usual household chores. They have seen their handicapped sibling shown favouritism, and given all that he wants. They feel resentment towards him: the nature of their holidays suffers as a result of him; and they feel ashamed of him when their school friends see them with him. The family's standard of living is lowered as a result of the extra cost of the handicapped child.

Parents

The parents feel disappointment, guilt, shame, embarrassment and resentment when they find that their child is handicapped. They may neglect the rest of the family. The mother and father may be unable to go out together because they will not or cannot leave the handicapped child. The mother may have a pathological attachment to the child. The parents overprotect and over-indulge him. They worry about his schooling and his future. They look round for a reason for the tragedy which has befallen them—blaming, perhaps, the doctor or the midwife, blaming themselves for some imaginary sin. A woman may ascribe the tragedy to something which she did in pregnancy, or to the use of the contraceptive pill, or to postponing pregnancy too long, or having one child soon after another. The parents' leisure activities are restricted. The father becomes jealous because of the excessive time and devotion which his wife gives to the child—and the marriage suffers. The mother is tired because of all the extra work which the child involves, and because of all the worries associated with the handicap—worries about schooling, about the child's health, his impending operations and the extra time which he takes.

These difficulties do not arise in all cases. It depends in part on parental personalities. In some homes there are no obvious problems; the handicapped child is a source of great pleasure and happiness.

EDUCATION

Whenever possible, handicapped children should attend an ordinary school. Whatever sort of school they attend, they will feel different from other children; but it is better for them if possible to mix with normal children rather than only with children with similar handicaps. Rosewell (1968) wrote as follows, 'to restrict a child's experience by allowing him to mix only with those who share his difficulties is usually a short-sighted view. It merely postpones integration on leaving school and makes it more traumatic.' It is important that affected children should not be overprotected at school. It may be necessary to make special physical arrangements for the children. Some may have to attend an ordinary school part time, and a special school for the rest of the time. Some will go to a special school at first and then graduate to an ordinary school later, when they have mastered reading and writing. An ordinary school may organise a special unit for handicapped pupils—for those with defective hearing or vision. Some, especially the blind, may have to attend a residential school (p. 211). One feels that every effort should be made to avoid adding an educational handicap to the physical handicap: and that they need the best possible education and the maximum degree of stimulation to achieve their best.

The child's personality and management at home will have a considerable bearing on his ability to adapt to special circumstances. Some children may be teased for their handicap and suffer acutely as a result. Much depends also on their level of intelligence. To achieve an average performance a handicapped child requires a better than average level of intelligence; unfortunately many do not possess this. The mean IQ of children with cerebral palsy and other congenital abnormalities is less than the average. In addition they are more likely than others to be absent from school; the rate of absenteeism is almost double that of normal children.

RESTRICTIONS FOR HANDICAPPED CHILDREN

Handicapped children should be subjected to a minimum of restrictions. The subject was discussed in the valuable book published by the American Academy of Pediatrics (1972). The American paediatricians suggested that contact sports (boxing, wrestling, football, hockey, basketball and lacrosse) should be avoided by

1   Children with only one eye: a history of retinal detachment:

congenital glaucoma. One must add that children with myopia (short sightedness) should not box, because of the danger of retinal detachment.

2 Children with heart enlargement from any cause. Aortic or pulmonary stenosis. Cyanotic congenital heart disease. Children with other forms of heart disease should regulate their own exertion, as they do, and they should not be restricted by the school. The risk of unrestricted sport in the case of aortic or pulmonary stenosis is sudden death.

3 Children with blood coagulation defects—e.g. haemophilia, Christmas disease.

4 Children with enlargement of any abdominal organ, such as the spleen, because of the fear of rupture.

They suggest that if a child suffers concussion in a game, he should leave that particular game on that day; if he suffers concussion twice, he should leave the game for the season.

If a child has epilepsy, restrictions should be kept to a minimum unless attacks are frequent. If he has had no fits for a year, he should be allowed to swim provided that there is supervision: he should not be allowed on to a high diving board, and in physical education he should avoid heights (e.g. rope climbing).

AFTER SCHOOL

According to the booklet by Tuckey and Parfit (1973) from the National Children's Bureau, between 7,000 and 8,000 children leave special schools each year. Of a sample of 788 handicapped school leavers, excluding seriously subnormal ones, only one per cent went on to some form of higher education. The report described the difficulties which these school leavers have to face and made sensible recommendations for action which would reduce these difficulties.

The following parents' associations give valuable help to parents and children:

British Diabetic Association, 3/6 Alfred Place, London WC1.
British Epilepsy Association, 3/6 Alfred Place, London WC1.
Cystic Fibrosis Research Trust, 1 Tudor Street, London EC4.
Haemophilia Society, 16 Trinity Street, London SE1.

Muscular Dystrophy Group, 26 Borough High Street, London, SE1.

National Deaf Children's Society, 31 Gloucester Place, London W1.

National Society for Mentally Handicapped Children, 86 Newman Street, London W1.

Spastics Society, 12 Park Crescent, London W1.

Association for Spina Bifida and Hydrocephalus, 112 City Road, London EC1.

References

American Academy of Pediatrics (1972) *School Health. A Guide for Physicians.* Evanston.

PECKHAM C.S. (1973) Preliminary findings in a national sample of 11 year old children. *Proc. Roy. Soc. Med.* **66**, 701.

ROSEWELL V.G.T. (1968) Special education—new trends? **57**, 4.

Statistics of Education (1972) Vol. 1, *Schools.* H.M.S.O.

TUCKEY L., PARFIT J. & TUCKEY B. (1973) *Handicapped School-Leavers.* National Children's Bureau. N.F.E.R. Publishing Co.

Other Reading

BERGGREEN S.M. (1971) A study of the mental health of the near relatives of twenty multihandicapped children. *Acta. Paediat. Scandinav.*, Suppl. 215.

BOWLEY A.H. & GARDNER L. (1972) *Educational and Psychological Guidance for the Organically Handicapped.* London, Churchill/Livingstone.

Carnegie United Kingdom Trust (1964) *Handicapped Children and their Families.* Edinburgh.

DINNAGE R. (1972) *The Handicapped Child.* London, National Children's Bureau.

Drug and Therapeutics Bulletin (1969) Helping parents with the handicapped child. **7**, 49.

FELDT R.H., EWART J.C., STICKLER G.B. & WEIDMAN W.H. (1969) Children with congenital heart disease. *Am. J. Dis. Child.* **117**, 281.

FREEMAN R.D. (1968) Emotional reactions of handicapped children. In CHESS S. & THOMAS A. *Annual Progress in Child Psychiatry and Child Development.* New York, Brunner Mazel.

KERSHAW K.D. (1973) *Handicapped Children.* London, Heinemann.

LOWIT I.M. (1967) Social and psychological consequences of chronic illness in children and their families. *J. Pediat.* **71**, 75.

McMICHAEL J.K. (1971) *A Study of Physically Handicapped Children and their Families.* London, Staples.

SPOCK B. & LERRIGO M.O. (1965) *Caring for your Disabled Child.* New York, Macmillan.

TALBOT N.B., KAGAN J. & EISENBERG L. (1971) *Behavioral Science in Pediatric Medicine.* Philadelphia, Saunders.

WOLF J.M. & ANDERSON R.M. (1969) *The Multiply Handicapped Child.* Springfield, Charles Thomas.

YOUNGHUSBAND E., BIRCHALL D., DAVIE R. & KELLMER PRINGLE M.L. (1970) *Living with Handicap.* London, National Bureau for Cooperation in Child Care.

SPECIFIC HANDICAPS

BLINDNESS

The causes of blindness are of prenatal or post-natal origin. It may be genetic—often in the form of a cataract. It may be due to rubella in early pregnancy. Cataracts are also due to certain rare metabolic diseases. Retrolental fibroplasia was one of the commonest causes of blindness 30 years ago: now it virtually never occurs, because it is preventable: it was due to administering high concentrations of oxygen to small premature babies.

Postnatal causes include ophthalmia of the newborn which was due to gonorrhoea, once an important cause of blindness, but in civilised countries it is now virtually unknown. Blindness is a rare complication of meningitis. In countries abroad blindness is caused also by trachoma, smallpox and vitamin A deficiency. It is a complication of rheumatoid arthritis, complicating about 10 per cent of all cases. It may also be caused by a drug previously used for the treatment of rheumatoid arthritis—chloroquine: it can be caused by chloramphenicol and other drugs. It may be due to injury of the eye by airguns, fireworks, catapults and bows and arrows. A rare cause is a malignant tumour—the retinoblastoma—sometimes seen in early infancy. Blindness in the squinting eye results from failure to treat a squint: the child represses the vision in the squinting eye in order to prevent double vision, and if this is not corrected by perhaps three or four years of age the child will be permanently blind in that eye.

The commonest cause of partial sight is severe myopia. Partial blindness occurs in albinism (in which there is also white hair). As Harcourt put it (1973) there is a blurred zone between blindness and partial sightedness.

The incidence of blindness is about 0·16 per 1,000 school children. There are just over 1,000 educable blind children aged 2 to 16 years in England and Wales. Of the 100,000 blind people, 3,000 are under the age of 14 (Kershaw 1973). In Peckham's analysis of 17,000 children born in England, Scotland and Wales in one week of March 1958, it was found that 78 per cent had normal vision, 10 per cent had doubtful vision and 13 per cent had a definite defect. Ten per cent had had glasses prescribed, but only a third of these were wearing them at the time.

The mean IQ of blind children is less than average: about a quarter are mentally subnormal. Others are apt to suffer 'pseudo-retardation' because of overprotection, and lack of the sensory stimuli which normal children receive. The Vernon Committee on the Education of the Visually handicapped (Department of Education and Science 1972) reported an increasing association of visual with other handicaps as a result of the surgical treatment of other handicaps and their greater survival rate; the number of children with uncomplicated visual handicaps is decreasing.

Myopia, short sightedness, occurs when the refractive media of the eye is too great and the rays of light converge in front of the retina. It is corrected by a minus lens which causes the rays of light to diverge so that they converge on the retina. A plus lens for long sight causes the rays to converge. Myopic children are more apt to suffer serious injury to the eye than other children, and boxing must be forbidden. In astigmatism the rays of light are not refracted equally in all meridians, so that the rays do not focus on a point in the retina. It is corrected by a cylindrical lens alone or with a plus or minus lens. A squint (strabismus) is due to muscle imbalance.

Some 8 per cent of boys and 0·4 per cent of girls have red–green blindness. It is little handicap. It is said that affected children can follow traffic lights by noting the position and luminosity of the light.

HISTORICAL

In our book *Lessons from Childhood* we referred to famous people who had a defect of vision. For the effect of visual defect on art, the reader should refer to the fascinating book by Trevor-Roper (1971). Famous people who had defective eyesight in early childhood include Kepler, the astronomer, who had a severe visual defect as a result of smallpox: Samuel Johnson, who was almost blind in one eye as a result of ophthalmia: Rudyard Kipling, who was in serious trouble at school and at his 'home' on account of a severe visual defect which for long passed unrecognised: and Helen Keller, who at 18 to 20 months of age lost both her sight and hearing. Louis Braille at three years of age was trying to cut a tough piece of leather when his knife slipped and penetrated his left eye. The opposite eye became blind (as a result of sympathetic ophthalmia) and he was totally blind by the age of five.

VISION TESTS

It must be emphasised that the child with a defect of vision cannot know that he cannot see properly: it is we, doctors and teachers, who must make the diagnosis. On external examination, without instruments or test objects, one can learn much about a child's eyes. A squint can be readily detected (though one might add that in infancy it is easy to suspect a squint when there is not one).

A cataract is easily detected by looking at the pupil. Almost all infants with more than a trivial visual defect have obvious nystagmus—the jerky movements of the eyes such as one sees when a person is looking through the window of a moving bus or train The occurrence of nystagmus when a baby is watching a moving object is the basis of a test in which a drum revolves with stripes on it: if the child can see he will show nystagmoid movements as he watches it (opticokinetic nystagmus). Doctors also test the blink reflex (when an object approaches the eye), the reaction to light (the pupil contracting) and vestibular reactions (eye movements on rotation).

A dangling ring, or a shiny metal instrument, is used for testing eye-following. One holds it above the baby as he lies on his back, and once it has caught his eye one slowly moves it first to one side, to an angle of 90 degrees from the couch and then to the other in order to determine how far he follows. By three or four months one places a one-inch cube in front of the child and later a pellet of paper, and it is easy to observe whether he sees it: by five months he will reach out and get the cube; by 10 months he goes for the pellet with the index finger and picks it up between the tip of the forefinger and the tip of the thumb. By the age of two Mary Sheridan's Stycar test can be used: the child has a set of toys—a car, a plane etc., and the examiner has a duplicate set. At a distance of 10 feet the examiner holds a toy and asks the child to match it with the corresponding one in his set. Later a Snellen chart or modification (e.g. that of Mary Sheridan) is used: the results are expressed as a fraction, the numerator being the child's distance from the chart (e.g. 20 feet) and the denominator the smallest line read (e.g. the 50 foot line—giving a result of 20/50).

The three-year-old with a vision of 20/50 or less, or a 4- to 5-year-old with a vision of 20/40 or less, should be referred to an expert—as should a child with a difference between the eyes of 2 lines or more on the Snellen chart, or a squint (Bowley and Gardner 1972).

For colour vision the ISIHARA test is used.

SOME EFFECTS OF VISUAL DEFECT

Blind children commonly poke their fingers into the eyes—presumably so that they see 'stars'—or coloured phosphenes. They often exhibit rapid symmetrical flapping of the hands, flexing or extending the neck, swaying the body, facial grimacing or jumping backwards and forwards (Williams 1968). They are prone to certain behaviour problems, as a result of feeling different from others, to experience fear reactions, to be submissive, to lack initiative and to be easily discouraged. They may adopt socially undesirable behaviour, because they cannot see how others behave. They may be spoilt, because too much is done for them, and they may be the object of favouritism. For other features of behaviour related to long or short sight, see Chapter 2.

Douglas (1968) found that short-sighted children achieve superior attainment scores but not verbal scores: they have 'higher job aspirations, and more academic hobbies'.

MANAGEMENT

I have no experience of the management of blind children, and shall mention only a few points. It is essential that they should not be overprotected: they must acquire independence and self confidence. A blind baby must be given solid food at the usual age—instead of depriving him of this because of the theoretical risk that he might choke. He must be given all the usual sensory stimuli—with special emphasis on tactile stimulation. He has to learn by sound and feel, instead of largely by vision.

He may need to go to a residential school at least at first; but many feel that once he has learnt special techniques in a special school he should attend an ordinary school where possible. A residential home (e.g. Sunshine Homes) may be necessary, particularly if he has other handicaps. He may learn Braille by about six years of age, but he is likely to read more slowly than a

H

normal child—a third or a quarter as rapidly. He may learn to type. The child should be encouraged to join Scouts or Guides. Independence should be encouraged—so that the child, for instance, can travel on a bus.

REFERENCES

BOWLEY A.H. & GARDNER L. (1972) *Educational and Psychological Guidance for the Organically Handicapped.* London, Churchill/Livingstone.
DOUGLAS J.W.B. (1968) *All our Future.* London, Peter Davis.
HARCOURT B.C. (1973) The association of visual and other handicaps in childhood. *Proc. Roy. Soc. Med.* **66**, 612.
ILLINGWORTH R.S. & ILLINGWORTH C.M. (1966) *Lessons from Childhood. Some Aspects of the Early Life of Unusual Men and Women.* Edinburgh, Churchill/Livingstone.
PECKHAM C.S. (1973) Preliminary findings in a national sample of 11 year old children. *Proc. Roy. Soc. Med.* **66**, 701.
TREVOR-ROPER P. (1971) *The World through Blunted Sight.* London, Thames & Hudson.
WILLIAMS C.E. (1968) Behaviour disorders in handicapped children. *Develop. Med. Child. Neurol.* **10**, 736.

OTHER READING

KERSHAW K.D. (1973) *Handicapped Children.* London, Heinemann.
LUNT L. (1965) *If You make a Noise I can't see.* London, Gollancz.
SHERIDAN M. (1960) Vision Screening of very young or handicapped children. *Brit. Med. J.* **2**, 453.
WILSON W. (1973) Experience with a multidisciplinary assessment team for visually handicapped children. *Proc. Roy. Soc. Med.* **66**, 616.

DEAFNESS

Famous people who suffered from deafness included Beethoven, Dean Swift, Goya and Toulouse Lautrec.

According to Bowley and Gardner (1972) approximately 1·7 per 1,000 school children have sufficient hearing loss to require a hearing aid—a total of about 12,500 school children. In addition there are children with other handicaps, such as cerebral palsy, who have hearing deficits. It is said that in the United States 7 per 1,000 school children have a hearing loss severe enough to interfere with normal progress at school (presumably unless supplied with hearing aids). It is calculated that 1,500 children are born in Britain with severe hearing loss each year. One in 1,000 need to go to special schools, and 2 per 1,000 need special help in order to attend an ordinary school. In Britain between 4,000 and 8,000 children under five have impaired hearing. About one per 250 school children has some high frequency deafness. Few are totally deaf.

CAUSES AND FACTORS

The causes of deafness are prenatal, natal and postnatal. Prenatal causes include rubella in the first three months of pregnancy and congenital syphilis; prematurity; and drugs taken by the mother during pregnancy—especially kanamycin, vancomycin, genta-micin, streptomycin, neomycin, quinine, thalidomide. There are numerous genetic conditions associated with deafness. They include Waardenburg's syndrome—in which there is a white forelock and a difference in the colour of the iris of the eyes, with congenital deafness. There is a slightly greater incidence of deafness amongst babies born prematurely. About half of all children with cleft palate develop deafness at school age. Children with cerebral palsy, especially if due to kernicterus, commonly have a hearing defect. Cretins are slightly more likely than others to be deaf. There is a slightly increased incidence of deafness in children with fibrocystic disease of the pancreas.

Prenatal factors are more related to high tone deafness than to other forms. The principal natal cause of deafness is severe anoxia. In the immediate postnatal period severe jaundice may lead to deafness, as a feature of kernicterus.

Postnatal causes of deafness are numerous. They include menin-gitis, especially in infancy; measles, mumps, head injury; drugs, notably streptomycin, capreomycin, vancomycin, neomycin, paromomycin, gentamicin, kanamycin, viomycin, colistin, quinine, salicylates, frusemide, nortriptyline and vincristine; adenoids; recurrent otitis media, leading to glue ears; loud noise; and in 30 per cent the cause is not known. Recurrent otitis media, if inadequately treated, may cause deafness, partly by causing a 'glue ear' in which there is tenacious fluid in the internal ear. It is treated by a 'Grommet', a device to allow the fluid to drain into the back of the throat. It is estimated that about 3 to 5 per cent of children aged 5 to 9 have some hearing loss due to glue ears.

There have been numerous articles on the danger of loud noise to the human ear. I have named several of those in the reference list. It has long been known that workers in certain industries (such as boilermaking) are liable to become deaf. It has been shown that the playing of 'rock'n'roll' music for a period of 88 hours over two months destroyed numerous cells in a guinea pig's inner ear. There is serious anxiety about the effect of loud music on the ears of the young. Lipscomb (1969) wrote that 'persons who expose themselves to high intensity music for a total exposure time exceeding 23 hours in a single two month period may suffer irreversible damage to cochlear sensory cells in the ear'. Elsewhere he wrote (1972) 'the fact that the hearing activity of a significant portion of American youth under 21 years of age is becoming reduced many years before such reduction should be expected leads to the fearful suggestion that this generation of young persons will encounter much more serious hearing problems in their middle years than the present group of 50- to 60-year-olds.' Krystor many years ago (1950) stated that brief exposures of about 100 decibels for up to an hour may cause deafness. Relevant factors (Glorig 1966) are the overall noise level, the composition of the noise, the duration of exposure during a single 24-hour period, and the total time of exposure during a work life. In one experiment (Dey 1970) it was shown by recordings of music played by a typical rock band in a discotheque that a noise level of 105 decibels was most damaging. Tape loops of this sound were played by earphone to 15 young people with normal hearing at levels of 100 to 110 decibels for 5 to 120 minutes. After listening for two hours 2 out of 100 recovered their hearing only slowly, while at 110 decibels 16 per cent would be adversely and probably permanently affected.

Many favour the concept of the child who is 'at risk' of certain abnormalities—meaning that he is more likely than others to have a particular handicap. For instance, if a mother has rubella (German measles) in early pregnancy, her baby is 'at risk' of deafness. This concept has led some to pay particular attention to certain children who are 'at risk': the danger is that they will not examine with sufficient care those not 'at risk'. Investigations have shown that 30 per cent of deaf children were not 'at risk' children; but that there is a 14 times greater incidence of deafness in the 'at risk' group which comprises about 15 per cent of all children. The 'at risk' group will include children born by mothers who had rubella in early pregnancy, those with a family history of hereditary deafness, severe jaundice in the newborn period, and children with cerebral palsy, mental retardation, speech delay or indistinctness, and multiple handicaps. When a mother suspects that her child is deaf, it is essential to take her suspicion seriously and test the child's hearing: she is likely to be right. It is or should be a routine to test the hearing of all children who are late in talking, or who speak indistinctly for their age. In many areas Health Visitors screen all children for deafness at 8 to 12 months and at 2 years.

TYPES OF DEAFNESS

By the term conductive deafness one means deafness which results mainly from involvement of the transmission of sound in the middle ear; it is so termed because it affects air conducted sounds and bone conduction of vibration (e.g. made by the tuning fork). This is due to disease of the middle ear; the hearing loss is more or less equal through the tone range, so that amplification provides balanced hearing. Perceptive deafness is due to inner ear disease and nerve deafness. This tends to be deafness more for high tones, so that a hearing aid, which at present amplifies all sound, is less satisfactory. Sometimes there is a mixture of both kinds of deafness.

The loudness of sound is tested in decibels. Mild hearing loss is that of 15 to 30 decibels; partial deafness is one of 30 to 65 decibels; severe deafness that of 65 to 95 decibels, and profound deafness is that of 95 decibels or more.

HEARING TESTS

The hearing must be tested in as quiet a room as possible. One can test the hearing of the newborn infant by a bell, crinkling paper, or by the voice. The reactions are a cry, blinking of the eyes, a startle reflex, quieting if crying, a catch in the respirations or inhibition of sucking. By the age of 3 to 4 months it is much easier to test the hearing, because by that age the normal baby turns his head to sound. He is tested by the crinkling of paper, or the ringing of a bell, for high tones, about 18 inches from the ear, on a level with the ear, and out of sight. The sounds PHTH or PS are high tone, and one can test him with these, making sure that one does not blow into the ear: the sound OO is satisfactory for low tones. At about 6 months he looks down to trace the source of sounds made 9–12 inches below the ear, and a month later he turns his head up to sound above the ear. Babies usually localise sound on the right before those on the left. Other tests include a squeaky doll, or a plastic cup and spoon scraped or tapped together. One notices not only whether he responds, but the rapidity with which he does so: the backward child responds more slowly than the average or bright one. After 9 months one tests with the sound source 3 feet from the ear. After 18 months one tests with simple toys—a ball, doll, car, cup and brick and after two adds a plane, ship, fork and knife asking the child (without being able to lip read) to show one the toy named. We are indebted to Dr Mary Sheridan for simple methods of testing hearing (e.g. with the Stycar test). By the age of three audiometry or conditioning tests can be used; for instance the child is told to put a brick into the box when the drum is beaten; the drum is then sounded out of sight. By the age of 4 the child can be tested by headphones fed by the audiometer, different tones being used. Hearing is also tested by 'evoked response audiometry' with the electroencephalogram.

It is essential to be aware of the difficulties of hearing testing and of mistakes which can be made. A child may see the shadow of the tester on the wall. The tester may make a draught by moving an object, or blow into the child's ear, so that he turns his head. The mother may show by her expression that she has made a sound. A test sound cannot be repeated more than two or three times; habituation would occur, so that the child would not respond. The child may fail to respond because he is tired or hungry. He should not be tested at the moment when he is preoccupied with something else. Any normal child may seem not to hear when he is preoccupied. Mentally defective children, being late in all aspects of development, are late in responding to sound: many children have been thought to be deaf when the correct diagnosis was mental deficiency. The danger is that the mentally subnormal child is more likely than others to be deaf: it is easy to miss a hearing defect in a child with cerebral palsy with mental subnormality, or with mental subnormality alone. Psychotic children, such as those with infantile autism, may appear to make no response to sound. An important but rare condition is congenital auditory imperception—in which the child can hear but cannot interpret what he hears—and he is therefore late in talking and reading. Finally, just as some children are late in sitting, walking, talking or controlling the bladder, due to delayed maturation of a specific part of the nervous system, an occasional child exhibits delayed auditory maturation—and is late in responding normally to sound. Some normal children are slow in maturation in all aspects of development, and are true 'slow starters'. It follows that when there is a defective response to sound, the child must be examined fully, so that his performance in all other aspects of development can be assessed.

THE RESULT OF DEAFNESS

Contrary to the statements made by some, the deaf infant does not vocalise less than normal infants until the factor of imitation enters: before that the nature of the noises he makes are developmental and not dependent on hearing. Then vocalisations become reduced. He begins to feel thwarted at being unable to make his wants known, and screams when he wants something, or wishes to express pleasure or annoyance. He may watch his parents unusually carefully in order to determine what they are saying. He fails to develop speech, and may develop behaviour problems because of thwarting and his inability to express himself. He uses an outburst of temper as a method of communication. Minor degrees of deafness may pass unnoticed even at school; he may be thought to be backward when the real trouble is a hearing difficulty. He may withdraw from company, and be forced into social isolation.

If his hearing defect is for high tones only, he misses mainly consonants in speech, and is therefore late in talking—and he cannot appreciate music.

The deaf child finds it difficult to participate in the usual activities of the family and friends. He is more dependent on others; he misses warning sounds—as in the street. He misses sensory input and suffers intellectual retardation unless special efforts are made to prevent this.

Approximately 22 per cent of deaf children leave the special school with intelligible speech, and 23 per cent without speech. 14 per cent are unable to read or write.

THE IMPORTANCE OF EARLY DIAGNOSIS

Early diagnosis is of great importance so that residual hearing can be utilised, by means of amplifying apparatus, so that speech can be learnt at the usual age. The greater the delay in making the diagnosis, the more difficult it becomes for the child to learn to speak: he passes the sensitive period and finally the critical period, so that it becomes virtually impossible to teach him to speak intelligibly.

It must be noted that some children hear normally at first and then develop deafness—as a result of a cleft palate or recurrent otitis media. Deafness due to the glue ear can be relieved by surgery. It is an advantage to the child to have learnt to speak before the deafness develops.

It cannot be emphasised too strongly that the child who has always had defective hearing cannot know that he cannot hear. It is we, doctors and teachers, who have to make the diagnosis.

TREATMENT OF THE DEAF CHILD

I have no personal experience of the management of the deaf child, and am indebted to many experts for the notes below. Few children are totally deaf; these have to depend entirely on lip reading. Those with partial deafness depend either on hearing alone, or on a combination of hearing and lip reading. Children may learn to lip read from about 20 months of age. As Ewing said, your words must meet his eyes, not his ears. The following are instructions commonly given to parents:

See that there is light on your face when you speak to him: the child has his back to the light.
Do not speak over four feet from him: speak on a level with him.
Use proper sentences and no baby talk: not single words.
Do not shout.
Do not mouth words in an exaggerated manner.
Speak more slowly and distinctly than usual.
Do not speak with a cigarette in the mouth.
Use short sentences.
Do not move the head when talking, or use gestures.
Let him touch your mouth as you speak; let him see you talk, feel you talk.
Go out of your way to talk to him, show him things, help him to develop interests.

Let him do things with you.

Repeat things over and over again. Read to him, show him pictures.

Talk about things which he can see—not so much about things which he cannot see.

Talk about things as they happen, so that he can associate what he has seen with your words.

Never give him reason to feel that you are talking about him or laughing at him. Never isolate him. Make him feel part of the family.

Always respond to his noises.

Give him love, security, acceptance, approval, but do not spoil him or show favouritism.

Teach him discipline just the same as any other child.

Teach independence: avoid overprotection.

Give him responsibility.

Remember that a deaf child can be greatly retarded by depriving him of normal stimulation. A good home will raise his IQ; a bad home will lower it.

SPECIALISED TREATMENT

The speech therapist has a vital role to play in helping a deaf child to talk: I shall not discuss here the methods used. Neither shall I discuss educational methods for the deaf in ordinary or special schools.

REFERENCES

BOWLEY A.H. & GARDNER L. (1972) Educational and Psychological Guidance for the Organically Handicapped. London, Churchill/Livingstone.

EWING A. & EWING E.C. (1964) Teaching Deaf Children to Talk. Manchester, University of Manchester Press.

GLORIG A. (1966) The effects of noise on man. J. Am. Med. Ass. 196, 839.

KRYSTOR K.D. (1950) The effects of noise on man. J. Speech. Hearing. Disorders, Suppl. 1.

LIPSCOMB D.M. (1969) High intensity sounds in the recreational environment. Hazards to young ears. Clinical Pediatrics, 8, 63.

LIPSCOMB D.M. (1972) Environmental noise is growing—is it damaging our hearing? Clinical Pediatrics, 11, 374.

SHERIDAN M.D. (1958) Simple clinical hearing tests for very young or mentally retarded children. Brit. Med. J. 2, 999.

SHERIDAN M.D. (1969) The development of vision, hearing and communication in babies and young children. Proc. Roy. Soc. Med. 62, 999.

Rupp R.R. & Koch L.J. (1969) Effects of too loud music on human ears. But, Mother, Rock'n' Roll HAS to be loud. *Clinical Pediatrics*, **8**, 60.
Whetnall E. & Fry D.B. (1964) *The Deaf Child*. London, Heinemann.

OTHER READING

Beagley H.A. & Knight J.J. (1967) The auditory evoked response as an index of hearing in practical audiometry. *J. Laryng.* **81**, 347.
British Medical Journal (1970) Deafening music. Leading Article, **2**, 127.
Crabtree N. (1972) Assessment and treatment in hearing impaired children. *Proc. Roy. Soc. Med.* **65**, 709.
Dey F.L. (1970) Auditory fatigue and predicted permanent hearing defects from Rock'n'Roll music. *New Engl. J. Med.* **282**, 467.

OVERACTIVITY AND BRAIN DAMAGE

Almost all children pass through a phase of 'overactivity'. The child of 6 or 7 cannot sit still: he constantly fidgets: he is always on the go: he finds it most difficult to walk along the street holding his mother's hand, for he must hop and skip all the time. He exhausts everyone but himself. As he gets older and matures he gets out of this overactivity—though in later years he may be more active (or less active) than others. His overactivity may be increased by boredom and poor teaching. It may be merely a feature of his normally ebullient personality (Werry 1968).

Troublesome overactivity is a problem which exhausts parents and teachers alike. Livingston (1969) defined it as a 'chronic sustained excessive level of activity which is the cause of significant and continued complaint both at home and at school'. The movements are more purposeless than merely increased in quantity. It is nine times more common in boys than in girls. In the preschool age the child shows boundless energy, incessant activity, is constantly getting into danger, and surprisingly requires less sleep than other children of his age. At school the overactivity causes his teachers to complain. The overactivity is commonly associated with poor concentration, a short attention span, easy distractibility, bad writing and clumsiness. In more severe forms there is impulsiveness, excessive talkativeness, and scatter in work, partly, perhaps, because he will not concentrate long enough to learn properly. He is apt to be regarded as badly behaved, odd, spoilt and badly brought up. He shows a marked discrepancy between verbal and performance tests. These and other symptoms are commonly ascribed to 'brain damage' or 'birth injury' (Millichap 1972).

The concept of brain damage or birth injury is highly popular with psychologists, and is used by some paediatricians. It causes great distress to parents, to whom it implies that the tragedy which has befallen their child and the family could have been prevented if the obstetrician, midwife or family doctor had been more careful at the delivery. If a tragedy should befall any of us, it is better that we should feel that it was unavoidable, than to feel that if care had been taken or some other action had been taken, the tragedy could have been avoided. Some psychologists include prenatal conditions in their use of the words brain damage; but parents and others will interpret the words brain damage as being the direct result of birth injury. Even if psychologists understand the words to include prenatal conditions, it would not be a good term, because in the majority of cases of mental subnormality, cerebral palsy and other neurological conditions the defect is of unknown origin; it may have been dependent on structural abnormalities of the brain including failure of a portion of it to develop normally, sometimes because of genetic factors; it may have been due to placental insufficiency, infections in pregnancy, drugs taken in pregnancy, or other conditions (Chapter 1).

No one can deny that brain damage may occur at birth; it may result from severe anoxia due, for instance, to prolapse of the umbilical cord. Usually, however, there is no such obvious cause of anoxia, and it would be naïve and unscientific to ascribe subsequent neurological abnormalities to anoxia at birth, convulsions in the newborn period, prematurity or abnormal delivery, instead of looking beyond these occurrences to the conditions which caused them. For instance, a breech delivery is commonly related to the fetus being small for dates: this in turn may be due to maternal toxaemia or other factors. It would be wrong to ascribe a child's subsequent abnormality to a breech delivery when there were important noxious factors operating during pregnancy. There is a five times greater incidence of breech delivery amongst babies with spina bifida: spina bifida has caused the breech delivery. In low birth weight babies there is an eight times greater incidence of congenital abnormalities than in full-term babies: something has caused both the congenital abnormalities and the prematurity. A paediatrician knows that when a baby is born it is exceedingly difficult and usually impossible to decide that the child's bad condition is due to brain damage in delivery, unless the child dies and an autopsy is performed. It is impossible to prove birth injury on neurological examination of the newborn, because abnormal neurological signs could just as well be due to prenatal causes, such as a developmental defect in the brain. It is extremely unlikely that examination of the cerebrospinal fluid would prove that there had been a cerebral haemorrhage, because blood in the cerebrospinal fluid may be due to the lumbar puncture needle. It is certain that neither neurological examination nor any special investigation in later weeks, months or years can provide any evidence that a child's difficulties are due to birth injury. If the paediatrician cannot prove in the newborn period that the child's brain has suffered damage in delivery, it is still less likely that a psychologist can prove in later years that the child's performance and behaviour is due to birth injury. In fact it is impossible for the psychologist to prove it: there is no psychological test which can do it. It may be added that in the great majority of cases of so called brain damage there was not even a history of an abnormality at birth.

Psychologists tend to defend their diagnosis of 'brain damage' because the child shows features similar to those of others who sometime after birth suffer a severe head injury or meningitis. But there are innumerable examples of a symptom being the end result of a wide variety of pathological processes: for instance vomiting can be due to hundreds of causes, and because one of them is head injury, it is hardly rational to argue that all vomiting is due to head injury.

Some avoid the words 'brain damage' and use instead the words 'minimal brain dysfunction'. This at least does not imply that one understands its causation: what the words mean, I do not know. Readers may find part of the answer in the extensive 396 page symposium edited by de la Cruz, Fox and Roberts (1973), with its 772 references. Numerous experts made useful contributions to the symposium. Both Eisenberg and Masland commented that there is no pathological basis for this condition—for it is not fatal, and one cannot therefore examine the brain of affected children. Omenn wrote about the genetic aspect of the condition. Bateman discussed the importance to teachers, concluding that 'medical classifications such as minimal brain dysfunction are as irrelevant to educational practice as educational classifications are to medical practice'. He added 'The educator's willingness to attempt to use the minimal brain dysfunction classification has had another result.

It has provided a seemingly sophisticated and respectable excuse for both non-teaching and poor teaching.' He regretted the fact that the term put a label on the child, so that he was regarded as abnormal. Masland wrote that minimal brain dysfunction is not a diagnosis: it merely groups together a number of children with certain characteristics in common. I agree with the comments of Kinsbourne, who wrote that 'The diagnosis of minimal brain dysfunction is based on findings that are abnormal only with reference to the child's age. If the child were younger, the child would be regarded as normal. They indicate a relative delay in some aspect of neurological maturation as a result of slowed evolution of cerebral control of the relevant activity.' Gallacher wrote of a study which indicated that up to 3 per cent of American school children aged 5 to 19 need special educational services for the condition. Three per cent would mean 1,800,000 children. In contrast Rutter, Graham and Yule (1970) in their Isle of Wight study, found that less than one per 2,000 school children were affected.

Wender (1971, 1973) wrote that 'minimal brain dysfunction is probably the single most common disorder seen by child psychiatrists'. He included in addition to the above symptoms, fidgeting, clumsiness, dyslexia, impulsiveness, destructiveness, stealing, lying, arson, bedwetting, faecal incontinence, sexual behaviour disorders, accident proneness, defective judgment, impulsive behaviour, stubbornness, obstinacy, negativeness, 'bossing', disobedience, aggressiveness, difficulties in right–left discrimination, temper tantrums, extrovert behaviour, resistance to social demands, unwillingness to follow the rules of a group, and mood fluctuations. He wrote that 5 to 10 per cent of the school population suffers this syndrome. I cannot agree with this hotch-potch: I think that it is absurd to ascribe all these common behaviour problems or features to 'brain damage'. Many of the children with these symptoms are reacting predictably to an unfavourable environment: and there are many other causes (Chapter 2).

Some 43 symptoms are ascribed to brain damage. They include in particular distractibility, poor concentration, overactivity, emotional lability and perseveration—a child persisting in his activity despite all efforts to stop him. These children are apt to be called bad-mannered, badly behaved, spoiled or badly brought up. Other children regard them as 'queer' (Birch 1964).

Roger Reger remarked that some or many of the 43 symptoms commonly ascribed to brain injury occur in any ordinary class at school. He wrote that 'most of what is assumed to be known about the brain injured child is folklore. There is no justification whatsoever to continue to call children "brain injured" if there is no reason to assume that these children have injuries to the brain.' 'The concept of the "brain injured child" will have a detrimental effect on special education in the long run, since it is a non-specific noneducational conception to begin with. The difficulties of explaining to parents the riddle of the brain injured who is not brain injured is itself enough to constitute a handicap to the profession. The flippant way the label of brain injury is tagged on to children by people who, frankly, do not know what they are talking about, is hardly likely to further the causes of the profession.'

The late Dr Birch in his excellent book on the subject made similar comments; he regarded the condition as a behaviour syndrome for which there is no evidence that brain damage is the cause.

There is some evidence that prematurely born babies exhibit at school some of the symptoms described above—especially the overactivity and short attention span (Drillien 1964). This is true when they are compared with children who were born at term, when other possible factors, such as social circumstances and IQ scores are equated. We do not know the reason for this.

Genetic causes are of the greatest importance. I have seen many children who had been termed by others 'brain damaged' yet whose parent or parents had exhibited exactly the same features. I saw a public school boy on account of these symptoms. Two psychologists had told the parents that the boy was 'brain damaged' —but that his IQ score was 124 to 130. The parents were very distressed and sought my opinion. It was immediately obvious that the boy took after his mother, and on questioning she said that she was exactly the same at his age. I saw another boy who on account of the most gross overactivity and extrovert behaviour had been expelled from four schools. His IQ score was 120. His mother had been exactly the same in her childhood. Overactivity is commonly an inherited personality trait.

In experimental animals excessive restriction in their early life causes overactivity when they are released. It may be that undue restriction in the early life of human beings will have the same effect.

That which is normal at one age is not normal at another. As overactive children mature, they lose much of their overactivity. In the meantime they may suffer from the attitudes of others and become worried by their ridicule. They may respond to the expectations of others by deliberately 'play-acting'; they are expected to behave oddly, and they do. A mentally subnormal child, being late in all aspects of development, is late in maturing and his over-activity lasts much longer than that of a normal child. Some children, having lost their overactivity, remain 'clumsy children'. Weiss et al. (1972) followed 64 of these overactive children for five years; while the overactivity diminished, they retained their poor concentration, learning difficulties and emotional immaturity.

There have been numerous articles about the treatment of these children. They need love and security, like other children, or more so. They need to be treated with tolerance, understanding and patience. They must not be ridiculed and care must be taken not to talk about their difficulties in front of them. They should be encouraged to take part in sport and other school activities. Every effort should be made to prevent them feeling different from other children. American workers commonly recommend drug treatment in the form of amphetamine, but British workers, fearing drug addiction, prefer not to recommend this treatment. Other drugs used include methylphenidate (Ritalin) and thioridazine. It should be noted that phenobarbitone is apt to make these children worse, making them even more overactive and irritable. All drugs have possible undesirable side effects: some of the side effects of drugs used to try to control overactivity are serious. In my opinion drug treatment has little place in the management of these children; I agree with the critical review by Sroufe and Stewart (1973) who wrote that in the United States the number of children being given drugs for these problems is rapidly increasing and exceeds 150,000. According to them 5 per cent of children in elementary schools are 'overactive' and 3 per cent have reading difficulties and these children are being given drugs in order to improve their performance. They wrote that it is now felt that these stimulant drugs do not actually sedate children, but that they do improve their concentration and performance: but they add the important comment that they do not improve their actual learning. It is to be hoped that this American practice of drugging children will be avoided in Britain.

REFERENCES

BIRCH H.G. (1964) *Brain Damage in Children*. New York, William Wilkins.
DRILLIEN C.M. (1964) *The Growth and Development of the Prematurely Born Infant*. Edinburgh, Churchill/Livingstone.
LIVINGSTON S. (1969) Overactivity. *J. Am. Med. Ass.* 208, 694.
REGER R. (1965) *School Psychology*. Springfield, Charles Thomas.
WEISS G., MINDE K., WERRY J.S., DOUGLAS V. & NEMETH E. (1972) Studies on the hyperactive Child. Five year follow up. In CHESS S. & THOMAS A. *Annual Progress in Child Psychiatry and Child Development*. New York, Brunner Mazel.
WENDER P.H. (1971) *Minimal Brain Dysfunction in Children*. New York, Wiley-Interscience.
WENDER P.H. (1973) Minimal brain dysfunction in children. *Pediatric Clinics N. America*, 20, 187.
WERRY J.S. (1968) Developmental hyperactivity. *Pediatric Clinics N. America*, 15, 581.

OTHER READING

DE LA CRUZ F.F., FOX B.H. & ROBERTS R.H. (1973) Minimal brain dysfunction. *Annals of New York Academy of Science*, 205, pp. 1–396.
MILLICHAP G. (1973) Hyperkinetic syndrome. *J. Am. Med. Ass.* 224, 920.
RUTTER M., GRAHAM P. & YULE W.A. (1970) *A Neuropsychiatric Study in Childhood*. Clinics in Developmental Medicine 35/36. London, Heinemann.
SROUFE L.A. & STEWART M.A. (1973) Treating problem children with stimulant drugs. *New Engl. J. Med.* 289, 407.

THE CLUMSY CHILD

Several famous people were notably clumsy. They included Beethoven, Napoleon Bonaparte, Oscar Wilde and G.K. Chesterton. Henri Poincaré, France's most famous mathematician, was ambidextrous, clumsy with his hands, and had visuospatial difficulties causing problems with geometry.

There is no exact definition of clumsiness. There is no dividing line between the normal and the abnormal. Some children are awkward with their hands, some are the opposite: some are awkward and clumsy on their legs, some nimble and graceful.

The clumsy child tends to write badly, to hold his pencil in an unusual way with the paper at an unusual angle. He is awkward when fastening buttons, doing his hair or fastening shoe laces. He frequently breaks objects: needle threading is unusually difficult. He falls a lot, misjudges distances, walks into things, particularly on going through a doorway. He throws a ball badly. He finds it difficult to stand on one foot, to hop or skip, and to walk in a straight line. He is bad at dancing and PE, at which, like G.K. Chesterton, he is teased and laughed at. He dislikes games. Gubbay (1972) used a variety of tests for these children—getting them to hop on a straight line, to tie a shoe lace, thread beads, to walk with the heel of one shoe placed in front of the toe of the other, to catch a tennis ball after throwing it into the air and clapping the hands. He tested spatial sense by asking the child to touch his left ear with his right hand, to cross the middle finger over the index finger, and to place objects into a small bag.

Most clumsy children write badly. They may speak badly and have more than usual difficulty with sums and spelling. In the WISC test they have a higher verbal than performance score. They do badly in the Goodenough draw-a-man test.

The condition is more common in boys than girls. Gubbay estimated that the description fitted about five per cent of the school population. These children are mentally normal—though mentally subnormal children are more likely to be clumsy than mentally normal ones. They have normal physical strength and unless tested by an expert are apt to be regarded as showing no abnormal neurological signs. Gubbay showed that there is no correlation with prematurity, postmaturity, illness in the newborn period or with abnormal delivery. There is commonly a family history of similar clumsiness. Some children grow out of it—so that in their case one would regard the trouble as one of delayed motor maturation; but others remain clumsy for life. To some extent it may be an emotional problem, but the clumsiness itself may cause emotional disturbance. If everyone expects him to be clumsy, he is likely to respond by clumsiness. In some cases there is evidence that it is due to minimal cerebral palsy. There is no evidence that it is due to birth injury. There are rare causes such as muscular dystrophy and various rare neurological diseases, mainly genetic in origin. Drugs given for the treatment of epilepsy or of emotional disturbance are important causes of clumsiness and may cause marked unsteadiness. Phenytoin given for epilepsy is a common cause: amitriptyline and chlordiazepoxide and other drugs may cause it.

Clumsy children are not only teased and ridiculed by their peers; they get into trouble with the teacher, unless he understands the problem. The teacher is likely to regard the child as naughty or careless, as 'not trying'. The child feels inadequate and worries, and the school work may suffer. I was asked to see a girl who played truant from school: fortunately she was found out on the first day of truancy and was referred to me. She was deeply worried at the constant reprimands which she was receiving at school and decided that she could not bear it any longer. I found that she had definite but minimal signs of cerebral palsy.

There is little which one can do to treat the condition. The essential thing is that the teacher should know that the child cannot help it, and that it is not the child's fault. When a teacher recognises this fact, and understands that the child is not being naughty and careless, the teacher will be kind and sympathetic and try to help the child, knowing that reprimands and criticism can only make the child worse by superimposing psychological problems on top of the organic difficulty with which the child has to cope. No medicine and no physiotherapy will help.

REFERENCES

GUBBAY S.S. (1972) The Clumsy Child. M.D. Thesis, University of Western Australia.
REUBEN R.N. & BAKWIN H. (1968) Developmental clumsiness. *Ped. Clin. N. America*, 15, 601.

CEREBRAL PALSY

DEFINITIONS

Cerebral palsy has been defined as 'a disorder of movement and posture resulting from a permanent non-progressive defect or lesion in the immature brain'. It is incorrect to describe all children with cerebral palsy as 'spastics', though most of them are. There are three principal types—spastic (70 per cent of all), athetoid (20 per cent), and ataxic; there are some other rare types. The spastic type is subdivided on the basis of its distribution. Spastic hemiplegia means that the child is spastic on one side of the body, e.g. left arm and leg. The leg may be either more or less affected than the arm. The affected arm and leg are usually shorter than the unaffected limbs. Spastic quadriplegia means that all four limbs are spastic. Spastic diplegia means that it is mainly the legs which are spastic, but that the arms or hands are slightly affected. Spastic paraplegia is rare; in this type only the legs are spastic. Spasticity in the legs of moderate or severe degree usually leads to toe walking and this may have to be corrected by an operation on the Tendo Achillis behind the heel.

The athetoid form of cerebral palsy is characterised by slow writhing movements of the whole body, especially when the child knows that he is being observed, and ceasing during sleep. There may be some stiffness—partly because the child may hold the limb stiff in an attempt to control the movements. The ataxic form consists of unsteadiness and clumsiness of movement.

In the case of all three types there are all grades of severity from the most trivial, which may be ascribed to naughtiness or carelessness, to the most severe, which in the case of the spastic form can be readily diagnosed in the first week.

INCIDENCE

In Britain every year about 2,000 children are born with cerebral palsy. About a third die before school age. The incidence of cerebral palsy in school children is approximately two per thousand. There are about 100,000 spastics in Britain, of whom 40,000 are under the age of fifteen.

CAUSES

The causes are prenatal, natal and postnatal; of these, prenatal factors are much the most important. Of the prenatal factors, probably the principal one is a failure of part of the brain to develop. The reasons for this are unknown. One cause may be genetic. The main known factor is prematurity. A third of all children with cerebral palsy were prematurely born: the lower the birth weight the greater the risk of cerebral palsy. About a third of the smallest premature babies (e.g. under 1,250g, 2¾lb) will be spastic. There are frequently several factors operating in one child. The age of the mother and her parity, and exposure to irradiation, are irrelevant. About 1 in 25 or 30 children with cerebral palsy have an affected sibling. One form of cerebral palsy, kernicterus, due mainly to blood group incompatibility, is now preventable.

Another important factor in the cause of cerebral palsy is multiple pregnancy: whereas the incidence of twins in Britain is 1·2 per cent, 10 per cent of children with cerebral palsy are members of twins. Usually only one of twins is affected. In Japan there was a serious 'outbreak' of severe cerebral palsy ('Minemata disease') as a result of a mercury-containing effluent from a factory entering the Inland Sea. Fish absorbed the mercury and pregnant women ate the fish. The result was a major disaster—the children of these pregnancies being mentally subnormal and spastic.

There are still some who regard birth injury as the main cause of cerebral palsy. It may be a cause, but in my opinion it is most unusual: the great majority of cases of cerebral palsy are of pre-natal origin, especially failure of part of the brain to develop normally. Nevertheless, severe anoxia at birth is a cause of cerebral palsy: actual birth injury (e.g. by forceps) must be an extremely rare cause. I have never seen a proved case.

Postnatal causes include encephalitis, meningitis or severe head injury.

THE HANDICAPS

(i) *The IQ*. It is a truism that if a handicapped child is to achieve an average performance at school, he needs an above average IQ. Unfortunately children with cerebral palsy with only occasional exceptions have a lower than average IQ. The incidence of mental subnormality in these children is 20 times that of the population as a whole. Fifty per cent have an IQ below 70, while only 3 per cent have an IQ above 110. The mean IQ of children with hemiplegia is seventy-five.

(ii) *Convulsions*. A third of all children with cerebral palsy have fits—often not until the school years. Almost one in two children with spastic hemiplegia has fits. Athetoid children are rarely affected.

(iii) *Speech problems*. Most athetoid children and about one in two spastic children have speech problems. They are due to several factors—the mental subnormality, the defect in the cerebral cortex, spasticity and incoordination of muscles of speech, and deafness.

(iv) *Deafness*. Most children with kernicterus and about one in five other children with cerebral palsy have a defect of hearing.

(v) *Visual defect*. Almost one in two has some visual defect. The defects consist of myopia (short sightedness), squint and other abnormalities. The smaller the child at birth the greater the incidence of visual handicap.

(vi) *Sensory and visuospatial difficulties*. Affected children have a variety of sensory defects. They commonly have visuospatial problems—including defects of body image. For instance, if a head is drawn on a blackboard, and the child is asked to insert the eyes, ears, nose and mouth, he does not know where to put them.

(vii) *Laterality*. There is commonly difficulty in establishing lateral dominance or handedness.

(viii) *Dental problems*. Dental caries is more common, partly because of difficulty in chewing and in taking a good diet with solid food. There may be enamel hypoplasia.

(ix) *Nutrition*. Spastic children around puberty are in danger of becoming obese, because of relative inactivity. Athetoid children do not become fat.

(x) *Incontinence of urine*. This is more common in children with cerebral palsy—partly because of mental subnormality.

(xi) *Drooling, slobbering*. Inability to control saliva is a common feature of children with cerebral palsy, especially the athetoids, largely because of spasticity and incoordination of the muscles around the mouth.

(xii) *Deformities of the limbs*. If a child has hemiplegia, the affected leg and arm (unless the arm is only slightly spastic) are shortened— not growing as quickly as the normal limb. The affected limb (except in a warm room) is cold as compared with the normal limb. Almost all children with moderate or severe spasticity develop toe walking and many will suffer dislocation of the hip unless steps are taken to prevent it (by operation). The toe walking in a hemiplegic child is due partly to shortening of the affected limb, partly to spasm of the muscle behind the heel and partly to other causes.

(xiii) *Poor concentration*. This is partly due to a low IQ, partly to a visual or auditory handicap, and partly to the defect in the cerebral cortex.

(xiv) *Psychological problems*. These are numerous. They include the effect of parental overprotection—for it is the natural reaction of the parents of any handicapped child to do everything for him instead of letting him learn slowly and painfully to do things for himself and acquire independence. This dependence on others is difficult for a child. They include the result of favouritism, for parents are likely to show favouritism to the affected child. Only rarely does the child suffer rejection by the parents: he is much more likely to suffer from an abnormal attachment of his parents to him—so that he is overdependent on the parents, who spoil him, show overanxiety about his health, and do not let him grow up emotionally. Children with cerebral palsy are likely to be lonely, because of difficulty in making friends, and when they reach puberty they have great difficulty in normal sexual relationships. Affected children suffer from feeling different from others, and often, as a result, from jealousy. At puberty and in adolescence it is a characteristic of normal children to want to conform with their age group; above all they do not want to be different. They may suffer from the attitudes of others, who may be unwise in their conversation in front of them, or who isolate them because of their handicap. They are apt to feel frustrated and depressed, to be tearful and to withdraw from the company of others. Later they suffer because of their difficulty in finding work on leaving school.

THE MANAGEMENT

The ramifications of cerebral palsy, and the diversity of the handicaps, mean that a large team is required for its management. It includes the physician, the orthopaedic surgeon, the psychiatrist, the psychologist, the ophthalmologist, the ear, nose and throat surgeon and audiologist, the dentist, the physiotherapist, occupational therapist, the speech therapist and the social worker. Hence treatment is extremely expensive. Residential management is even more costly, but for geographical reasons it is sometimes necessary: if a child is unable to attend an ordinary school, the distance to a suitable special school may be such that a residential school is essential. One has then to remember that such an arrangement involves separation from the parents, with resulting emotional problems. These are particularly relevant in the case of children with cerebral palsy, because of the low IQ of so many of them. For instance, if a spastic child of eight has an IQ of 50, his mental age is that of a four-year-old (though an abnormal one in many respects apart from his physical handicap). One would not normally arrange for a four-year-old to go to a boarding school.

The preschool spastic child, if living in a city, may attend a special nursery school. When he reaches school age, one has to decide whether he should attend an ordinary school, a school for physically handicapped children, a school for spastic children, or a school for educationally subnormal or seriously subnormal children. If the child's IQ is sufficient, the choice lies between an ordinary school and a school for physically handicapped and/or spastic children. Much will depend on the nature and extent of his physical handicap—and the associated handicaps. If a child's handicaps permit, and the structural character of the school permits, many feel that he should attend an ordinary school. He is bound to feel different from normal children: but he may feel even more different from other children if he has to attend a special school. The physical arrangements in the school may be a deciding factor: if there are awkward steps, and for various reasons a child could not go to the lavatory without help, or if there are insuperable transport difficulties, he may be unable to attend an ordinary school. From the educational point of view it is better for him to attend an ordinary school. In a school for handicapped children there may be fewer hours of instruction, and a wide scatter of age groups and IQ within a class, which make a high standard difficult to achieve. Educational progress is apt to be interfered with in any case by the tendency of affected children to start at school later than ordinary children, and by a greater absence rate for illness or other reasons.

It is most important that therapy should not be allowed to interfere with education if at all possible. The value of physiotherapy is in considerable doubt: research in Sheffield (Wright 1973) failed to demonstrate its value; the value of education is obvious, and it is most important that education should not be missed because of the highly doubtful value of physiotherapy. No one has assessed the value of speech therapy in these children.

Orthopaedic surgery can achieve a great deal for affected children, and is by far the most important part of treatment. An orthopaedic surgeon experienced in this field prevents the dislocation of the hip, deals effectively with toe walking, and can enable a child to walk, after muscle transplants or other means, when otherwise there would be no chance of the child walking unaided.

Above all children with cerebral palsy need to acquire independence—to sit, to walk, to talk, to feed themselves and to attend to their toilet needs. A good therapist can help much in this respect—not by physiotherapy, but by guiding and counselling the parents in the management of the child, and by advising with regard to special equipment—for instance, to help him to feed himself. Drugs have little place in the treatment of cerebral palsy except in the prevention of fits, though many drugs to reduce spasticity have been tried.

THE OUTLOOK

The outlook for affected children is grim, except in the case of children with a good IQ with only trivial handicaps. It will be difficult for them to secure employment. Very few will live independent lives. It is difficult to quote figures, because of the great variables involved, particularly the IQ, the severity and nature of the disability, and the associated handicaps. In an American study three of 89 *selected* children were independent in adult life. In a Swedish study of 159 selected children with a good IQ, needing residential care largely for geographical reasons, and followed for 20 to 45 years, 7 had a home of their own, 9 worked outside home, 4 did household work, and none of the others were earning a living.

THE SPASTICS SOCIETY

The Spastics Society has done a tremendous amount for spastic children and adults, and most spastic children belong to it.

BOOKS

The reference list includes recommended reading on the subject.

REFERENCES

FINNIE E. (1968) *Handling the Young Cerebral Palsied at Home.* London, Heinemann.

HAEUSSERMANN E. (1958) *Developmental Potential of Preschool Children.* New York, Grune & Stratton.

HOLT K.S. (1965) *Assessment of Cerebral Palsy*, Vol. 1. *Muscle Function, Locomotion.* London, Lloyd Luke.

HOLT K.S. & REYNELL J.K. (1967) *Assessment of Cerebral Palsy*, Vol. 2. *Vision, Speech, Hearing, Language.* London, Lloyd Luke.

INGRAM T.T.S. (1964) *Paediatric Aspects of Cerebral Palsy.* Edinburgh, Churchill/Livingstone.

WRIGHT T. & NICHOLSON J. (1973) Physiotherapy for the spastic child. *Develop. Med. Child. Neurol.* **15**, 146.

EPILEPSY

In our book *Lessons from Childhood* (1966) we listed some of the famous people who suffered from epilepsy. They included Moham-med, Buddha, Alexander the Great, Alfred the Great, Caligula, Petrarch, Julius Caesar, Pythagoras, Democritus, King Louis XIII, Charles V of Spain, King William III, Napoleon, Peter the Great, Archduke Charles of Austria, Nobel, William Pitt, Lord Byron, Swinburne, Van Gogh, Edward Lear, Dostoevsky, Molière, Charles Dickens, Pascal, Swedenborg, Paganini, William Morris, Flaubert and Richelieu. The latter in a fit believed that he was a horse and neighed and jumped; afterwards he had no knowledge of what had happened. Mary Baker Eddy suffered frequent hysterical convulsions.

Not all fits are due to epilepsy. It is often difficult for a teacher to distinguish a faint from a fit—and it is not easy for the doctor, who has not seen the episode, to make the diagnosis. Faints are more common in the older child. The usual place and time for a faint in school is the morning assembly: faints are extremely unlikely to occur if the child is not standing at the time or is not changing posture from lying to standing or possibly sitting to standing. A faint could occur if a sitting child suffers sudden pain, as when he cuts his finger: otherwise a faint would not occur when the child is sitting. Usually a child feels peculiar before he faints: then he subsides on to the floor, having lost his colour, and is normally limp and may be unconscious. A child (or adult) may twitch in a severe faint, especially if he is kept erect, and thus be thought to have epilepsy. If the bladder is full, he may wet himself in a faint. He is unlikely to fall asleep immediately after a faint, but a child commonly falls asleep after a major fit. When a person faints, there is a fall of blood pressure and the oxygen supply to the brain is reduced because of dilatation of vessels in muscle and constriction of vessels in the skin; it is this which may cause a child or adult occasionally to show convulsive movements in a faint.

Fits may be due to hysteria: they arise from the subconscious mind and are not feigned fits, as in malingering. An expert is required to establish the diagnosis, which may be difficult. Hysterical fits are confined to the older child. Fits may be due to a head injury, cerebral tumour or other intracranial condition: but at school age the commonest cause of fits is epilepsy. A fit in a diabetic child may be due to a low blood sugar, and treatment is urgent. If he is unconscious, he should be taken immediately to hospital.

The cause of epilepsy is unknown in most cases. It may follow head injury or a cerebral abscess or tumour. It is common in children with cerebral palsy or in mental subnormality other than mongolism. The incidence of epilepsy is about 4 to 6 per 1,000 school children. About 60,000 children in British schools have epilepsy; about 600 of these children are in schools for epileptic children, but the great majority are in ordinary schools.

There are many types of epilepsy. Petit mal epilepsy consists of short-lasting episodes in which the child rarely falls: attacks never last more than 20 seconds (by definition); there is no preceding aura; they are characterised by momentary staring, often upward movement of the eyes, a vacant expression and momentary loss of consciousness. The limbs do not twitch. If the child is speaking, he stops and stares, and on recovery from the attack has forgotten what he was saying. He may wet himself in an attack. Attacks may be very frequent, and there may be several attacks in rapid succession so that attacks for a time may be almost continuous. The specialist may precipitate an attack for diagnostic purposes by causing the child to overventilate. Petit mal attacks usually become less frequent in adolescence: they occur predominantly between the age of four to eight.

There are many varieties of grand mal. In the common form the child without warning becomes stiff, falls unconscious, twitches, often becomes blue, the eyes turn up into the head or into the corner, he may wet himself, and after a variable time recovers, often to fall into a deep sleep. He may vomit or have a headache, but usually recovery is complete. Occasionally there is weakness of the arm or leg for a few hours after a fit. The fit may last for a few seconds or minutes, and occasionally longer; a prolonged fit is termed status epilepticus and urgent treatment is required because it may damage the brain. Sometimes the fit ('Jacksonian epilepsy') affects only one side of the body, or one arm, and the child may not lose consciousness: it occurs particularly but not only in children with spastic hemiplegia. Other unusual forms of epilepsy include sudden severe headache or sudden severe abdominal pain —in each case followed by sleep. Major fits are sometimes caused by the flickering of light on a television screen or by other bright lights. Fits are sometimes precipitated by loud noise, by reading, by fever, psychological stress or other factors, and may be related to menstruation. Fits are particularly liable to occur when the child is falling asleep or awakening. Many fits are confined to the night. It may not be recognised that in an epileptic child wetting of the bed may be due to a fit.

Temporal lobe epilepsy may cause a variety of bizarre episodes. In one third there is a preceding aura consisting of peculiar stereo-typed movements, or sudden fear, anxiety, chewing, smacking movements of the lips, swallowing, peculiar taste or smell, noises in the ears or visual phenomena. The attack may consist of epileptic automatism—sleep walking, slurred speech, irrelevant speech or laughter, sudden overactivity or sudden unexplained unprovoked temper outbursts. I saw one boy who in his first attack walked fully clothed into a lake. One has seen many children who present as temper tantrums, but who were recognised as having temporal lobe epilepsy because the attacks were of sudden instantaneous onset without any provocation or discoverable reason. Sometimes the episode may last for several hours. There is no loss of consciousness in these attacks, and no twitching, so that the true diagnosis may pass unrecognised for a long time.

It is now known that even though a child does not have an overt fit, there may be subictal activity in the brain, as shown by the electroencephalogram. This means that electrical discharges are occurring, and though they are not great enough to cause a fit, they are sufficient to alter a child's behaviour, concentration and memory.

Epilepsy is frequently associated with psychological problems. The child may be overprotected by his parents and prevented from taking part in sport, such as swimming. Partly as a result of this he may become a hypochondriac. He may be rejected on account of the fits, and he may be excluded from school—or from the school of choice. He may be afraid of the aura or of the result of a fit, and he may receive injuries and bruises in fits. He may fear death. He is disturbed by feeling different from others, particularly if his activities are restricted. Other children may behave in an odd way towards him because of his fits. He feels insecure, and so may develop a wide variety of behaviour problems: he feels thwarted and depressed. Other behavioural features may be the direct result of the epilepsy, and they include aggressiveness, overactivity, stubborn behaviour, destructiveness, antisocial behaviour, lying or stealing. It is sometimes difficult to determine whether the undesirable behaviour is the result of his insecurity and his anxieties, or the effect of the epilepsy on the brain. In other cases the behaviour may be the effect of drugs taken for epilepsy. Phenobarbitone in particular may have the paradoxical effect of causing overactivity and irritability, especially if the blood level rises too high. The drugs may cause drowsiness and depression or other reactions. His behaviour may be further affected by a deterioration in his school performance.

Deterioration in school performance may result from several factors. It may be the result of absences from school. It may be due to frequent attacks of petit mal causing loss of the thread of discussions in class: but petit mal does not itself damage the brain, however frequent the attacks are. The deterioration may be due to the psychological problems mentioned above—and in turn it may cause those problems. It may be due to the effect of drugs taken for the epilepsy. All drugs taken for epilepsy may have untoward side effects, and frequent monitoring of the blood level of the drugs is often necessary—particularly as one drug may affect the blood level of another drug, one interacting with the other: commonly two or three drugs are given simultaneously. Some of the drugs may cause anaemia, which lowers the standard of work. The epilepsy may itself damage the brain, particularly if fits are long lasting.

Some children with epilepsy have certain learning disorders, depending on the site of the focus in the brain from which the electrical discharges responsible for the fit arise (Stores 1971). The fits may cause impaired verbal ability, defective memory, visuo-spatial disability and poor concentration. This latter difficulty may be aggravated by phenobarbitone, which itself may reduce the child's power of concentration.

There are many problems which the child, the parents and his family have to face. The mean IQ of epileptic children is less than the average, because there is a high incidence of fits in mentally subnormal children and children with cerebral palsy, though most epileptic children have an average IQ and some are mentally superior. Whenever possible the child should attend an ordinary school and be treated as a normal child. He may have to be excluded from those athletic sports in which sudden falls would be dangerous. He should be allowed to swim, as long as fits are under control, and as long as there is supervision, but he should be dissuaded from diving from the highest diving board, or from rope climbing in the gymnasium. Provided that the fits are properly controlled, there should be virtually no restriction, if there is restriction at all. Judgment must be used, and calculated risks have to be taken.

Treatment is normally continued until the child has been free from fits for two or three years: the drugs are then discontinued, but in about a quarter there is a recurrence of fits within a few years.

When a child has a major epileptic fit in class, there is little to be done except if possible to see that he does not injure himself. It is a mistake to try to wedge something into his mouth to prevent him biting his tongue. If the fit lasts more than about 10 minutes it is urgent to get him to hospital for treatment.

REFERENCES

ILLINGWORTH R.S. & ILLINGWORTH C.M. (1966) *Lessons from Childhood: Some Aspects of the Early Life of Unusual Men and Women.* Edinburgh, Churchill/Livingstone.
STORES G. (1971) Cognitive Functions in children with epilepsy. *Brit. J. Hosp Med.* **6**, 207.

OTHER READING

BOWER B.D. (1969) Epilepsy and school athletics. *Develop. Med. Child. Neurol.* **11**, 244.
LIVINGSTONE S. & PRUCE I.M. (1972) *Comprehensive Management of Epilepsy in Infancy, Childhood and Adolescence.* Illinois, Charles Thomas.
ROSS E.M. (1973) Convulsive disorders in British children. *Proc. Roy. Soc. Med.* **66**, 703.

SPINA BIFIDA AND HYDROCEPHALUS

The subject of spina bifida has attracted a great deal of attention in recent years because of the vast amount of time which has been put into the study of affected children in Britain and abroad. The largest centre in Britain has been that at Sheffield, where Mr Robert Zachary and Mr James Lister have been responsible for the surgery, Mr John Sharrard for the orthopaedic surgery, and Dr John Lorber for the medical management of these children, each with a team of assistants.

Spina bifida consists of a malformation in the spine and spinal cord, between the neck and the sacrum. A meningocele is a defect which does not involve the spinal cord, and causes little or no disability. A meningomyelocele involves the spinal cord, and is associated with varying degrees of weakness of the legs and other symptoms. Four out of five children with spina bifida also have hydrocephalus and without proper treatment the head may grow to an enormous size. Spina bifida affects about 2 per 1,000 births: but a quarter are stillbirths or die soon after delivery.

Hydrocephalus is due to obstruction of the flow of cerebrospinal fluid. The fluid is formed in the ventricles and passed to the outside of the brain and down the spinal cord. Obstruction is caused by congenital malformation or postnatal meningitis: the fluid dilates the ventricles which therefore compress the brain tissue. It is treated in all but the mild cases by passing a valve from the ventricle into the heart: if the valve becomes blocked the child becomes poorly and is apt to vomit and have a headache.

INCIDENCE

Approximately 1,500 children are born with spina bifida in England and Wales every year: about half survive into later childhood. About 600 children each year reach the age of five. In a city of a million people, one would expect about 40 births a year with the condition. It is more common in some parts of the world than in others. It is more common in Ireland and Wales than in England.

The cause is partly genetic and perhaps partly environmental—due to factors in utero, but the knowledge of those factors is slender. When a child is born with spina bifida, the chance of another child being born with the same or a similar defect is approximately one in twelve. Hydrocephalus alone may be genetic in origin or due to infections in utero, such as toxoplasmosis. It is basically an obstruction to the pathways of the cerebrospinal fluid.

THE HANDICAP

Almost all children with meningomyelocele are handicapped. The extent of the handicap depends on the site of the lesion: those with the defect in the lumbar region are the worst affected: those with the defect in the neck, between the shoulder blades or over the sacral area, are less affected. A severely affected child has completely or almost completely paralysed legs: he has sensory loss below the lesion, so that he cannot feel pain, touch or heat. A lumbar meningomyelocele usually causes incontinence of the bowel and bladder, and means that the child is prone to urinary tract infection. He cannot empty the bladder voluntarily, and the bladder has to be expressed by hand—before each feed in infants and four or five times a day in older children. The child has no bladder sensation and does not know when it is full: there is constant dribbling of urine. Owing to lack of movement, not only is obesity apt to occur, but the bones become decalcified and fractures of the legs are very common: many children have six or more fractures of the femur—fortunately painlessly, because of lack of pain sensation. Owing to lack of sensation in the legs, burns and scalds are apt to occur. Pressure sores are a constant danger. Dislocation of the hip is common. Deformity of the spine, with severe twisting (scoliosis) or bending (kyphosis) occurs.

The IQ of 362 children with hydrocephalus with or without spina bifida, and of 113 children with spina bifida alone, was found by Dr John Lorber at Sheffield to be as shown in Table 16.1.

TABLE 16.1

IQ at school age	Hydrocephalus ± spina bifida	Spina bifida alone
120+	1·9	4·4
110–119	5·5	16·8
90–109	30	47·8
80–89	20	15·9
51–79	28	11·5
Less than 50	14·8	2·6
Total number of children	362	113

The problem of education is an important one, because so many of these children have an IQ within the normal range. It is useful for them to attend a nursery class, if there is one available. At school age it is desirable that the school should be as near to the child's home as possible, so that he can get home at lunch time: he may have to have his bladder expressed at home. He may have to go to a school for physically handicapped children, or a residential school if the home is in the country: but if he can go to an ordinary school, it is preferable: but one essential is that a wheelchair can be used, and that there are no steps: and he must be able to get to the lavatory. The advantage of a special school is that appropriate therapy can be given, there is regular medical supervision, the physical arrangements in the buildings are suitable and classes are small. It is estimated that in London 60 per cent of those reaching school age will need special education for physically handicapped children and that 10 per cent will need to go to a school for educationally subnormal children. Some affected children may go to a school specially designed for children with spina bifida. The provision of such schools is expensive. Leach (1970) pointed out that if Britain were to provide special schools for every spina bifida child now being salvaged, it would have to build one with 50 places each and every month for the next 15 years.

Children with meningomyelocele are likely to have numerous operations—in connection with the valve in the neck, the bladder problem and orthopaedic difficulties. These operations involve long absences from school, which add to the handicap: they are often dreaded by children as they get older.

THE OUTLOOK FOR THE CHILD WITH A MENINGOMYELOCELE

The outlook is gloomy in the extreme. The question of whether they will be able to walk is dependent on the state of the legs at birth: if they are completely paralysed at birth it is unlikely that they will ever walk. Of all cases of meningomyelocele, approximately one third will never walk and will be chairbound, one third will be able to walk a little with difficulty (and the help of appliances), and one third will be able to walk with little help. Urinary tract infection is always a serious problem, and is commonly the eventual cause of death.

Many feel that badly affected children should be allowed to die in the newborn period, as most would if untreated. If they are caused to survive by operative methods, they are certain always to be handicapped (Lorber 1972). Eliot Slater wrote (1971) 'these children are now beginning to come into puberty and adolescence, when their sufferings will really begin. Only the most miserably impoverished social life will be open to them; they will be equipped with normal sex drive but no sex function; all around them they will see the normal, the vigorous and the healthy. Will they really be grateful to the fates, the all too human fates but for whose intervention they would have died before their miseries began?' The parents suffer 'years of servitude, of tortured love, trying to make up to him for all his disadvantages'.

REFERENCES

LEACH G. (1970) *The Biocrats*. London, Cape.
LORBER J. (1972) Spina bifida cystica. Results of treatment of 270 consecutive cases with criteria for selection for the future. *Arch. Dis. Childh.* **47**, 854.
SLATER E. (1971) Health service or sickness service? *Brit. Med. J.* **4**, 734.

OTHER READING

Department of Health and Social Security (1973) *Care of the Child with Spina Bifida*.
LAURENCE K.M. & TEW B.J. (1971) Natural history of spina bifida cystica and cranium bifidum cysticum. *Arch. Dis. Childh.* **46**, 127.
LAWSON J.S. (1968) Ethical problems associated with the management of congenitally handicapped newborn infants. *Australian Paediat. J.* **4**, 186.
LIGHTOWLER C.D.R. (1971) Meningomyelocele; the price of treatment. *Brit. Med. J.* **2**, 385.
LORBER J. (1971) Results of treatment of myelomeningocele; an analysis of 524 unselected cases with special reference to possible selection for treatment. *Develop. Med. Child. Neurol.* **13**, 279.
LORBER J. (1972) *Your Child with Spina Bifida*. Association for Spina Bifida and Hydrocephalus.
LORBER J. (1973) *Your Child with Hydrocephalus*. Association for Spina Bifida and Hydrocephalus.
WALKER J.H., THOMAS M. & RUSSELL I.T. (1971) Spina bifida—and the parents. *Develop. Med. Child. Neurol.* **13**, 462.
ZACHARY R.B. (1968) Ethical and social aspects of treatment of spina bifida. *Lancet*, **2**, 274.

I

CHAPTER 17
COMMON SYMPTOMS AND DISEASES

ABDOMINAL PAIN, ACUTE

Acute abdominal pain lasting for more than two or three hours must be regarded as an emergency: the child must be seen by a doctor forthwith. It may be due to appendicitis: the pain commonly begins in the mid-abdomen and later settles in the lower part of the right side of the abdomen (right iliac fossa). There is usually vomiting and fever. Pain is often experienced in the right iliac fossa when there is right lower lobe pneumonia. Often pain in the abdomen is due to a virus infection. Pain in the abdomen may be experienced when a child has a urinary tract infection or torsion of the testis. Severe vomiting, coughing or diarrhoea itself causes pain. Abdominal pain is also caused by hypoglycaemia (low blood sugar) or diabetic acidosis. In West Indian children the pain may be due to sickle cell anaemia. Various medicines may cause abdominal discomfort.

ABDOMINAL PAIN, RECURRENT

The problem of the school child with recurrent abdominal pain faces every paediatrician. In a Buckinghamshire survey of 6,000 school children (Shepherd *et al.*, 1971) recurrent abdominal pains were experienced by 4 per cent of girls up to 10 years of age, 15 per cent of 12 and 13 year-olds and 25 per cent of 14 and 15 year-olds. Apley (1959) in his study of 1,000 Bristol school children, found that one in every nine had recurrent abdominal pain: in not more than one in 20 was there evidence of organic disease on full investigation. In half the cases there was a family history of abdominal pain: the father may constantly complain of his ulcer, and the child in imitation or subconscious fear of suffering in the same way develops recurrent pains. Not all the recurrent abdominal pains are psychological. Fears and psychological stress are a cause: but there are other causes of which we do not know and which we do not understand. The pains may be exaggerated if the mother shows anxiety about the child's symptoms, showing excessive sympathy and concern.

The pains are usually central and periumbilical: if they are always in another part of the abdomen organic disease is more likely. The pains may be momentary or last for a day or two. There may be associated headache or fever, and in that case merge into the picture of the periodic syndrome or migraine (p. 257). The more severe the pains are, the less likely they are to be due to disease. On follow-up a third in about 10 years are free from symptoms: others may continue to have pains or else to have migraine.

The difficulty facing doctors, teachers and parents is the fact that it is impossible to assess someone else's pain. Though abdominal pain or headache can be feigned, it is unwise to assume that they are feigned unless one is certain—and one can hardly ever be certain. Even though the pain is non-organic, it is probably almost always genuinely felt. Excessive sympathy will make it worse: but one has to avoid going too far the other way and being too unsympathetic. Children should rarely miss school for more than a day on account of these pains unless there is also vomiting and fever.

A doctor has to investigate recurrent abdominal pains if they are frequent and severe. He has to be certain that there is no kidney disease. In countries abroad, but not England, the doctor looks for roundworm infection. Constipation is almost certainly *not* the cause of the pain.

ACNE

Acne, a feature of adolescence in boys and girls, may be disfiguring to the face and psychologically traumatic. It consists of spots mainly on the face and trunk. It is due to increased sebum production with obstruction of the sebaceous ducts with consequent infection: bacterial decomposition of the sebum produces irritant substances and inflammation results. Further infection results from scratching. The increased sebum production is dependent on hormones which cause the physical features of puberty: but certain drugs, notably corticosteroids, iodides and certain anti-epileptic drugs may be responsible.

We cannot at present reduce the production of sebum: but obstruction of the ducts by sebum may be prevented by regular soap and water, a special soap containing sulphur and salicylic acid being used: many other preparations are used including 'Brasivol' ointment. Ultraviolet light, sufficient to cause desquamation, may help. When there are infected spots, tetracycline is useful.

ANAEMIA

Anaemia has to be distinguished from pallor. Pallor may be a familial feature, or the result of hunger, a stuffy room, or lack of fresh air and exercise. Anaemia, diagnosed by blood tests, can be caused by numerous conditions. The common cause in a school child is iron deficiency, due to a poor diet with too little protein. It could also be due to blood loss—from nose bleeds, or from taking aspirins (which may cause bleeding from the stomach). It may be due to chronic infections, due to hereditary blood diseases, and in coloured children who have lived abroad it may be due to hookworms (which cause loss of blood from the duodenum). In West Indian and other negro children it may be due to sickle cell anaemia—in which there is an abnormality of the haemoglobin with chronic excessive destruction of the red cells: there is anaemia, and often attacks of pain in various parts of the body, including the bones or fever and thromboses: it is a hereditary disease, affecting about 10 per cent of all negroes in the United States.

ASTHMA

It is estimated that about 14,000 British school children suffer from asthma.

Asthma is a condition characterised by paroxysmal difficulty in breathing with wheeze and cough, commonly worse at night, caused by allergy to substances, especially those in dust. There is spasm of the bronchi and additional obstruction by viscid mucus. Some three to five per cent of school children have it. A third of all asthma begins in the first ten years. It commonly develops in children suffering from eczema. Sometimes it is confined to the hay fever season, and is associated with hay fever. There is usually a family history of allergy. There are three main components of asthma—allergy, infection and psychological stress: attacks commonly follow a cold and wheezing is characteristically precipitated by exertion. Numerous substances may cause the asthma: a common one is a mite, the dermatophagoides pteronyssinus, which lives on the human skin and in dust—on the bedclothes, carpet, mattress and elsewhere.

An asthmatic child presents a serious problem to the family, especially the parents. They spend many sleepless nights with him, and many suffer fatigue and domestic friction as a result. They become apprehensive and frustrated; their activities are restricted. The asthmatic child is apt to be overprotected; the parents constantly warn him not to get his feet wet, not to catch a cold, not to get tired or excited, and to be careful of what he eats. He is kept off school when he has the slightest wheeze and put to bed. The child responds by becoming anxious about his health and worries about missing school, and so he wheezes all the more. He becomes loath to be separated from his mother. He is apt to become depressed, unduly jealous of his siblings, and to develop other behaviour problems. It is not clear why parents think that he will wheeze less if he misses school; the reverse is often the case, and asthma is a major cause of school absence.

Unless the asthma can be controlled by treatment, the child develops a chronically overdistended chest and he is usually small in height. The treatment includes an attempt to remove offending allergens, particularly dust in the bedroom. It includes an effort to reduce the overprotection and smothering effect of parental overanxiety, and to reduce school absence. Attacks can often be prevented by the regular use of an inhalation of 'Intal'—disodium cromoglycate, three or four times a day. Most children lose their asthma by late adolescence, only about 10 per cent continuing to have troublesome asthma after that.

ATAXIA, UNSTEADINESS OF GAIT

The development of ataxia in a previously normal child is a serious symptom and should be investigated. It is a very common side effect of the drug phenytoin, used for epilepsy, but can be caused by several other medicines. It may be due to solvent sniffing (Chapter 4). Ataxia may be an early symptom of degenerative diseases of the nervous system, cerebral tumour and other serious diseases.

CONSTIPATION

There are still mothers who worry about their children's bowels—presumably because they fear that something dreadful will happen if there is not a daily bowel action. They are probably anxious about their own bowels. The British drink 30,000 gallons of liquid paraffin a year, obtain 3,500,000 prescriptions for laxatives and spend £5,000,000 on laxatives from the chemist. How much of this is consumed by children, we do not know: all we can say is that sensible mothers do not know whether their children have daily bowel actions or not: it just does not matter. The only reservation is that when a small child withholds all faeces, deliberately or otherwise, he may soil the pants (see encopresis, faecal incontinence); if he (or anyone else) consistently ignores the call to defecate, the rectum becomes so loaded that sensation of fullness is lost and the child cannot empty the bowel if he tries.

COUGH

The usual cause of a cough is a cold or 'upper respiratory tract infection' causing tracheitis or bronchitis: but it may not be due to disease at all; it may be a habit, a 'tic', an attention-seeking device, or the result of smoking—or of smoking by parents (Colley, 1974).

A cough with a wheeze in a school child is almost always due to asthma. A cough which is worse at night and which repeatedly makes a child sick is due to whooping cough until proved otherwise. A cough which only occurs at night when the child lies down is likely to be due to a postnasal discharge—the end of a cold, or the result of an antrum infection or of adenoids. Tuberculosis in Britain is now an extremely rare cause of cough. A serious disease of which a cough and serious lung infection are a feature is cystic fibrosis of the pancreas.

CYSTIC FIBROSIS OF THE PANCREAS

Cystic fibrosis of the pancreas, also called fibrocystic disease of the pancreas or mucoviscidosis, is a serious recessively inherited condition affecting one in 1,500 live births. As it is a recessive, the gene is carried by both parents; it is only when each of a couple carries the gene that children are affected. If one child has it, there is a one in four risk that further children will have it. Both sexes are equally affected. The features of the condition are chronic lung disease, malabsorption from the intestine causing excessive amounts of fat in the stools, the result of disease of the pancreas, and an excessive amount of sodium in the sweat. Other organs are commonly involved. An important feature is the thick tenacious mucus secreted from the bronchi and elsewhere. There is clubbing of the ends of the fingers if there is serious lung involvement.

Many affected children die in infancy, but with modern treatment many now survive into adolescence or later. Death is usually from lung disease.

DENTAL CARIES

It is said that skulls of Neanderthal man, who lived 50,000 years ago, showed dental caries. In Egypt in 3000 BC caries was much more frequent in the wealthy upper classes than among their slaves—presumably because of the nature of the foodstuffs which they ate. For at least 3,000 years it was believed that caries was due to gnawing by worms. According to Ryan (1973) the Babylonians regarded toothache as a visitation of divine displeasure and prescribed prayers and propitiatory incantations for its cure. Pliny the Elder recommended for its treatment the insertion into the ear of drops of oil in which earthworms had been boiled.

The role of refined carbohydrates in the production of caries cannot seriously be disputed. In Australia Fanning and colleagues (1969) studied the incidence of caries in 2,468 school children; there was a statistically significant excess of tooth decay in children attending schools which sold sweets in the canteen, as compared with controls from schools not selling sweets. Rodents fed by stomach tube remain caries-free: fed by the mouth, they do not. The worst offender among sweets is toffee, probably because of its prolonged contact with teeth. There is little correlation between the amount of sugar taken and caries; more important is the frequency with which sugar is taken, particularly between meals. Fruit drinks and other carbonated beverages have a bad effect on teeth. Amongst preschool children the use of a 'dinky feeder' filled with a sweet substance, such as rose hip syrup, used as a pacifier, has a disastrous effect, causing gross caries. Fruit syrups act by their high sugar content, with high viscosity, low pH and the chelating action of citric acid.

Microorganisms of the group streptococcus mutans are an essential factor in caries production. They form polysaccharides from carbohydrates and contribute to the adhesiveness of micro-organisms and to plaque formation (Bowen 1972); and they also form acid. Experiments with vaccines are being made: a group of monkeys has been successfully vaccinated against dental caries.

Overcrowding of teeth predisposes to caries by making proper cleaning between teeth difficult or impossible: and it follows that adequate dental care includes the treatment of overcrowding and malocclusion.

Fluoridation of water supplies is the most effective single measure for the prevention of caries; it causes a 60 to 90 per cent reduction in caries. It is officially endorsed by the World Health Organisation, the United States Public Health Service, the American Medical Association, the American Dental Association, the American Academy of Pediatrics, and the American Society of Dentistry for Children. The addition of fluoride to toothpaste is thought possibly to be of some value.

A new development in the treatment of caries consists of the use of cyanoacrylate to seal off fissures: the site is thoroughly cleaned, etched with phosphoric acid, rinsed, dried and then filled with cyanoacrylate.

DIABETES MELLITUS

Diabetes is a hereditary disease, usually recessive, affecting one out of every 250 births or about one in every 3,300 school children aged 5 to 17. When a mother has diabetes, there is approximately a one in eight chance that her children will develop it—though not necessarily until adult life. Only about 0·2 per cent will develop it before the age of 10, and 0·7 per cent before twenty. It is calculated that in the United States there are about three million diabetics, of whom about four per cent are below the age of fifteen. It is due to a deficiency in the beta cells of the pancreas resulting in insufficiency of insulin with resultant accumulation of glucose in the blood and related metabolic problems.

Almost all diabetic children develop symptoms of diabetes in an acute fashion: the usual symptoms are thirst, the passage of large quantities of urine (polyuria) and loss of weight. Sugar is found in the urine, often with acetone: the expert smells acetone in the breath. The response to treatment is immediate: the amount of insulin needed is determined in hospital and the child returns to school. Though there is still some difference of opinion, the usual diet is a 'free diet' but with no excess of sweets or carbohydrate. In the early days children were put on to a rigid weighed diet, but from the psychological point of view this is most undesirable; children will not adhere to the diet; and we now know that this rigidity is unnecessary. One reason for severe restriction of the diet was the serious fact that there is a high incidence of degenerative vascular disease within ten to twenty years of the onset: within 20 years 85 per cent have arteriosclerosis: but it has been proved repeatedly that dietary restrictions, apart from being unpleasant and a nuisance to all concerned, do nothing to improve the outlook. Physical growth proceeds normally if the diabetes is adequately controlled. Children are encouraged to take normal exercise.

The insulin requirements are affected by a variety of factors, particularly exertion and infection. Exercise decreases the need and infection increases the need: unknown factors alter the need, so that the symptoms of diabetic acidosis (pre-coma) and of too low a blood sugar (hypoglycaemia) must be known. The symptoms of pre-coma are mainly drowsiness, vomiting, abdominal pain and overbreathing with a dry skin and dry mouth. Acetone may be smelt in the breath and there is much sugar and acetone in the urine. The symptoms of hypoglycaemia (due to an overdose of insulin) are hunger, weakness, sweating, pallor and restlessness with dilated pupils; some children become lachrymose, some euphoric, and some aggressive; when the blood sugar drops further they pass into coma or have major convulsions. Symptoms commonly develop some 3 to 8 hours after ordinary insulin or 8 to 24 hours after slow acting insulins. The symptoms disappear immediately when the child takes a lump of sugar, or a sweet fruit drink, or a tablet of glucagon.

While adults may take certain preparations by mouth to control their blood sugar, children require insulin. Injections of insulin may cause atrophy of the underlying fatty tissue, or areas of induration: the latter may be due to infection at the site of injection or a sensitivity reaction to the brand of insulin used. In order to avoid skin atrophy children are instructed to use a different site for each injection, varying from one arm to the other, and one leg to the other, or using the skin of the abdomen for the site of injections. Each injection is given not nearer than half an inch from the previous one. Children have to learn to keep the skin clean.

DIARRHOEA

The usual cause of diarrhoea is bacterial infection (see Gastro-enteritis, p. 276): but diarrhoea can be due to emotional problems —worries and fears. Many medicines cause diarrhoea. In young children there is a condition called spurious diarrhoea in which there is gross constipation with the escape of liquid material round the edge of a huge mass of faeces in the bowel; the liquid leaks out, so that there is constant soiling of the pants. A serious chronic condition affecting children and adults is ulcerative colitis. There is diarrhoea and often blood and mucus in the stools. It can often be controlled by a drug (sulphasalazine), but not always, and surgical treatment is sometimes required. Expert treatment and supervision is essential.

EAR PAIN AND EAR DISCHARGE

Ear pain is most likely to be due to otitis media (middle ear disease), but it could be due to a boil in the ear. Pain in the ear may arise from an erupting or carious molar tooth. It is most important that otitis media should be treated promptly (by penicillin).

The commonest ear discharge is wax: but if the ear discharge is purulent, medical treatment is urgent.

ECZEMA

Eczema is a common allergic rash beginning in infancy and sometimes persisting for several years. It often occurs as a familial feature. In 40 per cent it is later accompanied by asthma. It is more common in babies given cow's milk preparations rather than breast milk. It commonly begins on the face and scalp—with redness and an irritating itching rash. Scratching makes it worse and often leads to infection and sometimes to impetigo. It is aggravated by sweating. It may become crusted or oozing. Later it may be confined largely to the flexor surfaces of the elbow, knee and wrist. It is not usually possible to determine which substance causes the eczema. It is a source of much misery to the child and the parents are apt to be worried or even embarrassed by the child's condition.

For its treatment one tries to stop the child scratching and a medicine may help; ordinary soap may be replaced by a skin cleanser. Numerous applications have been tried with limited success. Corticosteroid ointment may be used for a few days, but if used longer may damage the skin.

The child with eczema cannot be vaccinated against smallpox, for a fatal vaccinia may occur, but he is immunised against other infectious diseases.

FLAT FOOT

The foot appears to be flat in small children because the pad in the sole of the foot obscures the normal concavity. Provided that the foot is painless and movements of the ankle joint are full, treatment of any kind is never necessary. Only if there is pain, which is rare, and the inner side of the heel of the shoe is worn, would one fit a $\frac{3}{16}$in wedge on the inner side of the heel of the shoe.

FREQUENCY AND URGENCY OF MICTURITION

When the normal young child, aged 18 months to 30 months, is learning to control the bladder, he has great urgency when he feels the desire to pass urine: he cannot wait and at first wets himself. In a very few weeks his nervous control has matured sufficiently for him to hold out until he can reach the lavatory: and in a few more weeks this primitive urgency no longer occurs. But many bed wetters retain this primitive urgency for many more months. Ten per cent of children are still wetting occasionally when they start school, and many of them, if not most, have some of this urgency. It is cruel to prevent them going to the lavatory when they want to: they cannot help it: many of them are much disturbed when as a result of not being allowed to go to the lavatory they wet themselves.

Apart from this urgency some children have frequency of

micturition. This may be due to a urinary tract infection, and it should be eliminated by the doctor, because it is important that if there is an infection, it should be treated. Frequency may be merely an attention-seeking device, or a desire to get out of a distasteful class; but it could also be due to diabetes mellitus. It may be nothing more than a habit or a behaviour problem related to insecurity. The child should be seen by a doctor.

Polydipsia, drinking a lot of fluid, may be a habit, but it may be due to diabetes or other causes. The child should be seen by a doctor.

FUNNEL CHEST

A funnel chest (pectus excavatum) is a depression in the middle of the sternum. It is usually a familial feature: in some it is due to a short central tendon of the diaphragm. In other cases the funnel chest is the result of respiratory obstruction (as in asthma) or rickets. Treatment, which is surgical, is recommended only in the extremely severe cases—and then largely for psychological and cosmetic reasons.

GLANDS (LYMPH NODES), ENLARGED

Enlarged glands may be due to local infection or to certain general diseases.

In the neck, the usual cause of enlarged glands is a throat infection, such as tonsillitis. Tuberculosis used to be a common cause of enlarged neck glands, but as a cause of this it is virtually non-existent in Britain now, for tuberculous neck glands were usually due to bovine tuberculosis, acquired from infected milk. Thanks to pasteurisation this does not now occur.

Glands in the neck may be enlarged as the result of an infection in the skin of the face, behind the ear or scalp: they are enlarged in chronic eczema. They enlarge in glandular fever: and the glands at the back of the neck are enlarged in German measles.

Glands in the axilla enlarge as the result of an infection in the skin of the arm, or eczema, or the result of smallpox or BCG vaccination. They may enlarge in glandular fever.

Glands in the groin are always palpable. They enlarge as the result of an infection in the lower limb or in the skin around the anus. They enlarge in chronic eczema and sometimes in glandular fever.

HAEMOPHILIA

Haemophilia is a rare disease, occurring in 1 in 25,000 births. It is a sex-linked recessive defect resulting from a mutation of a gene in the X chromosome. If another child is born to the family and he is male, he will have the disease: if the child is female, she will carry the disease, and there is a one in two chance that her sons will have haemophilia, and her daughters will be carriers. The sons of a father with haemophilia will not have it, since they carry his Y chromosome, but his daughters will carry it so that half her sons will have it and half her daughters will pass it on to her sons. The daughter of a mother who is a carrier does not know whether she is a carrier or not unless she gives birth to an affected son. The sister of a man with haemophilia has a one in two chance of being a carrier, and if she is, half her sons will have it and half her daughters will pass it on. There is a family history of haemophilia in two out of every three cases. Much has been written about the historical aspect of haemophilia: the eighth child of Queen Victoria, Leopold, suffered from it.

The bleeding tendency is due to a deficiency of one of the factors (Factor VIII) necessary for the clotting of blood. Bleeding may follow a trivial graze or other injury, an injection for immunisation, the extraction of a tooth, or a knock on the nose, causing persistent nose bleeding. Haemorrhage into a joint is common; it may result from a trivial knock or for no apparent reason: the joints may become permanently stiff. Christmas disease is a closely allied condition due to a deficiency of a different factor.

Haemophilia does not shorten life, provided that blood transfusion and other appropriate treatment can be given when necessary. Blood transfusion is necessary only when there has been severe blood loss: when bleeding cannot be stopped by pressure, an injection of plasma or of a derivative of plasma, such as cryoprecipitate, is given to stop it. Even major operations can be performed provided that the child is properly prepared for it by the necessary injections: but even trivial procedures, such as the extraction of a tooth, must be carried out in hospital.

Every effort should be made to enable an affected child to lead as normal a life as possible. He carries a haemophilia card, so that the condition is known if he is injured. Special care has to be taken to avoid knocks to the knee and other joints which are prone to injury. Some children wear pads over their knees for this reason. Special care is taken of the teeth, so that extractions can be avoided: but if they are necessary, bleeding can be prevented by a suitable injection beforehand. After puberty an electric razor is preferred for shaving. Children are encouraged to swim, run, play tennis and later golf, but to avoid sports such as football. The aim is to enable them to grow up psychologically sound and to earn their living normally.

HEADACHES AND MIGRAINE

Not all headaches are due to migraine, but many are. Headache may be the result of an ill-ventilated room, hunger, stress, an impending thunderstorm or premenstrual tension. It is commonly a feature of fever for any cause. It may be an attention-seeking device. Teachers are aware of the so-called 'headache of convenience' in the arithmetic class. It may be due to worry, bullying or any other cause of unhappiness and insecurity. It may be caused by a variety of drugs. It is an unusual sequela of head injury; headaches and other sequelae of head injury are unusual unless the head injury was very severe, with laceration of the brain. The occurrence or absence of sequelae of head injury is otherwise dependent on hereditary, personality and environmental factors, especially the attitude of the parents. Headaches are most unlikely to be due to eye strain—unless the short-sightedness is so severe that it is obvious to anyone: and headaches are most unlikely to be due to a chronic antrum (sinus) infection: but they may be due to an acute sinus infection, in which case the child is obviously unwell.

In a Scandinavian study of 2,178 school children, it was found that 20·6 per cent had recurrent headaches. Bille found that 39 per cent of 1,085 Swedish seven-year-olds had headaches: and at Uppsala the incidence of headaches in 8,993 children aged 7 to 15 was 58·6 per cent. Dr John Apley in his study of recurrent headaches, abdominal pain and limb pain in 1,000 Bristol school children, found that 1 in 12 had recurrent headaches. Vahlquist in

Sweden found that 4·5 per cent of 1,236 school children aged 10 to 12 years had migraine and 13·3 per cent in addition had non-migrainous headaches.

There is no strict dividing line between 'ordinary' headaches and migraine.

Migraine

The word migraine is derived from the Greek meaning half a head —the implication being that a migraine headache is characteristically unilateral. That may be, but it is by no means always so: it is often just a frontal headache, and not confined to one side. Migraine was described by Hippocrates. Famous victims of migraine included Charles Darwin, Lewis Carroll, Alexander Pope, Sir William Herschel, Guy de Maupassant, George Eliot, Frederic Chopin, Peter the Great, Peter Tchaikovsky, Leo Tolstoy and Thomas Jefferson.

Some patients know when an attack of migraine is imminent. Some adolescents and adults (but rarely children) see 'fortification figures' in front of their eyes at the beginning of an attack—zigzag or similar designs. Some have tingling in the hands or feet, feel irritable or experience blurring of vision. Some note an increase in weight immediately preceding an attack. Some pass less urine than usual before an attack, and more after one. Some have aphasia— inability to speak or to pick out the right word at the beginning of an attack, often as the first symptom. More commonly a headache is the initial feature. The headache is often severe and becomes throbbing in character. Vomiting is common. Young children often experience vomiting, abdominal pain and fever, with little or no headache, and headache develops in attacks as the child gets older. Occasionally there is weakness of an arm or leg lasting a few hours after an attack (hemiplegia). In the first stage there is pallor with vascular constriction, and this is followed by vascular dilation, throbbing, and often suffusion of the face.

Migraine is precipitated by a variety of causes: these include particularly fatigue, hunger, emotional stress and tension, conflict at home or school, the contraceptive pill, and certain foods. It is thought that about 30 per cent of all cases are due to a metabolic error in the way of defective conjugation of tyramine, or of serotonin metabolism, due to a genetic enzyme deficiency. Many patients have found that an attack of migraine follows 4 to 48 hours after eating tyramine containing foods, of which the chief offenders are chocolate and cheese—especially Cheddar and Stilton (Dalton 1972). Others have an attack after eating citrus fruit, raspberries, certain wines, onions, cucumber, tomatoes, nuts, pork, fried foods, fish, broad beans, game, yeast, pickled herring, or after tea or coffee. Nitrite preservatives in cured meat (Henderson and Raskin 1972) and monosodium glutamate (in Chinese restaurants) have sometimes been incriminated. Meteorological conditions and high altitude have precipitated attacks. Other factors responsible for attacks of migraine include water retention, menstruation, loud noise, bright light, television, infections or exertion. Attacks last from an hour or two to three days.

Migraine can begin at any age. It has been described in infants under a year old, when it presents as vomiting and pallor. It is common in children (Friedman and Harms 1967, Friedman 1972, Rigg 1972). Thirty-five per cent of 800 adult sufferers had begun in childhood. It is more common in boys than in girls. It has been stated that migraine is more common in the more intelligent children, but there is probably little truth in this. It is said that migraine is more common in shy, anxious, sensitive readily frustrated children, with particularly ambitious, efficient, perfectionist parents. In three-quarters there is a family history of migraine. Amongst children with migraine there is a higher incidence of travel sickness. Follow-up studies have shown that in about six years 40 per cent of children have ceased to have attacks, and about 30 per cent have less severe attacks.

Treatment has not been very satisfactory. If foodstuffs are found to cause the attacks, it helps greatly to avoid them. Ergotamine preparations, successful for adults, are useful only for children with infrequent attacks: doctors are afraid of reactions to the ergot. Clonidine ('Dixarit') is often useful in preventing attacks. For an acute attack, an aspirin or tab. codein co ('veganin') is useful. The importance of psychological factors must be remembered: as little anxiety as possible should be shown about the attacks, and absence from school, though necessary in an attack, should be kept down to a minimum.

HEART DISEASE

One in 250 live born children has a congenital heart abnormality.

Approximately 6,000 children are born each year in Britain with congenital heart disease and 3,000 of these survive. The cause is usually unknown. The main known cause is German measles in the first three months of pregnancy: but there is a genetic factor, for if a child is born with congenital heart disease, not due to German measles in pregnancy, there is a slightly increased risk that another child will be affected. The extent of the risk varies with the different types of defect.

There are numerous types of congenital heart disease, the commonest being a communication between the two sides of the heart ('hole in the heart'), which has not closed as it should do by the time of birth. Usually the blood passes from the left side (oxygenated blood, which has been through the lungs) to the right side, so that the child is not blue (cyanosed): but if there are other defects in the heart the blood may go the other way, so that unoxygenated blood passes into the circulation and the child is blue (a 'blue baby'). These holes may close spontaneously anytime up to 20 years of age or more: but they may put a strain on the heart and cause permanent damage, so that the surgeon may decide to close the gap. Another common type of abnormality is the patent ductus arteriosus, between the aorta and pulmonary artery. This too should close by the time of birth. It is closed relatively early by the surgeon.

Many congenital heart defects are associated with other congenital abnormalities in other parts of the body (for instance deafness in the case of the German measles syndrome). The mean IQ of children with congenital heart disease is slightly less than the average—though many children will have a higher than average IQ. Most of the congenital heart conditions are associated with some stunting of physical growth. There is a risk that when teeth are extracted or tonsils are removed organisms liberated at the time of the operation may settle on the abnormal part of the heart and cause a serious infection (subacute bacterial endocarditis), and this is prevented by giving penicillin immediately before and after the operation.

It is wrong to restrict the activities of children with congenital heart disease, except those with aortic or pulmonary stenosis, or cyanotic forms (Chapter 16). They should be allowed to regulate their own activities and decide themselves how much they can do without becoming breathless.

Many children with these conditions are completely free from symptoms, the abnormality being found on routine school medical examination.

HEART MURMURS

About one in every two children when carefully examined is found to have a heart murmur. The great majority of these are of no significance and do not signify any disease or abnormality. They are termed 'functional murmurs'. Their exact origin is uncertain.

RHEUMATIC HEART DISEASE

In Britain rheumatic fever has almost completely disappeared, thanks to improved nutrition, the prompt treatment of strepto-coccal tonsillitis with penicillin and other factors. It used to be a major cause of heart disease, and still is in many developing countries. Rheumatic fever is a reaction to the haemolytic strepto-coccus, a common cause of acute tonsillitis, predominantly after the age of five. In many cases a week or two after the tonsillitis the child becomes unwell and may have inflammation of a joint—the wrist, elbow, knee or ankle. He may be feverish and develop a heart murmur indicative of carditis. Relapses are liable to occur in later months or years, but these can be largely prevented by daily penicillin taken for several years. On recovery from an attack there is no need to restrict the child's activity in games or other pursuits.

IMPETIGO

Impetigo is an infectious skin condition due mainly to the staphylococcus or streptococcus. It begins as fluid containing spots (vesicles) with surrounding redness and itching. The lesions then crust and commonly coalesce. The relevant glands often become enlarged. Impetigo usually follows injury to the skin, as by bites, burns, abrasions, nits, scabies or eczema.

A small area is treated by an antibiotic cream, but a large area or severe impetigo by an oral or injected antibiotic. It is infectious, but a child with a small patch of impetigo would not be excluded from school.

KNOCK KNEE

Knock knee is normal at two or three. Almost all children lose their knock knee by the age of six. No treatment is needed unless there is abnormal shoe wear, in which case an orthopaedic opinion should be sought.

LASSITUDE

It is not easy to distinguish lassitude, a complaint of tiredness, from a mere personality trait—a reluctance to take part in energetic pursuits—perhaps just a preference for reading rather than physical activity. The development of lassitude at early puberty is a common source of anxiety: the child who has been always on the go and apparently never tired is now easily tired and lacks energy. It is important to ensure that there is no organic disease in such cases, but in the majority nothing is found: it is merely a passing phase, though the physiological or pathological basis for the fatigue is unknown. Lassitude may be due to insecurity, to lack of adequate sleep or to overwork; but it may be due to disease— tuberculosis, a chronic urinary tract infection, or an unrecognised anaemia. The doctor should see the child.

LIMPING AND LIMB PAIN

The most common cause of the sudden development of a limp is an uncomfortable shoe, a painful area on the limb or an inflamed gland in the groin. A sprained joint or fractured bone should be readily recognised. Other causes include disease of the hip joint, particularly transient synovitis of the hip—in which the child develops a limp: it settles down within seven or eight weeks, particularly if weight bearing is avoided. Another hip condition is Perthes' disease of the hip—a condition of uncertain origin, probably non-infective, causing necrosis of the head of the femur. Some treat this by prolonged bed rest, while others think that bed rest is unnecessary. In the young adolescent, particularly an obese one, there may be a slipped femoral epiphysis, causing a limp usually without much pain, and requiring surgical treatment. Pain in the knee is sometimes pain referred from the hip joint. Bone pain may be a symptom of certain serious diseases, and should always be investigated by a doctor.

Apley (1968) found that one in 25 Bristol school children had recurrent pains in the legs, mainly the calf and thigh muscles, mainly at night. Some term these 'growing pains', but this is an inept term because they are not principally at the period of maximum growth—in early puberty. They are more apt to occur in the child of about seven to twelve. They are not due to disease: there may be a psychological factor and as little attention as possible should be made to them.

In a Scandinavian study of 2,178 school children aged 6 to 19, 12·5 per cent of the boys and 18·4 per cent of the girls had growing pains: at the age of 11, the peak age, 20 per cent of the boys and 30 per cent of the girls had them. 22 per cent of those with growing pains also had recurrent abdominal pain and 28 per cent had headaches.

The hula-hoop game and certain modern dances put a strain on the spine and joints and may cause vague back or limb pains.

MOUTHBREATHING

Mouthbreathing may be a habit: but it may be due to nasal obstruction (e.g. a deflected septum) or postnasal obstruction by adenoids. The ear, nose and throat specialist should see the child who is a chronic mouthbreather.

MUSCULAR DYSTROPHY

This is a rare tragic condition affecting about one in every 20,000 children. It is hereditary, but there are several types with different modes of inheritance. The commonest type—the Duchenne-type —is a sex-linked recessive, so that a male sibling has a one in two chance of being affected, and a female sibling a one in two chance of carrying the disease. As it is a recessive, the disease only occurs when by tragic coincidence a couple with the gene for muscular dystrophy marry. Only boys are affected. Walking is often delayed, but the initial symptom is usually a difficulty in climbing steps, or in running or hopping. There is a waddling gait, frequent falling and an increasing difficulty in getting up. When placed on his back the boy turns over on to his abdomen and holding his legs with his hands 'climbs up' into the vertical position. There is early weakness in the muscles of the hip and spine. By the age of 8 to 12 most affected boys are no longer able to walk: they live a wheel chair existence, with rapid deterioration if they have an illness which confines them to bed: they develop contractures and normally die in the late teens from respiratory infection. About 40 per cent have a low IQ score, and the mental backwardness often antedates other symptoms. The disease is probably primarily a neurological one rather than primarily muscular. No specific treatment is available. The development of scoliosis (twisting of the back) is prevented by splinting when the child is no longer ambulant.

There are other forms of muscular dystrophy: in the limb girdle variety the initial weakness is in the pelvis or shoulder muscles, starting in the teens, and involving both boys and girls. In another form, the facio-scapulo-humeral type, there is weakness of the muscles of the face, arm and shoulder. In another form there is progressive wasting of muscles, including those of the tongue.

NASAL DISCHARGE

The obvious cause of a nasal discharge is a cold: but a clear discharge in the hay fever season, or all through the year, when accompanied by much sneezing, is likely to be due to allergic rhinitis.

A yellow purulent nasal discharge is a common feature of a cold, but in between colds a yellow nasal discharge denotes an antrum infection. A unilateral nasal discharge would suggest a foreign body in the nose.

NAUSEA

A feeling of sickness, nausea, is a common indication of distaste for school. Apart from this it is often a symptom in normal children on getting up in the morning. It may be an attention-seeking device. It occurs in migraine, or on change of posture (standing up after sitting down), or as an initial symptom of an infection. Numerous medicines cause it.

OEDEMA OF THE FACE

Some children are naturally rather puffy under the eyes. Puffiness of the eyes may be due to crying.

Puffiness may be due to rubbing the eyes, as in hay fever. A more severe form, commonly allergic, but sometimes due to a hereditary enzyme deficiency, is angioneurotic oedema. Oedema may be due to a skin infection near the eyes. Various drugs, notably aspirin, may cause puffiness of the eyes. Puffiness of the eyes may be due to an acute antrum infection, the onset of glandular fever or acute nephritis.

PEDICULOSIS

Pediculosis capitis, the common form, is due to the louse. This feeds on blood. The eggs (nits) hatch and become glued to the hairs. They reach maturity in two to three weeks. The nits are readily distinguished from scurf, in that when the single hair with the white patch is passed between finger and thumb, scurf is not attached to the hair, while the nit is firmly adherent. There is itching of the scalp and often infection as a result of scratching. It is treated by benzyl benzoate emulsion or gamma benzene hexachloride, one application at night followed by a shampoo.

Pediculosis pubis affects the pubic hair or the eyelashes.

PIGEON CHEST

A pigeon chest consists of prominence of the sternum and the cartilaginous parts of the ribs, with depression of the thorax at each side. It occurs in normal children and is often a familial feature. It may result from congenital heart disease or chronic respiratory obstruction.

PRURITUS (THE ITCH)

The common causes in children are scabies, eczema, urticaria and chickenpox. Itching of the scalp may be due to pediculosis (nits). Itching of the trunk may be due to sensitivity to wool next to the skin, or to nylon, or to a sweat rash. Itching between the toes is caused by ringworm, and in cold weather itching of the hands and feet is caused by chilblains. Itching around the anus and vulva may be caused by threadworms, particularly in the evening and night (when the threadworms emerge from the anus and lay their eggs). Some medicines cause itching as a side effect.

RHEUMATOID ARTHRITIS

Rheumatoid arthritis occurs in childhood at two peak periods—age two to four and nine to fourteen. It is more common in girls than boys, and there is often a family history of the same complaint. There may be swelling and pain in one joint, especially the knee, or the joints of the fingers may be involved as in adults. There is commonly stiffness in joints often with neck stiffness on getting up in the mornings.

The disease often runs a prolonged course. Eventually a third recover completely, a third are left with severe disability, and the remainder with only slight handicap. The younger child is more likely to do well than the older one. Fifteen per cent suffer complications in the eye (iritis or cataract).

RINGWORM INFECTIONS

Ringworm of scalp (tinea capitis) in the school child is due usually to the fungus microsporon audouini, but sometimes to trichophyton. In the former case there are scaly circumscribed patches on the scalp with loss of hair. It is treated by griseofulvin.

Ringworm of the body (tinea corporis) consists of round red scaly patches. Ringworm of the foot (tinea pedis) consists of maceration and fissuring, with pin-sized vesicles, between the third and fourth and fourth and fifth toes. It is extremely common, and is spread in the swimming bath and the sports pavilion. It responds rapidly to Whitfield's ointment (benzoic acid compound ointment).

SCABIES

Scabies is due to the mite sarcoptes scabei: the impregnated female mite burrows into the skin and lays eggs there; the larvae emerge to the surface as adults. The female becomes impregnated and starts a new cycle. Intense itching occurs and there are characteristically lesions between the fingers, on the palms of the hands, the flexural surface of the wrist, the folds of the axilla, the areola of the breast in girls, and on the penis.

It is treated by a hot bath and wash with soap and water, followed by rubbing in gamma benzene hexachloride cream (Lorexane) or benzyl benzoate emulsion for two consecutive days over the whole body, except the face and scalp, followed by a bath. On the third day underwear, bedclothes and blankets are changed and disinfected by thorough washing. The whole family has to be treated.

TINNITUS (BUZZING IN THE EARS)

Tinnitus is a subjective symptom, like vertigo, which only the sufferer can assess. Anyone can hear noises in the ears, but normal people take no notice of them. Tinnitus can be an emotional symptom: but it can be caused by several drugs, notably salicylates and quinine.

TONSILS AND ADENOIDS

There are about 160,000 tonsillectomies each year in Britain. Like the operation of circumcision, there is a social gradient, there being much more in the upper than in the lower classes. Many years ago it was shown that there are striking geographical variations—children in some towns being many times more likely to have the tonsils removed than those living in other towns. It was shown, for instance, that a child living in Leeds was ten times more likely to have his tonsils removed than one living in Sheffield; one living in Rutland was 19 times more likely to have them out than one living in Cambridgeshire: and one living in Bexhill was 27 times more likely to have the operation than one living in Birkenhead: while one living in Huntingdonshire was 70 times more likely to have the operation than one living in Dewsbury. These variations are indicative not of increased needs in some towns but rather of differences of opinion. I have discussed these differences of opinion elsewhere (Illingworth 1961). In Newcastle the strange fact emerged that boys who were circumcised are more likely to have the tonsils removed than were uncircumcised boys. In New York there was a study of 1,000 eleven-year-old children: 610 had had the tonsils removed. The remaining 390 were referred to ear, nose and throat specialists, who advised that all but 65 of the remainder should have the operation. Muller (1953) examined the throats of 640 children aged 5 to 16 in one school: he reported that in only 14 per cent were the tonsils normal: but he did not appear to realise that he had not defined what he meant by the word 'normal'—and that perhaps the majority might be 'normal'.

Many paediatricians think that far too many tonsils are taken out (Bolande 1969). It is an accepted fact that of those children who are put on to the waiting list for tonsillectomy, and whose names are reached some two years later, less than half are found still to need the operation. It is normal for tonsils to be large at around the age of five—and tonsils should not be removed unless they are so large that they obstruct the airway, which is rare: in a few years they become smaller: furthermore, large tonsils are no more likely to be infected than small ones. Tonsils should never be removed because of frequent colds; their removal makes no difference to this problem. Children commonly acquire frequent colds and throats when they start school—and the age of five to six is the peak age for tonsillectomy: but in two or three years children acquire considerable immunity to these infections without tonsillectomy. Sometimes frequent tonsillitis can be prevented by continuous prophylactic penicillin throughout the winter—and this is more pleasant than tonsillectomy. If a child has had a quinsy (peritonsillar abscess) the tonsils should be removed. They should be removed if a child is having frequent tonsillitis with fever (every two or three months), which cannot be prevented by continuous prophylactic penicillin.

Adenoids should be removed if they are causing nasal speech, obstructed breathing, recurrent middle ear disease or deafness.

TUBERCULOSIS

Tuberculosis is due to the mycobacterium tuberculosis. Tuberculosis is now rarely seen in British children, thanks to improved social circumstances and good preventive measures. The incidence is lowest in those with the highest living standards. When an adult is found to have tuberculosis his children, or other children likely to come into contact with him, are skin tested to determine whether they have already been infected, and if negative they are protected by BCG vaccine. This vaccine is given to newborn babies if there is anyone in the family who has or ever has had tuberculosis, whether or not the tuberculosis is said to be inactive. All British children are skin tested for tuberculosis at the age of 11 to 12 years, and if negative they are given BCG. Bovine tuberculosis has now been largely eradicated because of the pasteurisation of milk supplies and other measures, though it has been found that badgers may spread the disease among cattle. There is no such thing as hereditary tuberculosis: but a child may have congenital tuberculosis: that is, he is born with it, having been infected through the placenta. It is now extremely rare.

Two to ten weeks after a child's exposure to tuberculosis the child becomes allergic to the infection and therefore has a positive skin test. The infection is commonly in the lung, but may involve almost any organ of the body, including the kidney, bone or brain. This is termed the primary infection: the infection spreads to the related lymph glands and may spread through the blood stream to any part of the body. Commonly the infection is subclinical— meaning that there are no symptoms: the body has mastered the infection, but it is detected by the positive skin test—which shows not that there is active tuberculosis, but that the child has been infected in the past. Nevertheless, any positive reactor is investigated (e.g. by X-ray of the chest) to ensure that there is no active process. There is a variety of modern drugs which are highly effective in treatment—so that the outlook for infected children is now excellent.

URTICARIA

Urticaria is one of the principle itching rashes. Urticaria, consisting of wheals, is an allergic response to foods, inhalants, drugs, infections or bites. Psychological factors are sometimes significant. I myself had an attack of generalised urticaria an hour after being nearly drowned.

Papular urticaria consists of numerous itching papules and may persist for weeks. It is usually due to sensitivity to the bites of fleas, lice, bedbugs, mites, midges, mosquitoes, or other insects. Animals in the house are the most likely source of the trouble. Cats should be dusted with pyrethrum or rotenone, and dogs with dicophane (DDT). The child's clothes are dusted with dicophane. The animal's sleeping quarters are sprayed with dicophane or rotenone.

VERTIGO (DIZZINESS)

Vertigo, like pain, is a subjective symptom whose severity others cannot assess. It is potentially an important symptom which should therefore always be investigated. It commonly precedes a faint, or occurs on sudden change of posture. It is a feature of a low blood sugar in a diabetic child. It can be caused by a variety of medicines.

Sometimes vertigo is due to a virus infection, and occurs in epidemics. There is a sudden onset of nausea and vomiting with vertigo; the child recovers in a few days.

A condition termed paroxysmal vertigo sometimes occurs in children aged about two to seven. There are instantaneous attacks of intense vertigo, lasting a minute or two. The cause is unknown. Attacks cease by the age of six to seven.

VOMITING

All children vomit, some more readily than others. It commonly occurs without disease—as a result of distaste for school (the vomiting occurring on getting ready for school), fears, anxiety, excitement, or as an attention seeking device. Migraine as a cause of vomiting has been described on p. 256.

Travel sickness affects children of all ages from infancy onwards. The condition is related to receptor cells in the vestibular apparatus of the internal ear, chiefly in the utricle. It does not occur in deaf mutes. It can be 'conditioned'—so that symptoms develop before a boat moves from dock—the mere smell or sight of the boat causing the child to vomit. The best prophylactic is hyoscine ('Kwells'). This has been proved by several workers who conducted research for the armed forces in connection with World War Two. Hyoscine cannot be used for more than a day or two, because its effect is cumulative and would be toxic. Antihistamines (e.g. Marzine) are used by some for the purpose.

Vomiting is commonly the initial symptom of an infection, especially tonsillitis, scarlet fever, middle ear disease, gastro-enteritis or even meningitis. It is a feature of whooping cough, in which there is a spasmodic cough which repeatedly makes the child sick and which is worse at night. Vomiting may be due to medicines. It may be a feature of diabetic acidosis or hypoglycaemia (p. 251). It may be a feature of acute surgical conditions, notably acute appendicitis (which usually begins with central abdominal pain, fever and vomiting) or torsion of the testis.

VOMITING OF BLOOD (HAEMATEMESIS)

Vomiting of blood is unusual in children. Probably the commonest cause is swallowed blood from a nose bleed or rupture of a vein in the throat in acute tonsillitis. It may be due to aspirin—an important cause of bleeding from the stomach in child or adult. It could be due to poisons or to a peptic ulcer.

WARTS (VERRUCAE)

Warts represent an overgrowth of epithelial cells in the skin as a result of papova virus infection. Some are thread-like structures (filiform warts) while others are flat: on the sole of the foot (plantar warts) they cause considerable pain. Some undergo spontaneous disappearance, but others last for years. They are mildly infectious.

Filiform warts are best dealt with by touching them with an applicator with cotton wool attached and soaked in liquid nitrogen. This is painless. One application is enough. Plantar warts are rendered largely painless by wearing a ring pad, or by a metatarsal bar on the shoe, so that pressure is taken off the wart. They are also treated effectively by formalin foot soaks or a plaster of salicylic acid. The child is allowed to continue to go to the swimming baths with a plantar wart if he wears Plastisoks.

WEIGHT LOSS

Loss of weight is always a serious symptom in childhood—unless it is the result of deliberate planned slimming in obesity. It may be due to severe infection, such as tuberculosis: to chronic diarrhoea or vomiting; to diabetes mellitus; or other serious disease. It could be due to severe emotional disturbance. In any case, it is a symptom which needs urgent investigation.

WORMS

Threadworms (Oxyuriasis)

The threadworm is the commonest of the worm infestations in Britain. Studies have shown that more than half of all school children have the infection. Fortunately it is almost always symptom-free, though an occasional child has itching around the anus or vulva mainly in the evenings and night when the female worm emerges from the anus and lays her eggs.

The worm is 2 to 10mm long. It grows in the caecum and appendix, maturing over a period of about seven weeks, and then the female worm in the evening emerges from the anus and lays about 10,000 eggs. The child scratches or rubs the skin, or contaminates the fingers by contact with the bedclothes or pyjamas: the fingers are taken to the mouth, the eggs are swallowed and hatch out in the intestine. They do not multiply within the bowel. The threadworm eggs are ubiquitous; in one investigation it was found that there were on an average 119 eggs per square foot of the school dining hall, 305 threadworm eggs per square foot of the wall of a classroom, and 5,000 per square foot of the wall of a lavatory. Eggs adhere to soap or the fur of animals. The eggs are spread around by a vacuum cleaner. If a child has the infection, it can be safely assumed that the other members of the family also have it.

The diagnosis is made by swabbing the perianal skin with adhesive cellulose tape and examining it under the microscope. It is unusual to see the threadworms in the stools.

Treatment is unnecessary unless there are symptoms: the condition is likely to recur.

Roundworm (*Ascariasis*)

The roundworm lives in the small intestine: the female lays about 200,000 eggs each day, and they are passed in the faeces. The infection is widespread in the tropics and many developing countries; it is spread by dirt and often from fruit and vegetables. In many countries the majority if not all of the children are infected. The diagnosis is made by finding the ova in the stools.

Roundworm may cause pneumonia, abdominal pain and other symptoms related to the alimentary tract.

Tapeworm

Tapeworm infections are spread from infected improperly cooked meat and pork. The tapeworm is 5 to 15 feet long. Man is infected by eggs taken into the mouth: the diagnosis is made by finding the eggs or segments of the worms in the stools.

Other worms

Man may be infected by other worms via the faeces of dogs and cats. The hookworm, which causes bleeding from the duodenum, reaches the child by infected soil in contact with the skin.

REFERENCES

Abdominal pain

APLEY J. (1959) *The Child with Abdominal Pain*. Oxford, Blackwell.
DAVIDSON M. (1971) Recurrent abdominal pain. *Am. J. Dis. Child.* **121**, 179.
SHEPHERD M., OPPENHEIM B. & MITCHELL S. (1971) *Child Behaviour and Mental Health*. University of London Press.

Asthma

BERMAN S. (1967) The psychological implications of intractable asthma in childhood. *Clin. Proc. Children's Hospital Dist. Columbia*, **23**, 210.
BURTON L. (1968) *Vulnerable Children*. London, Routledge & Kegan Paul.
MANSMANN H.C. (1968) Management of the child with bronchial asthma. *Pediatric Clinics N. America*, **15**, 357.

Cough

COLLEY J.R.T. (1974) Respiratory symptom in children and parental smoking and phlegm production. *Brit. Med. J.* **2**, 201.

Dental Caries

BOWEN W.H. (1972) Dental caries. *Arch. Dis. Childh.* **47**, 849.
FANNING E.A., GOTJAMANOS T. & VOWLES N.J. (1969) Dental caries. *Med. J. Australia*, **1**, 1131.
RYAN P. (1973) Decadent teeth. *New Scientist*, **58**, 770.

Haemophilia

Scientific American (1965) The royal haemophilia. August, p. 88.

Knock Knee

FARRIER C.D. & LLOYD-ROBERTS G.C. (1969) The natural history of knock knee. *Practitioner*, **203**, 789.

Limb Pains

APLEY J. & MACKEITH R. (1968) *The Child and His Symptoms*. Oxford, Blackwell Scientific Publications.
ØSTER J. & NIELSEN A. (1972) Growing pains. *Acta. Paediat. Scandinav.* **61**, 329

Migraine

APLEY J. & MACKEITH R. (1968) *The Child and His Symptoms*. Oxford, Blackwell Scientific Publications.
BILLE B. (1962) Migraine in school children. *Acta Paediat. Scandinav.* **51**, Suppl. 136.
DALTON K. (1972) Migraine. *Practitioner*, **209**, 835.
FRIEDMAN A.P. (1972) Migraine headaches. *J. Am. Med. Ass.* **222**, 1399.
FRIEDMAN A. & HARMS F. (1967) *Headaches in Children*. Maryland, Charles Thomas.

HENDERSON W.R. & RASKIN N.H. (1972) Hot dog headache: individual susceptibility to nitrite. *Lancet*, **2**, 1162.

RIGG C.A. (1972) Migraine in children and adolescents. *Clin. Proc. Children's Hospital National Medical Centre*, **28**, 297.

VAHLQUIST B. (1961) Migraine in children. *Triangle*, **5**, 89.

Muscular Dystrophy

DUBOWITZ V. (1965) Muscular dystrophy and related disorders. *Postgrad. Med. J.* **41**, 332.

DUBOWITZ V. (1969) Muscle disorders in childhood. *Brit. J. Hosp. Med.*, p. 1627.

Tonsils and Adenoids

BOLANDE R.P. (1969) Ritualistic surgery—circumcision and tonsillectomy. *New Engl. J. Med.* **280**, 591.

ILLINGWORTH R.S. (1961) The tonsillectomy problem. *Proc. Roy. Soc. Med.* **54**, 393.

MULLER E. (1953) Large tonsils. *Deutsche. Medizinische. Wochenschrift.* **78**, 1017.

Warts

TURNER T.W. (1971) Whither warts? *South Australian Clinics*, **5**, 270.

FURTHER READING

ILLINGWORTH R.S. (1973) *Common Symptoms of Disease in Children*. Oxford, Blackwell Scientific Publications.

CHAPTER 18

COMMON INFECTIOUS DISEASES

Probably all children acquire some of the acute infectious diseases: but some of the diseases can now be prevented by immunisation. Table 18.1 lists the common infections, together with the incubation period and duration of infectivity.

TABLE 18.1

Disease	Incubation period (Days)	Period of Infectivity
Mumps	12–26 (especially 18)	2 days before swelling, till swelling has gone down.
Chickenpox	14–18	1 day before rash to 6 days after start of rash.
Measles	8–11 (for onset of symptoms), 12–15 (to onset of rash)	5–6 days before rash till 5 days after temperature becomes normal.
Rubella	10–21 (especially 18)	1 day before rash till 2 days after start of rash.
Whooping Cough	7–10	2 days before start, 5 weeks after start.
Poliomyelitis	7–14	3 days before symptoms start to 2 weeks after onset if temperature is normal.
Enteric group	7–21 (especially 14)	2 days before symptoms, till stools and urine negative.
Scarlet fever⎫ Diphtheria ⎬	2–5	Till swabs negative.
Infective Hepatitis	15–60	16 days before jaundice to 8 days after start.
Glandular fever	33–49	Uncertain.

The notes concerning the duration of infectivity are important. In my opinion many children are kept away from school far too long, particularly for chickenpox and rubella.

CHICKENPOX

Chickenpox is a virus infection spread by droplets from the nose and throat. It is the same virus as that which causes herpes zoster (shingles) in adults. Infection is at its height in the period just before the rash appears, and by the time the spots have crusted it is not infectious. In the early stages of the infection it is extremely infectious. Second attacks are rare, but most adults with 'shingles' have had chickenpox.

The first symptom may be slight malaise for a few hours before the rash, or the rash may be the first symptom. The rash appears rapidly, as red papules which soon become clear fluid—containing lesions or vesicles. These then dry and scab. Crops of lesions commonly appear for three or four days. The rash begins on the trunk and abdomen and spreads to the face and scalp and there are commonly vesicles in the mouth. New spots appear for up to a week. The rash itches. There is varying fever; in mild cases the elevation of temperature is only trivial.

When one child in the family has chickenpox, there are seven chances out of ten that other children will develop it. It is futile to separate a child from his siblings. About 60 per cent of children have had it by the age of about eight. No treatment is needed and confinement to bed is unnecessary.

COLDS

The common cold, coryza, is the result of infection by any of numerous viruses. It is highly infectious, and is spread either by droplets from the nose and throat, or, in the case of the rhinovirus, a common cause of 'colds', by skin contact—the infection being carried to the nose or mouth by the hands which have been infected by another person. The peak age for colds is the age of five to six; after this age children acquire some degree of immunity to them. The infection is self limiting, meaning that no treatment is necessary, for it cures itself, though an annoying cough, middle ear infection or wheezing may follow a cold. Antibiotics should never be given for the treatment of a cold, for viruses are insensitive to them, and confinement to bed is unnecessary. The removal of tonsils has no effect in reducing the incidence of colds: neither does any medicine affect them. No effective vaccine has been developed, largely because so many viruses, numbering dozens, are involved.

K

DIPHTHERIA

Diphtheria is virtually non-existent in Britain now, as a result of immunisation. It is usually a throat infection, which may be complicated by heart disease, laryngeal obstruction, difficulty in swallowing and weakness of the limbs; full recovery is the rule provided that the child survives the acute stage. It is due to a bacterium spread by droplet infection.

DYSENTERY

Dysentery is a common infection in Britain, and about 20,000 cases are reported in England and Wales each year. It is usually mild in Britain, causing diarrhoea only, but abroad in the Middle and Far East it occurs in more serious form. It is spread by flies contaminating food, or by infected water or by careless handling of food by carriers. In Britain it is a self-limiting disease and clears up rapidly without treatment.

THE ENTERIC GROUP

This includes typhoid fever and paratyphoid infections, and is due to organisms of the salmonella group. In Britain it usually results from holidays in the Mediterranean seaboard particularly Spain, Tangiers, Morocco and Tunisia. It is spread by contaminated water or food; contamination is by infected urine or faeces, and may result from the careless handling of food by carriers of the infection, or from a contaminated water supply.

GASTROENTERITIS

Gastroenteritis is due to contamination of food by bacteria or chemical poisons. It is often called 'food-poisoning'. Travellers to Spain and other countries commonly ascribe their diarrhoea to 'rich food', or 'the sun', whereas it is almost certainly due to viruses or bacteria. The organisms include staphylococci and pathogenic E.coli, and reach the food by a contaminated water supply, or by those who handle the food. Failure to wash the hands after defecation is a potent cause. A staphylococcal or streptococcal lesion on the neck or elsewhere can readily infect a food handler's hands as a result of scratching, and so infect the food. The staphylococcus produces enterotoxins when it grows, and these are heat resistant, so that within an hour or so of eating the food the victim develops nausea, vomiting, abdominal pain and then diarrhoea. There may be elevation of temperature. Foods particularly liable to be affected include prepared meats, ham, chicken, salads, whipped cream and custards, especially when prepared in large quantities. When the symptoms are due not to the enterotoxin, but to the growth of the organism, the onset of symptoms is a few hours later. The attack is self limiting, usually lasting for 12 to 24 hours.

When on holiday in countries where hygiene is poor children should avoid all unboiled milk or water—and should not even brush their teeth in unboiled water: ice in drinks is potentially dangerous. They should avoid salads, ice-creams, cream cakes, shellfish or prepared meats. Water should be boiled (preferably), or a tablet of halazone is added to a litre of water, shaken, and allowed to stand for 30 minutes before use.

GERMAN MEASLES (RUBELLA)

Rubella is due to a virus and is spread by droplets from the nose and throat. The initial symptoms are usually trivial and may not be noticed at all. There may be slight malaise and fever. The characteristic sign is then enlargement of the glands at the back of the neck; the glands are tender. The throat may be a little red. About 24 hours after the glands have begun to enlarge, a rash appears on the face and behind the ears and spreads to the trunk and limbs. The rash usually disappears by about the third day. In mild cases there is not even a rash. No treatment is required and confinement to bed is unnecessary.

A second attack is extremely rare. It is moderately infectious. If a child in a house has German measles, there is a one in two chance that the other children will develop it. About one in four children have had it by the age of eight. In adults arthritis may complicate rubella, but it is very rare in children.

Many rashes resemble that of rubella, and without laboratory tests (which are not usually necessary), one cannot often be certain of the diagnosis.

GLANDULAR FEVER (INFECTIOUS MONONUCLEOSIS)

This is a common infection in school children—but it is diagnosed more often than it should be, for without laboratory tests the diagnosis is indefinite: many children said to have glandular fever have nothing more than an ordinary throat infection with enlargement of the glands in the neck as a result. It is a virus infection spread by droplets from the nose and throat.

Glandular fever commonly presents with fever, sore throat (with exudate on the tonsils), enlargement of the glands in the neck and axilla, enlargement of the spleen, sometimes swelling (oedema) around the eyes, and often a rash. The rash commonly develops four to ten days after the onset, but only one in five to ten children get it. It is mainly confined to the trunk, and usually resembles measles or scarlet fever. A variety of other symptoms may occur: they include jaundice and neck stiffness. The course in children is usually a mild one of a few days, but it may last longer. No treatment is available and bed rest, except when there is high fever, is unnecessary. It is unwise to give an antibiotic; it would be useless and might well do harm.

It is not highly infectious: when a child at home has it, it is unusual for other children to develop it: but outbreaks in schools have been described, though they are rare.

INFECTIVE HEPATITIS

This is the common cause of jaundice in children. It is due to a virus, which can be isolated from the blood and faeces of infected patients. It sometimes occurs in epidemics, but when one member of a family has it second cases are unusual. When several cases occur in a school it may be due to infection from someone with a mild attack who handles the food.

The early symptoms are malaise, nausea, vomiting and perhaps fever. The urine becomes dark and stools pale. The attack may last a few days or several weeks. It is infectious mainly in the early stage of the disease, especially in the period before the jaundice becomes obvious; for this reason isolation of a child from his siblings is useless—for it is too late.

MEASLES

Measles is a virus infection spread mainly by droplets from the nose and throat. It is highly infectious, and 90 per cent of children exposed to measles in the family will acquire it unless they have been immunised. Measles occurs in epidemics of about two to four year intervals. About 90 per cent of unimmunised children have had it by the age of eight.

The symptoms of measles occur in two stages, beginning with fever, a 'cold', sore throat and cough, these lasting for up to seven days, before the second stage when the rash appears, beginning over the side of the neck below the ears and the hairline, and then over the face spreading over the body and limbs. The rash begins as faint non-raised macules. In the early stage there are always 'Koplik's spots' in the inside of the cheek (the buccal mucosa); these are whitish dots with a rim of red round them. The fever commonly persists until the rash reaches the legs and feet (usually within two days). As the rash reaches the feet it fades on the face.

The infection is not carried by contacts not suffering from the disease. It is infectious mainly in the early stage of the disease before the rash appears, and isolation of a child from his siblings is useless: it is too late.

MUMPS

This is due to a virus which can be isolated from the saliva, throat and cerebrospinal fluid: the infection is spread by contact with another child or by droplets in the air. It commonly begins with fever, malaise and febrile aches and pains and pain over the angle of the jaw or in the ear. Within 24 hours of the onset one or both parotid glands enlarge and are painful, particularly when eating or when saliva flows. The swelling reaches its maximum in one to three days. The swelling subsides in three to seven days; if only one side is affected at first, the other side may be affected in a day or two. An interval of more than three days between the swelling of the two sides is unusual. There may be swelling of the salivary glands immediately below the jaw. Sometimes there is abdominal pain, nausea and vomiting. Before puberty swelling of the testis (orchitis) is rare, but after puberty one out of five develop it— sometimes on both sides, and it may be followed by testicular atrophy. In 30 to 40 per cent the infection is 'subclinical', and there are no symptoms at all, but blood tests show that infection has occurred. The condition is not nearly as infectious as measles:

when a child develops mumps there is a one in four chance that other children in the family will develop it. About a third of all children develop it by the age of seven. It is useless to separate a child with mumps from his siblings: if his siblings are male it is better for them to have it before puberty because of the risk of orchitis if they get it later.

POLIOMYELITIS

This is virtually non-existent in Britain, as a result of immunisation. It is a virus infection. The initial symptoms are fever and often headache, vomiting and neck stiffness.

SCARLET FEVER

Scarlet fever is a throat infection, caused by the streptococcus, with a rash, which is commonly followed by peeling. It is no more infectious than the common streptococcal tonsillitis. The symptoms are mainly headache, fever, sore throat and vomiting. The rash consists of a diffuse redness, made up of pinpoint red spots, with characteristic pallor around the mouth; it begins 12 to 72 hours after the onset of symptoms, starting around the neck, in the axillae and groins, spreading later to the trunk and limbs.

WHOOPING COUGH (PERTUSSIS)

Whooping cough is due to a bacterium or to a virus. It commonly begins with a cold, mild fever and cough. In a few days the cough increases. Spasms of coughing then develop, and the cough repeatedly makes the child sick: the cough is worse at night. Only after a week or two does the whoop develop—a long indrawing crowing sound on breathing in after a series of coughs. In mild cases, in infants or in children who have been immunised the whoop may never be heard. The spasmodic phase may last for four weeks or more; the cough may persist for 10 or 12 weeks, and sometimes there is an exacerbation when the child has almost recovered.

Whooping cough is highly infectious: if one child acquires it at home, there is a more than 90 per cent chance that the other children will develop it unless they have been immunised. About

60 per cent of unimmunised children have had the infection by the age of about eight.

PREVENTION OF INFECTIOUS DISEASES

Immunisation

The following is the routine immunisation programme:

Diphtheria, whooping cough, tetanus—3 months, 5 months, 11 months. A booster dose of diphtheria and tetanus is given at 5 years. A booster dose of tetanus toxoid is given at 15 to 19, or when a relevant injury occurs provided that the child has not been given the toxoid in the previous five years, when it is unnecessary.

Poliomyelitis—3 months, 5 months, 11 months. A booster dose is given at 5 years and at 15 to 19 years.

Measles—13 months, one dose.

Rubella—girls who have not had rubella and who are shown by blood tests not to have had it are given rubella vaccine at 10 to 12 years. Joint pain or limb weakness is an occasional sequel to the immunisation.

Smallpox—only for children about to go to certain countries abroad.

Tuberculosis (BCG)—children are skin tested at 10 to 13 years, and if negative are given BCG. Possible contacts of tuberculosis are given BCG at any age.

Typhoid (TAB—Typhoid, Paratyphoid A and B)—only for children about to travel to certain areas abroad.

Cholera—at any age, only if about to travel to certain places abroad, e.g. India. The vaccine is a combined one with TAB.

Yellow fever—at any age, only if about to travel to certain places abroad, e.g. Central Africa.

Infective hepatitis—an injection of gamma globulin is given only if about to travel to certain places abroad, e.g. Africa. It protects for about three months only.

The prevention of tetanus

All children (and adults) should be immunised against tetanus. When a child has been immunised, and he receives a dirty wound, the doctor gives not tetanus antitoxin, which frequently gives serious and dangerous side effects, and which cannot be effectively used twice (i.e. for a subsequent injury), but tetanus toxoid, which has no serious side effects, and usually none at all, provided only that it is not given too frequently. If a dose of toxoid has been given in the previous five years, a further dose should not be given; it is unnecessary and increases the risk of side effects.

An important part of tetanus prevention is thorough cleaning of the wound. Sometimes an antibiotic is given as well.

Quarantine

It is now recognised that quarantine—the isolation of contacts of a case of infectious disease—is useless, except for smallpox (and possibly poliomyelitis). R.E. Smith at Rugby School drew attention to the uselessness of quarantine. He wrote that over a 16-year period, 203 boys who had been exposed to infectious disease were allowed back to school, and only one developed the disease: there were no secondary cases. If there had been strict quarantine, 4,224 school days would have been lost. If only the susceptible boys had been quarantined, 2,123 days would have been lost.

Quarantine was not successful in the past when it was practised. One reason is that children cannot carry most of the infectious diseases (e.g. measles, rubella, chickenpox, whooping cough) to school. If they have had the infection, it is very rare for them to have it a second time, so that quarantine would be unnecessary. If one does quarantine a child, it is impossible to prevent him coming into contact with friends out of school hours. Children are not infectious in the early part of the incubation period. There is much to be said for children acquiring in childhood those infections not at present prevented by immunisation. It is desirable for boys to develop mumps before puberty, because of the risk of orchitis if mumps occurs after puberty. Chickenpox and whooping cough are often much more severe in adult life than in childhood.

Quarantine is not now practised in British or American schools except for smallpox.

Reference

Smith R.E. (1963) Quarantine. *Brit. Med. J.* 2, 374.

CHAPTER 19
ACCIDENTS AND FIRST AID

GENERAL

Accidents are the commonest cause of death in children after the first birthday, causing a third of all deaths in childhood. They cause more than twice the number of deaths than do all the acute infectious diseases combined, including poliomyelitis and tuberculosis. Accidents kill 15,000 children a year in the United States and cause permanent injury to 50,000 or more. About 15 million children are seen by doctors in the United States each year on account of accidents. Over 6,000 American children under the age of 15 die each year from motor accidents. In Britain about 2,000 children suffer fatal accidents, a third of them on the road, and a further 10,000 to 50,000 are injured. Every fifth to tenth child in Britain suffers a serious accident every year. About 21,000 school children are admitted to hospital in Britain each year on account of head injuries. In Newcastle upon Tyne 14 per cent of all admissions to paediatric wards were due to head injuries. In Sheffield one in every six children is taken to the Accident and Emergency Department of the Children's Hospital. A report by the American Federal Trade Commission indicated that in the USA 700,000 children are injured each year by defective and dangerous toys.

Each year about 30,000 children are admitted to hospitals in England and Wales for poisoning. In the United States 600 children die each year from poisoning, while a further 600,000 recover. Hundreds of different poisons are taken by children; there are at least 300,000 toxic household poisons available. The commonest usually are aspirins, iron tablets, tranquillisers or sedatives, contraceptive pills, berries, cleaning agents, pesticides, disinfectants, petroleum products, laxatives and heart tablets. In Sweden the commonist poison is said to be swallowed—cigarettes.

A serious form of poisoning is that due to lead; it is serious because it damages the brain and may cause lead poisoning. It is much more common in the United States than in Britain, largely because of the strictness of British laws concerning lead in paint. In America slum children eat paint off window sills and other places. In New York City 7,000 children have significant levels of lead in the blood, and in Chicago 3,000 cases of lead poisoning are reported each year.

THE FACTORS INVOLVED

Most if not all children suffer an accident sometime in the early years, but most accidents are trivial and require no medical attention. Others are more severe, and the child is seen by a doctor —either the family doctor or the doctor in the Casualty department ('Accident and Emergency Department') of a hospital. Recurrent accidents, amounting to accident-proneness, are essentially a behaviour problem—and behaviour problems, as already stated, are usually the result of the interaction of the child's personality and developing mind with the personality and attitudes of parents, teachers and friends. Not all accidents can be prevented, and parents and teachers commonly receive blame which they do not deserve. On the one hand if a child is overprotected he may fail to learn from painful experience or rebel against over-protection and become accident prone. The end result may be the same if he is brought up with excessive strictness. When a mother constantly remonstrates with her child, saying 'don't do this, don't do that'—the child takes no notice and then when an emergency occurs, as on crossing the road, the child as usual takes no notice of his mother and an accident occurs. On the other hand a child brought up with too little discipline, or with no protection against danger, is equally likely to be accident prone. A happy mean is desirable, but that is most difficult to attain and impossible to define. Calculated risks have to be taken—but they should be taken by persons with the necessary experience and judgment to know what risks are involved.

Those taking calculated risks with children (as all parents have to) must take into consideration the child's age (especially his mental age) and his personality. The parents have to provide complete protection to the child in his first year: but thereafter gradually, in the light of the child's mental age, they have to allow him to learn painful lessons, and cause and effect, and eventually to acquire complete independence. In the meantime, before independence is acquired, various environmental factors may be responsible for the breakdown of effective control: they include a change of house, illness of the mother, absence of the mother for a confinement, illness of siblings or an accident to a sibling occupying the mother's time and attention, the mother's preoccupation with household routine, the mother being out at work, the mother's worries, premenstrual tension, or domestic friction. Factors in the home relevant to childhood accidents include parental alcoholism, psychoses or neuroses, punitive management, rejection, overcrowding, lack of play space, parental ignorance of the ability of children to get into trouble, carelessness with the storage of poisonous material or of material liable to cause accidents—matches, flammable material, damaged toys, opened tins with jagged edges, or carelessness with boiling or hot water, or with pans or other cooking utensils: an open upstairs window: or a depressed grate in the garden drive when a child has a bicycle.

Features in the child which are relevant to accidents include overactivity, dare-devil exploratory behaviour, impulsiveness, aggressiveness, attention-seeking, insecurity, a desire for more independence, inattentiveness, day dreaming, clumsiness, carelessness and recklessness, failure to think of the consequences of an act, lack of self control, showing off and extroversion. Important factors are hunger, fatigue and boredom.

Children may have accidents in revenge against their parents or siblings, to seek sympathy or to avoid an unpleasant task. The accident may be a conscious or subconscious self injury because of a feeling of guilt. Children frequently involved in accidents are often unable to tolerate stress or frustration like normal children. Accident prone children are often anxious children, in conflict with their parents, often suffering emotional deprivation which is aggravated by dominating punitive discipline. As Lindy Burton wrote, the child who is insecure is apt to make substitute relationships with other children, and so to become involved in dangerous escapades. Accident proneness is 'part of a lengthy pattern of disturbed behaviour on the child's part, behaviour which in fact is directed towards wresting adequate attention and affection from the mother'—and it is only one problem of many—the child showing many other problems such as temper tantrums, disturbed sleep and unpopularity at school.

PREVENTION

Wise management and loving firm discipline at home are the most important aspects of the prevention of accidents. This includes the setting of a good example, for children are imitators, and it is important that the parents should always set a good example, avoiding dangerous practices which the child will copy.

Parents (and teachers) must always stop dangerous practices—playing on the stairs, putting a plastic bag over the head, playing with cord round the neck, hitting children on the head, running about with sharp objects in the mouth (or an object in the mouth such as a plastic trumpet which would be sharp if the child fell and broke it), playing with fire, throwing peanuts into the air and catching them with the open mouth (the danger being that the peanut is then inhaled into the bronchus). They should be aware of the danger of the swing (another child running behind the swing and receiving concussion), and the danger of polished floors. They must be aware of the danger of airguns, bows and arrows and catapults—all causes of severe injury to the eye. They must stop the door-banging game before a finger is trapped. They must be aware of the danger of fireworks—never allowing a child to put a firework into the pocket, to throw a firework, or to bend down over one when lighting it, or to put a firework into a milk bottle. All chemical substances must be kept out of reach—and all medicines must be locked up and the key kept in a safe place: but it is easier to say that all chemical substances should be out of reach than to achieve this. Old eye drops should be discarded because they become heavily infected. Aspirins which have begun to crumble or to smell sour should be discarded, as should medicine whose colour has changed or has developed a residue at the bottom.

Children must be allowed to ride a bicycle if they wish, but the dangers must be recognised. One danger consists of allowing a raincoat to become caught in the spokes: the drain hole in the drive is a danger to the child on a cycle. High rise bicycles are a particular danger. Craft et al. (1972) found that of 16 head injuries arising from cycle accidents, 11 involved the 'high rise' type of bicycle.

In the car, children should never be allowed to stand in front of the front seat—and still less on it, when the car is in motion. They should wear seat belts. The rear door should have a safety catch on the inside. Presumably all schools now teach children about road safety.

Children must learn safety on the water and safety in the water. The Lake District National Park publishes a leaflet about this. It advises all children in boats to wear the British Standards Institute approved life jacket; to avoid overloading the craft; to stay with the craft if it capsizes; and it warns adults to watch the wind and weather, to heed navigation rules, to check buoyancy equipment, and not to overload the craft. Older girls water skiing must wear rubber wet suits, or rubber pants to prevent water being forced up the vagina. Standard swim suits do not prevent the entry of water into the vagina under high pressure (Tweedale 1973). Other water skiing accidents include rope burns, ruptured ear drums, sinusitis and injury by the boat propeller. An underwater swim should not be immediately preceded by overventilation (Craig 1973), for it may result in sudden death. All children should learn to swim: they should watch the depth: they should be told about the under-tow at the seaside and about currents; they must be aware of the danger of cold: they must not shout for help in fun. They should know about the danger of the lilo floating out to sea.

The Central Council for Physical Recreation publishes a booklet on Safety on Mountains, and older children who climb in the hills should read and digest it. They should be told, for instance, that they must not be afraid of refusing to climb a section if they are afraid: it requires more courage to refuse than to attempt to climb —and the attempt will involve much inconvenience and perhaps danger to others if an accident occurs.

Children should be given positive instruction not only with regard to road safety, water safety and mountain safety, but to safety in the correct handling of carpentry and other tools.

HEAD INJURY

Head injuries to children are exceedingly common. In a Scandinavian study it was found that about nine per cent of school children received such injuries. A high proportion have suffered previous accidents and previous behaviour problems. Head injuries must be taken seriously if there is evidence of concussion—that is if the child cannot remember exactly what led to the injury. The child is then referred immediately to the nearest casualty department of a hospital, where he is admitted for 24 hours' observation—in case signs of a cerebral haemorrhage should develop.

Very few children have any after effects of concussion. It is only if the head injury is very severe, and there is prolonged coma, indicating laceration of the brain, that there is a material risk that there will be sequelae. Even after a long period of unconsciousness recovery is often complete. The symptoms which may follow severe injury are headache, fits, poor concentration, overactivity, aggressiveness or emotional behaviour. In a Scandinavian study (Nylander and Hjern 1964) it was found that 10 per cent of children who had severe head injuries suffered some sequelae but all of them came from an insecure family background. Except in these severe cases, symptoms after a head injury were also present before the injury. Headaches otherwise are most unlikely to follow a head injury in which there have been no indications of brain laceration or haemorrhage. Various studies (*British Medical Journal* 1972, Harrington and Letemendia 1958) have shown that important factors are the child's pre-existing personality and management and his management after the injury. If parents assume an overprotective attitude after an injury, the child is more likely to suffer symptoms: and the more severe the injury the more likely it is that parental attitudes and management will be undesirable and therefore harmful. After a head injury the child should lead a normal life—without restrictions of any kind—except only when brain damage has left neurological sequelae and that is rare.

TREATMENT

ABRASIONS AND CUTS: BLEEDING

An abrasion is cleaned with soap and water and if possible left without a bandage. If a dressing is applied, cotton wool must be avoided, because it adheres to the damaged tissues and causes pain when it is removed. A dry dressing is all that is required.

If there is bleeding from a cut, it should be stopped by pressure over it. In the case of severe bleeding, it is a help to elevate the limb.

BITES

Bites are treated like any other penetrating wound: the site is thoroughly cleaned. Sometimes a doctor will prescribe penicillin or other antibiotic and if necessary give a booster dose of tetanus toxoid.

BLEEDING NOSE OR TOOTH SOCKET

The cause of nose bleeding is usually unknown, because usually the nose is not examined. If there is recurrent nose bleeding, the specialist should see the child: it may be due to a bleeding point which can be treated by touching it with a cautery.

Nose bleeds may be due to injury to the nose, picking it or inserting a foreign body. It may result from whooping cough or blood diseases. It may be due to hereditary telangiectasia—an abnormal collection of blood vessels in the nose, on the face or elsewhere.

The usual source of bleeding in epistaxis (bleeding nose) is the front part of the septum: hence a rational approach is to apply pressure on the nose between forefinger and thumb in the long axis of the nose—keeping the pressure for not less than five minutes. It is a mistake to release the pressure at intervals in order to determine whether bleeding has ceased: it merely starts again. If bleeding still continues, the child is referred to the family doctor or casualty department.

If a tooth socket is bleeding after an extraction, the child is referred back to the dentist (if he is available) or to the family doctor or casualty department. If there is troublesome bleeding, the clot should be removed by a swab and then a gauze roll is applied over the bleeding area and the child bites on it: he must maintain the bite pressure for at least five minutes: if at intervals he releases the pressure in order to determine whether it is still bleeding, the bleeding is likely to start again.

THE BROKEN TOOTH

When a school child breaks a tooth, or loosens it by injury, he should be taken to the dentist immediately. If the fracture is slight and confined to the enamel, he may merely smoothen the fractured surface. If the fracture is more extensive, he will cover it with a special paste and if necessary a stainless steel cap, or fix a crown. If the tooth is not fractured but has been loosened, it is splinted to the adjoining teeth for some weeks. Even though the tooth has been completely knocked out of its socket, the tooth should be preserved in damp cotton wool and taken *immediately* to the dentist (*not* next day), for he may be able to replant the tooth.

Injury may jolt the developing permanent teeth out of position, so that a tooth may erupt almost horizontally. Hence the dentist must see the child straight away, so that the appropriate treatment can be given.

BURNS AND SCALDS

A good immediate step is to insert the burnt part immediately into ice cold water. A small burn is treated by cleansing with cetrimide (1 per cent), applying a dry dressing, and applying an adhesive dressing (e.g. Surgifix tubular bandage). The part is kept dry and the dressing is left intact for a week. For larger burns the doctor will probably apply Tulle Gras or Viocutin. Ointment or butter must *not* be applied. A blister is normally left intact, though a painful one on the palm or sole may be opened by the doctor with a sterile needle.

FOREIGN BODY IN NOSE, EAR, EYE

Unless the object can be readily removed, it should be left and the child referred to a doctor: inexpert efforts to remove objects commonly lead to their being pushed further in and made more difficult to remove. A doctor may remove a foreign body in the ear by gently syringing. Gentle downward pressure along the nose may displace and expel a foreign body.

A foreign body on the eyelid is readily removed, but if it is on the surface of the eye it can often be washed off. If that fails a moist cotton wool applicator may remove it. If there is a suspected metallic foreign body (if, for instance, the child were using a hammer) the child should be referred immediately to a hospital casualty department.

It should be noted that particles of glass in the tissues are detectable by X-rays.

If a chemical gets into the eye, the safest step is to bathe the eye immediately in a copious supply of cold water, unless it is carbolic, in which case it is swabbed off immediately with cotton wool (protecting your own hands). The child is then taken immediately to the hospital casualty department.

POISONING

The child who has swallowed poison should be taken to the hospital immediately: it is a mistake to waste time telephoning to the doctor or hospital. It may be wise to make the child sick, if possible, by a spoon applied to the throat: this must never be done if the child has inhaled a petroleum derivative. In the case of some poisons (especially salicylates, iron medicines and diphenoxylate(lomotil)), there is a latent period between the ingestion of the poison and the onset of symptoms: this is dangerous, and may give a false sense of security.

The child should be taken to hospital in the prone ('spank') position, because if he is sick in this position, he is less likely to inhale it.

STINGS

There is no specific treatment for bee or wasp stings. If the sting can be seen, it should be pulled out. Any soothing application, such as calamine lotion, may give some psychological help.

REFERENCES

Accidents—General

BURTON L. (1968) *Vulnerable Children.* London, Routledge & Kegan Paul.
CRAFT A.W., SHAW D.A. & CARTLIDGE N.E.F. (1972) Head injuries in children. *Brit. Med. J.* 4, 200.
CRAIG A.B. (1973) Some hazards of aquatics. *Am. J. Dis. Child.* 125, 643.
ROYAL SOCIETY FOR PREVENTION OF ACCIDENTS, Terminal House, 52 Grosvenor Gardens, London S.W.1. *Safety in the Water, Safety on the Water, Water Safety Code, Safety Afloat.*
TWEEDALE P.G. (1973) Gynecological hazards of water-skiing. *Can. Med. Ass. J.* 108, 22.

Head injuries

British Medical Journal (1972) Head injuries to children. Leading Article, **1**, 196.
HARRINGTON J.A. & LETEMENDIA F.J.J. (1958) Persistent psychiatric disorders after head injuries in children. *J. Mental Science*, **104**, 1205.
HJERN B. & NYLANDER I. (1964) Acute head injuries in children. *Acta Paediat. Scand.*, Suppl. 152.
RUNE V. (1970) Head injuries to children. *Acta Paediat. Scand.*, Suppl. 209.

OTHER READING

JONES J.G. (1969) Preventing poisoning accidents in children. *Clin. Pediatrics*, **8**, 484.
MEYER R.J. & KLEIN D. (1969) Childhood injuries, approaches and perspectives. *Pediatrics*, **44**, 791–896.

CHAPTER 20
PSYCHOSES AND PSYCHONEUROSES

Autism is a form of psychosis which is said to affect one in about 2,000 to 4,000 children; it is said that there are about 3,000 autistic children of school age in England and Wales. Figures given for its incidence are difficult to interpret because, subsequent to Leo Kanner's original description in Baltimore, some have included under the term autism mentally defective children who show certain autistic features.

The symptoms are usually first noticed in early infancy. The mother begins to think that the baby is unusual. He does not smile at her and does not want to be picked up. He may hardly ever cry, or cry continuously unless he is rocked. He is unresponsive and may be a slow feeder. Apart from his failure to smile his milestones of development are likely to be normal: but he shows no interest when people talk to him. In infancy and later childhood he is likely to look normal: but it is soon found that he is not developing speech, and appears not to hear or to understand what is said to him: he shows no response to sound and is liable to be thought to be deaf. He may indicate his needs by gesture.

After infancy there is a striking absence of speech, or if there is some speech it is inappropriate. He is apt to show peculiar mannerisms—flapping the hands, flicking the fingers in front of the eyes, toe-walking, unusual repetitive play, rocking and spinning objects. He exhibits characteristic gaze aversion—refusing to look at people in the eyes. He dislikes change and may have a temper tantrum if an adult attempts to distract him, but his power of concentration, except on a particular toy, is poor. He mixes badly with other children, preferring to be alone. There is a striking lack of interest in people, and he prefers toys. He rarely smiles or laughs, but if he does laugh it is inappropriate. He may show inappropriate fears. There is little variation in facial expression.

He shows no appreciation of danger, and is liable to run into the path of a moving car. He is overactive, and may have an inverted sleep rhythm. Self injury is common.

In summary, the child is interested in things, not people; he lives in a world of his own, cutting himself off from others: he refuses to look one in the eyes: his speech is severely delayed. He may look normal and unless he is mentally defective his other milestones of development are normal. He appears not to hear. The autistic features are the same whether the child has a high or low IQ.

The cause of autism is unknown. It used to be held that it was related to emotional deprivation, but this view has now been discarded. Rimland (1965) described an autistic child as one who is 'handicapped by a basic inability to integrate visual and auditory experiences into the meaningful patterns which form a basis for the normal child's developing understanding of the world'. Others have described it as a developmental perceptual disorder, in particular a defect of language and of comprehension.

Infantile autism is not the same condition as schizophrenia. Rutter has described some of the essential differences. Autism is four times more common in boys than girls, while in schizophrenia there is no sex difference. In schizophrenia there is a genetic factor, and therefore often a family history of it, but this is not true of autism. Unlike schizophrenia, autism is more common in the middle and upper classes. The signs of autism are present from early infancy, or at least in the first two years, while those of schizophrenia are not present before the age of three or four, and schizophrenia is rare even then. The mean IQ is higher in schizophrenia (though it is difficult to test in an autistic child because of his unresponsiveness). Hallucinations occur in schizophrenia, but not in autism. Schizophrenic children respond better to treatment: there is no medical treatment for autism, though teachers may cause an improvement in his behaviour.

Rutter and Lockyer (1967) have carried out a long term follow-up study of 63 autistic children for five to fifteen years. About 14 per cent were able to live a nearly normal life: 29 were without useful speech: two out of 38 over the age of 16 had jobs. Twenty-one had never attended school. Some cease to be autistic but very few lose their ritualistic or compulsive behaviour: none were heterosexual. Most of them were easier to manage. Ten of the 63 developed fits in adolescence, and some underwent mental deterioration. The outcome was related to the severity of the autism, the severity of the speech defect and the IQ: those without speech at five had the worst prognosis.

SCHIZOPHRENIA

Schizophrenia is rare in children: the features which distinguish it from autism have been described in the previous section. It is characterised by withdrawal from company, resistance to change, panic reactions, inappropriate behaviour, failure to use language for ordinary communication, and hallucinations. The child is remote, and one cannot get through to him. There may be echolalia—the repetition of words in parrot fashion. The child may show impulsive or unpredictable behaviour.

Those interested should read the fascinating and tragic account of a schizophrenic boy in the book by Wilson L. (1969) *This Stranger My Son*, London, Murray.

HYSTERIA

Hysteria is occasionally seen in older school children. As in adults, it may show itself in a variety of ways—aphonia (causing the child to speak in a whisper), convulsions, tremors, paralysis of a limb, blindness, deafness, difficulty in swallowing, walking with the back bent or with other bizarre gait—which the expert recognises immediately as hysteria, in that the gait could not be caused by organic disease—over-ventilation (forced deep breathing leading to tetany, with peculiar sensations and spasms in the hands and feet), or peculiar coughs. These symptoms arise from the sub-conscious mind, and are not feigned: but all these symptoms *could* be feigned, and therefore malingering. It can be extremely difficult for an expert to distinguish hysteria from malingering: but it is important to recognise that the symptoms of hysteria are genuine and not feigned.

Hysteria is a serious mental disturbance which is difficult to treat. It is a matter for the expert.

REFERENCES

RIMLAND B. (1965) *Infantile Autism*. London, Methuen.

RUTTER M. (1968) Concepts of autism: a review of research. *J. Child. Psychol. Psychiat.* **90**, 1.

RUTTER M. (1971) *Infantile Autism: Concepts, Characteristics and Treatment.* Edinburgh, Churchill/Livingstone.

RUTTER M. & LOCKYER L. (1967) A five to fifteen year follow up study of infantile psychosis. *Brit. J. Psychiat.* **113**, 1169, 1183.

OTHER READING

CHURCHILL D.W., ALPERN G.D. & DE MYER M.K. (1971) *Infantile Autism.* Springfield, Charles Thomas.

ROWLANDS P. (1972) *The Fugitive Mind. The Early Development of an Autistic Child.* London, Dent.

WING J.K. (1966) *Early Childhood Autism.* London, Pergamon.

INDEX